Reiner Weichhardt
Editor

Deputy Director
NATO Economics Directorate

 **NATO**

Privatization in NACC Countries: Defence Industry Experiences and Policies and Experiences in Related Fields

Colloquium
29-30 June, 1 July 1994
Brussels

 **OTAN**

Privatisation dans les pays du CCNA: expériences et politiques des industries de défence et expériences dans les domaines connexes

Colloque
29-30 juin, 1er juillet 1994
Bruxelles

Editorial support and coordination: Michael Devlin, Editorial Services, Brussels

First edition 1994
ISBN 92-845-0079-6

This is the latest in a series bringing together papers presented at the NATO colloquia organised by the NATO Economics Directorate and Office of Information and Press on economic issues in the former USSR and Central and East European countries. For further information please write to the Director, Office of Information and Press, 1110 Brussels, Belgium.

The articles contained in this volume represent the views of the authors and do not necessarily reflect the official opinion or policy of member governments or NATO.

100274 5173

Privatization in NACC Countries: Defence Industry Experiences and Policies and Experiences in Related Fields

Privatisation dans les pays du CCNA: expériences et politiques des industries de défence et expériences dans les domaines connexes

NOTE ON THE NORTH ATLANTIC COOPERATION COUNCIL
(NACC)

The North Atlantic Cooperation Council was created as an initiative by the Heads of State and Government of the NATO Allies meeting in Rome in November 1991 and includes presently the following members: Albania, Armenia, Azerbaijan, Belarus, Belgium, Bulgaria, Canada, Czech Republic, Denmark, Estonia, France, Georgia, Germany, Greece, Hungary, Iceland, Italy, Kazakhstan, Kyrgyzstan, Latvia, Lithuania, Luxembourg, Moldova, Netherlands, Norway, Poland, Portugal, Romania, Russian Federation, Republic of Slovakia, Spain, Tajikistan, Turkey, Turkmenistan, Ukraine, United Kingdom, United States, Uzbekistan.
The Colloquium is an element of the NACC Work Plan.

Contents

Contents

Contents

9

Contents

Preface

Dr. Reiner Weichhardt
Deputy Director
NATO Economics Directorate

The 1994 NATO Economics Colloquium was one of the items included in the economic chapter of the annual Work Plan of the North Atlantic Cooperation Council (NACC). Under the Chairmanship of M. Daniel George, NATO's Director of Economic Affairs, the conference brought together a broad audience of specialists from governmental bodies, the business world and academia. Thirty-one authors and speakers from Allied and Partner countries and International Organizations discussed in five panels pertinent privatization issues in NACC countries with a particular focus on defence industrial problems. The keynote speaker was Romanian Deputy Prime Minister and President of the Council for Economic Coordination, Strategy and Reform, Professor Mircea Cosea. A guest lecture was delivered by OECD's Assistant Secretary General and Director of the Centre for Cooperation with the Economies in Transition, Mr. Salvatore Zecchini.

Many experts argued that defence industry privatization is to be considered as a part of overall industrial privatization. However, there are also specific elements to be taken into account. One is that the privatization and conversion potential of the defence industrial sector has to do with excess production capacities. These are capacities which go beyond core defence production needs, as determined by a country's security requirements. However, the demarcation line between core and excess capacities is not always easy to draw.

There was general agreement that Partner countries, having inherited a large-scale defence sector, are faced with serious social problems in the process of defence industry privatization and conversion. No doubt, successful transformation depends on the full support of citizens, especially the defence industry workforce. Because defence production is such a major component of these economies, the millions of workers and managers in this complex can be a formidable lobby against continued economic and social adjustment. But there is no alternative to change. Few markets remain for these millions of manhours of production, and there is little money left for government subsidies. Moreover, foreign capital will only be made available if there are economically viable restructuring projects.

Another interesting theme highlighted during the conference was that defence industry restructuring is also a Western challenge. The same issues of over-production, job loss and problems to compete effectively on the world market are concerns that also plague defence producers in the United States and the European Union. Western governments are finding that the down-sizing of their defence sector is a painful but necessary process. Admittedly, industrial adjustment and diversification is facilitated by the fact that Western firms are operating in well-established market economies. NATO's Partner countries certainly have a far greater challenge ahead, but their change must progress at its own pace.

This book contains all the Colloquium papers. Since only a few up-dates have been made during the editing process, they reflect as accurately as possible the state of information available at the time of the conference. The views expressed by the experts have offered many new insights to the problems and challenges of defence industry privatization and conversion in Allied and Partner countries. The NATO Economics Directorate is therefore confident that the conference results will stimulate and fertilize future work in the field.

I wish to thank Michael Devlin, Editorial Services, Brussels, for his most valuable editorial support and coordination in producing this book, as well as for the preparation of brief summaries introducing each paper.

Welcoming Address by the Secretary General of NATO
(as delivered by the Colloquium Chairman)

I very much regret that I am unable to join you all this morning for the opening of the 1994 NATO Economics Colloquium, but let me extend, through your Chairman, my warm welcome and best wishes for a successful meeting. I also want to thank all the speakers who have come from a number of near and distant places to share their thoughts on this important topic with us. The Colloquium has now become a regular activity under the Work Plan of the North Atlantic Cooperation Council and the increasing participation of speakers from Cooperation Partner countries greatly enriches the discussions and increases the benefits which participants take away.

NATO's cooperation with the states of the former Soviet Union and other Central and East European countries is dynamic and constantly takes on new aspects. This is in the interest of all parties involved. Our aim is to use the framework of the NACC to facilitate and promote work on common problems, like defence conversion, where each country can bring to the table the benefit of their experience and take away knowledge gained from others. As NACC Ministers affirmed after their meeting in December 1993:

"We aim to advance our practical cooperation on defence conversion and on security-related economic issues, including those related to defence budgets."

This conference is an important activity in this regard. Its focus, as suggested by the Colloquium's title, will be on defence industries, as this is an area of particular security interest where NATO nations have a great deal of expertise and experience. But there can be no isolation of this area of industrial activity from general privatization policies and overall economic reform. A viable market framework must be set up if the privatization and conversion to civilian goals of defence industry is to be successful.

It seems clear that privatization of economies is an important, perhaps a key, step towards the establishment of market economies. Beyond the purely economic aspects, however, there are the broader political and social implications. History has shown that a nation of property owners, with widespread vested interests, is more likely to be imbued with strong democratic attributes and greater stability and internal security. This does not mean that one model exists for all to follow. The road to a market economy may vary from one country to another and the final results may differ, with some countries opting to maintain a greater part of the economy under state ownership than others do. But few would argue for a system of complete, or near-complete, state ownership. Thus I am sure that each of you will carry away from these discussions this week some new ideas on privatization which will be of benefit in the design and implementation of your own national programmes.

Thank you all once again for joining NATO in this cooperative venture, and I and my colleagues will look forward to the published results of your deliberations.

THE POLICY FOR PRIVATIZATION AND RESTRUCTURING OF THE ARMAMENTS INDUSTRY IN ROMANIA

Mircea Cosea

"Social engineering", not industrial re-engineering, is the first and most important step toward successful defence privatization, says Professor Mircea Cosea. In September 1994, the Romanian government launched its fast-track privatization programme of some 3000 state-owned enterprises, but none of these were in the state armaments sector. Because defence conversion is a very sensitive demographic, labour-related and political issue, careful social planning is required to ensure a smooth and successful transition. Romania begins its defence conversion process in mid-1995.

Professor Mircea Cosea is Deputy Prime Minister of Romania and President of the Council for Coordination Strategy and Economic Reforms.

Analysts have the tendency to grant Romania a special place within the process of transition and reform which is carried out in Central and Eastern Europe. In many cases it is considered that Romania has a certain delay as compared to its neighbours Hungary, Poland or the Czech Republic, due to the fact that it has chosen a type of gradual reform which, in their opinion, has resulted in a much too slow staging of some basic elements of transition such as privatisation and restructuring. Irrespective of the more or less accepted schemes of the theories of shock therapy or gradual therapy, one must highlight the fact that at the beginning of 1990 Romania embarked upon its way towards reform in totally different conditions, as compared to all the other countries in transition. These special conditions resulted in a great lag for Romania, as compared to the other countries. The starting conditions for transition are due either to the heritage of the former communist regime or to the special manner through which Romania has done away with it.

Therefore, one must be aware that the communist regime was, until its last moments, totally different from those that the neighbouring countries were still having. It was only in Romania where a totalitarian, unipersonal, despotic and absurd communist regime still existed, which was trying to establish a society meant to be a copy of the communism of North Korea. The totalitarianism based on the principle of excessive centralism and on the political and cultural insulation of the country was the reason for which, at that time, Romania was not prepared to confront transition, both from the point of view of the mentalities and of the managerial behaviour. As a matter of fact, in Romania, until the very last day of the regime of Ceausescu there had been no concern to prepare for a change, the conceptual immobility of the communist leadership forced the entire population to live not only in economic autarchy, but also in educational autarchy.

Another reason which contributed to Romania's initial lag in embarking upon transition was the fact that the removal of the communist regime was made in a violent manner, not by means of "velvet revolution", as in the other countries. The violent revolution meant not only human victims but also the disintegration, in a few days only, of the whole political, economic and administrative system, of the hierarchal structures and of the balance of values which, altogether, led to a total political and social void.

That is why Romania started to move towards transition with a considerable lag, over two years being necessary for the settling and stabilising of society and economy within a structure able to be reformed.

Under these circumstances the macrostabilisation effect of the reform were felt in early 1993, when the subsidies were completely eliminated, the Value Added Tax was introduced and a financial and monetary policy was introduced, which aimed at cutting off inflation and at achieving a positive economic trend. In the first half of 1994 Romania succeeded in signing a standby agreement with the International Monetary Fund and the World Bank. The exchange rate was stabilised and a serious reduction of inflation was achieved.

The privatization process cannot be considered separately from the general economic and social context. That is why the dynamism and size of this process have followed closely the general evolution of the transition.

The process of privatising the companies constituted by enforcement of Law 15/1990 began in 1991 with the promulgation of Law 58. The State Ownership Fund and five Private Ownership Funds have thus been set up. All the citizens of Romania - being entitled to - received ownership certificates representing, in fact, titles on 30% of the authorised capital of the companies administered by the Private Ownership Funds. The rest, of 70%, has been turned over to the State Ownership Fund.

The major goal of the privatisation process is the actual transfer of property, capable of generating a responsible behaviour in the new shareholders and having, as a result, efficient, competitive and more dynamic economic units with an increased capacity of adjustment to domestic and international competition.

The actual development of the reform process has up to now emphasized a persistence, if not a deepening of the economic imbalances, should they be with respect to raw materials, finance and currency, labour market, etc. These have been in themselves a result of the changes occurring in the structure of domestic consumption as well as in that of the export market, in most unfavourable conditions, largely due to recession and to protectionist policies.

In this wide framework, the complex and time-consuming processes of privatisation and restructuring have been, and continue to be, influenced by a series of constraining elements, such as:

* the financial blockage due to the fact that unprofitable companies are still maintained in the economic circuit, and due to some monopolistic tendencies;
* the absence of domestic capital for investments, both from the point of view of its volume and of its qualitative structure - institutional investors, financial markets;
* the absence of an organised market of capital (Stock Exchange), to have a multiple role, the educational and informational sides included;
* the state budget deficit which does not allow the financial support of the restructuring and privatisation process;
* the interest of investors, the foreign ones in particular, in buying shares from the state-owned companies had been relatively low, as a result of their perception regarding the lack of political and economic stability in Romania after December 1989;
* a certain policy of restrictive crediting, with negative impact, under the circumstances of the macro economic stabilisation and of a still insufficient reorientation of the banking activity;
* the privatisation process has been marked by the lack of development/restructuring studies on the respective domains/sub-domains of activity to be elaborated by ministries and departments. In their absence, there was no clear image - both at the macro- and micro-economic levels - of the domains considered strategic for privatisation, from the viewpoint of dimensions and perspectives - to be attractive for the foreign investors;
* obtaining of property titles on the land, an essential condition for privatising a company, is a relatively slow process, all along the chain of approvals.

Nevertheless, as the organisational and preparation process of privatisation, in all its aspects have been achieved, the process itself has been started. In the first trimester of 1993, and up to the end of that year 270 companies were privatised (out of which 250 are small companies), their authorised capital being over 64 billion lei and having 76,000 employees.

Up to now, 450 small companies (out of a total of 3,100 small companies) of a total of 6,200 commercial companies, 36 (out of 2,500) medium-sized companies and 3 (out of 700) large companies have been privatised.

Consequently, about 8% of the commercial companies have been privatised, with a capital which represents 3% of the total capital; by carrying out the Privatisation Programme approved for 1994, the social capital of the privatised companies will not exceed 10% - although the number of the privatised companies may rise to 38%.

Due to the fact that the privatisation process has been carried out much too slowly so far, the Government of Romania has decided to embark upon a rapid mass privatisation plan, starting from September 1994, which includes over 3,000 enterprises. The industry of armament is not included in the plan for mass privatisation, none of the 3,000 enterprises being armament producers or a producer of materials which could be considered as armament (we are referring here strictly to the production for defence purposes without including the enterprises from the civilian industry which are able to supply goods to be used in equipping the army).

The privatisation of the industry of armament in Romania is a process which is still in the field of action of some restrictive factors, such as:

a. The fact that several persons in the leading circles of the industry of armament think that privatisation of this industry would be a threat to national security and to the confidentiality which is specific to the activities of endowing and supplying of the army.

b. The present situation of the armament industry is characterised by a severe decrease in its production and a partial use of its productive resources, which are due to the loss of certain traditional markets (the former members of the Council for Mutual Economic Advantage or Countries which are under embargo) and also to an important decrease in the internal demand.

c. The reduced span of the programmes for reconverting and restructuring the military production.

d. The absence of foreign capital and a certain lack of interest of the foreign investors for the privatisation of any military production units.

e. Difficulties in finding foreign partners in order to cooperate with them in producing military technology or equipment.

f. The existence of an extremely well trained labour force, which is also extremely specialised, which leads to great difficulties in restructuring or in re-orientating the labour force.

g. The existence of such a type of management at the level of the productive units which combines - in most cases - civilian staff and military staff, which calls for management methods and techniques of a military type.

Although all the above-mentioned elements result in a difficult privatisation process, the Government intends to pay special attention to this industrial sector, starting from the idea that the privatisation of the armament industry is necessary both because of the necessity to make it efficient and to the necessity to consolidate macroeconomic stability. It has been agreed that the first elements of privatisation of the armament industry are to be included in the second stage of the mass privatisation programme, which will start in the second half of 1995.

In order to prepare for this moment, the Government has started restructuring activities, trying to adapt armament production to the actual demand of the market. Consequently, starting from January 1, 1994, the Inter-Ministerial Council for the restructuring of the defence industry has already undertaken feasibility studies and has adopted a short- and medium-term strategy for the restructuring and the reorientation towards an activity of turning a military industry into a civilian one.

Romania considers the Partnership for Peace as highly important.

Romania was the first country to sign the partnership agreement, therefore it hopes that the economic component of this partnership will improve. It is in this way that Romania understands the activity of privatisation and restructuring the defence industry. At present Romania needs the assistance of the countries which are members of NATO in order to find some economic solutions for the military system. Therefore, the economic component of the partnership for peace could be sensed, at the level of the needs of Romania, at least by the following issues:

    a. The countries members of NATO could provide Romania with technical and financial assistance for the speeding-up of the restructuring process and of the reconversion of the defence industry.

    b. The countries members of NATO could produce, in co-operation with defence Romania industry some equipment or elements of military technique.

    c. Romania might be appointed as the exclusive centre for producing certain equipments or elements of military technique.

    d. The countries members of NATO might provide technical assistance for elaborating some reconversion programmes for the labour force used in the military industries.

PANEL I

National Approaches to Privatization: Comparative Assessment

Chair: Daniel George, Director, NATO Economics Directorate

Panelists: Marvin Jackson
Éva Ehrlich
Gediminas Rainys
Wolfgang Vehse
Bülent Gültekin

CRITICAL ISSUES IN PRIVATIZATION: THE CENTRAL AND EASTERN EUROPE EXPERIENCE

Marvin Jackson

All the countries in Central and Eastern Europe have embarked on some kind of mass privatisation programme. The problem is that everyone has different expectations, and each chosen method brings different results, says Marvin Jackson. Vouchers mean a quick sale, but companies can have too many shareholders and weak management. Centralised programmes are slow. They rely on expensive consultants and give an unpopular head start to the managers in post. The most successful method seems to be where there is one big investor, or where there are owner-managers.

Professor Marvin Jackson is the Director of the Leuven Institute for Central and Eastern European Studies at the Department of Economics, University of Leuven.

The pillars of transition in Central and Eastern Europe are democratization, "marketization", and privatization. Of course, there are other essential elements such as the rule of law, protection of human rights, economic stabilization and international security. Our paper focuses on privatization.

An immense literature has already been generated on this subject and the number of possible issues is large enough to fill several tomes. We shall try to restrict our survey to how much privatization has been done, what forms of privatization have proven successful, and what accounts for the record.

Among the other issues that remain important are: what has been the impact and what should be the likely future impact on economic performance; how can privatization measures be improved; what are the current political issues of privatization; and what is likely to be the future of privatization in the region.

Essential Dimensions of Privatization

It might have been better if we would have started with a different word than "privatization" because the essential dimension of the process is more general than that suggested by giving natural and capital assets to "private" individuals or households, although this is the essence of the matter. We are concerned with at least three essential and potentially separable rights: control, usufruct, and disposition. Also, we are concerned with changing the ill-defined nature of such rights (who had them) under the old system to a system where the legal and physical personalities who hold such rights and the conditions in which they hold them are clearly specified. Therefore, privatization is best seen in two steps: as a specification of ambiguous rights and as an assignment of those rights ultimately to physical persons.

There are several distinctly different processes of privatization that have been going on in Central and Eastern Europe. We turn aside from new start-ups or freshly established private companies that have been the success stories in all of the transition countries. Our focus is on the main problem: the privatization of former state-owned enterprises (SOEs).

A main form of clarifying the poorly defined property rights of the former system is the conversion of the legal form of an enterprise from the laws or regulations regarding SOEs to a form, typically a joint-stock company, that is permitted in the commercial code of the country. There may, of course, be other laws defining the status of enterprises, including special joint-stock company laws.

The immediate result of such a conversion is typically a joint-stock company, whose shares are "owned" by the state, and some state agency, a ministry or a holding company, is the nominal owner of shares and, therefore, can undertake control of the company according to the rights of shareholders in the charter and constitution of the company (the corporate body as a legal person).

After conversion, various means can be used to transfer shares (and the property rights of shareholders) to non-state owners. It is this transfer that constitutes privatization in the narrow sense.

Forms of Privatization

It is not easy to give a simple list of the forms of privatization. We think the following categories identify the essential differences.

- Classic centralized privatization - preparation by government experts or consultants of an individual company or a small group of related companies, possibly including restructuring, for sale by tender, auction or through a stock market.
- Self or decentralized privatization by liquidation or conversion and sale upon petition of employees or investors - government experts limit themselves to establishing general guidelines and general approval of projects that are proposed and detailed by the enterprise insiders or other investors.
- Mass privatization - the simultaneous or near simultaneous obligatory preparation (including possibly conversion) of a large number of enterprises for auction, sale or give-away (usually) accompanied by mass distribution of the means of acquisition (vouchers or subsidized credits).

- Covert privatization - from the general public point of view, the unintended or hidden transfer of assets through distorted pricing arrangements, in the simplest cases as sales of assets from SOEs to private companies and individuals or more subtle forms such as wage payments in excess of productivity, underpricing of sales through a front company, or overpricing of supplies from a front company.

Forms of resulting ownership can be any form permitted in the commercial code while ownership configurations can be highly concentrated in a single investor or highly distributed among more or less equal owners, as in an employee-owned co-operative. Minority shareholding by the state or other public bodies also occurs.

Country Records of Privatization

We have prepared a record covering 14 transition countries in which we attempt to give a highly simplified report of the record of privatization in terms of both the extent of privatization and the main form or forms of privatization that have been used.

This is a difficult task because there are no common statistical standards for reporting privatization. We are quite aware of them. But in this short paper they will be not be discussed. According to our calculations, in the spring of 1994 the following rates of privatization of former SOEs have been achieved:

TABLE I - COMPARATIVE PRIVATIZATION 1994

Country	Share of Private Sector 1992(93)[b]	Share of SOEs Privatized 1994.I	Comments
Czech Republic	20(55)	42	First wave
		58	Second wave
Russian Fed.	(+50)[c]	63	(Loginov 1994)
Lithuania		67	All enterprises: (Rainys 1994)
Estonia[a]		20	(Agency 1994; Kell 1994)
Hungary[a]	38(50)	27	15% by assets
Poland[a]	45(58)	27	
Belarus[a]	8	15	Rough estimate
Ukraine[a]		15	Rough estimate
Romania	25(30)	5	
Latvia[a]		4	
Bulgaria[a]	15(20)	1	

[a] Mass program with vouchers not important up to now.
[b] In GDP. [c] Chubais 1994.
Source: Jackson and Bilsen 1994.

We have written research reports that support these estimates. Also, we have prepared a survey record of the main techniques and problems of privatization from which was extracted the following short summary for each country.

A few comments are necessary to explain the difficulties of compiling the table. Basically one can measure the rate of privatization of SOEs as the share of enterprises privatized or the share of assets privatized. Across countries there is no common baseline definition of the minimum sized enterprise to include in the reported statistics. This is important because the smaller the enterprises the easier it is to privatize them (notice this could be a problem in the case of Lithuania in the table). A problem with the share of enterprises is that the base figure for "total SOEs that could be privatized" changes because large SOEs have been broken up into several smaller enterprises before and during privatization. A problem with the share of assets is that asset evaluations are terribly inaccurate.

The Czech Republic (and former Czechoslovakia)

In the former CSFR out of 7187 state and co-operative enterprises, there were some 6000 enterprises in 1991 that were considered eligible for privatization, of which 3100 entered the first wave and 1491 offered their shares in the voucher scheme. The respective figures for the Czech Republic alone were 4400, 2210, and 988. The second wave of voucher privatization just started will put another 860 companies in the process.

Conversion to joint stock companies accounted for 24% of enterprises and 43% of capital of enterprises privatized in the Czech Republic, of which 23% and 40% respectively were sold through vouchers. Other forms of privatization in the first wave were public auction, public tender, direct sale and free transfer.

Russian Federation

The essence of Russian privatization is based on three steps:the large-scale conversion of SOEs to joint-stock companies; the selection by employees of one of three variants of closed subscriptions of shares; and a voucher auction.

Enterprises subject to privatization are required to set up a commission to develop a privatization plan. Employees of larger firms (more than 200 employees and/or assets of more than R 1 million) are given a choice of three variants of acquisition:
- Workers could have 25% free, non-voting shares and managers 5% at nominal prices, with both eligible for another 10% in an ESOP arrangement.

Workers and managers together can buy up to 51% at a nominal price of 1.7 times the July 1992 book value and workers can pay in cash, vouchers, or special retained earnings accounts with workers and managers also able to obtain another 5% under the ESOP arrangement.

- Managers can buy up to 40% at low prices on the condition that they do not go bankrupt.

According to one sample study, the second variant has been used about 80% of the time.

Approximately one-third of the vouchers was used by the workers and managers in the closed subscriptions. About half of the enterprises that were required to convert to joint-stock forms turned to the general voucher auction process and in these cases an average of not more than 30% of the shares have been auctioned for vouchers. These included about 20% by private individuals and 30-50% by investment funds.

Poland

Poland's multi-track privatization law of 1990 provided a centralized "capital track" for commercialization and sale either to single buyers or a public offer where the Ministry of Ownership Transformation played a dominant role and a decentralized "liquidation" track where the founding organs (voivods and ministries) played a key role and the assets were turned over to insiders through sale, donation or leasing. In mid-1991 changes were made to open up privatization of small and medium enterprises to public auctions, including the employees along with domestic and foreign investors. A mass voucher-based system was also expected to be on line by the second half of 1991, but it still has not been realized even though a new form of it is expected from the present government.

The most common form of transformation has been by liquidation, mostly under the Privatization Act of 1990, but also under the Enterprise Act of 1985. Liquidations usually result in employee companies based on leasing of assets and often involve joint ventures with founding bodies and even outside investors. Most have less than 200 employees and are outside of industry.

Hungary

The State Property Agency (SPA) was set up in Hungary in 1990 to oversee and direct privatization. The Act on Asset Protection, also in 1990, required the SPA to be notified and to approve sales or new organizations over a limit amount by state-owned companies. In late 1992 a State Asset Management Company was also set up and put in control of strategic companies, leaving the SPA to concentrate on privatization. It first stressed centralized privatization, launching three batch programs in late 1990.

In an effort to push privatization, two decentralized programs were introduced. Investor-initiated privatization was announced in February 1991. Interested investors initiate offers to the SPA which, in turn, usually calls for a competitive tender (either closed or open). A feature of Hungarian privatization has been the high share of foreign sales.

"Self-privatization" started in June 1991 and was recently discontinued. It permitted an enterprise to initiate its own privatization under an independent consulting and property evaluating company which was chosen from a list approved by the SPA. The consulting companies were compensated by a bonus dependent on the sale price and the speed of privatization.

Other means provided are restitution vouchers, which can be exchanged for certain designated state properties. Since 1992 the "E-loan" program provides preferential rediscount through commercial banks for share buyers, but commercial banks have not been attracted. Employees with more than six months tenure can purchase shares through ESOPs with the programs eligible for E-loans. Extended leasing with buyout has been available since 1992 to managers of enterprises with a book value of less than HUF 1000 million after there is an unsuccessful tender.

A much-discussed Hungarian version of mass privatization was introduced on the eve of elections by the previous government. It was then suspended and its fate under the new government is not known.

The Baltic States

Lithuania seems to have gained an early head-start over the other two countries. It has made use of auctions with vouchers since 1992. Still, the program has encountered political problems and some 40% of the vouchers still are unredeemed.

In 1992 Estonia's first privatizations were management-employee buyouts. Subsequently a system emphasizing centralized multiple tenders succeeded in raising the number of enterprises sold. Now new approaches are being developed which include public offerings with a shift from emphasis on sales prices to the quality of the business plan. Estonian capital will receive preferential treatment in competition with the possibility of a hire-purchase scheme. The possibility of using compensation vouchers in privatization has also been considered.

Latvia has been seen as a laggard. While the use of vouchers was approved in late 1992, their distribution was not scheduled until mid-1993 and they do not yet appear to have played an important role. A new privatization law was passed and put into force in February 1994. It provides that both money and vouchers can be used to purchase state property and sets a minimum of 25% vouchers.

Bulgaria

A law on privatization was passed in April 1992 after a long political discussion going back to 1990. Since the law was passed there has continued to be much quarrelling over specific programs and personnel. The law envisaged centralized auctions and tenders. In 1993 the government adopted a mass privatization program which is not yet underway and is subject to great debate. Bulgaria's first privatization cases have involved major foreign investments.

Romania

The organizational framework for privatisation includes the National Agency for Privatisation (NAP), the State Ownership Fund (SOF), and five Private Ownership Funds (POFs). The NAP is the main organizer of privatisation, including organizing the sale of "assets" and whole companies and some oversight functions with respect to the SOF and POFs.

Romania's government introduced a voucher-based privatization program in 1992. The State Ownership Fund has become the ownership agent for 70% of the shares of state-owned commercial companies, concentrating on very large companies. It is required by law to liquidate its holdings in seven years. Five Private Ownership Funds are assigned to manage, as "mutual funds", the remaining 30% of shares which has been distributed to citizens under the mass privatization program. They are semi-specialized by branch of industry (some branch holdings are assigned to all five) and their focus is more on medium-sized companies. They also manage the "mass privatisation" program in which "certificates of ownership" have been distributed to more than 15 million Romanians. Each certificate has five coupons or claims on each of the five POFs. The coupons can be sold for cash or invested in a POF or one of its constituent companies. The certificates can be offered, for example, for up to 30% of a company in a MEBO (management-employee buyout), which has been the most common form of privatization so far.

Belarus

A first privatization law permitted workers' collectives to purchase their companies at highly discounted prices. A new law on privatization was introduced January 1993 which provided that 50% of enterprises would be sold and put in the budget and 50% sold to the public through lease/options, commercialization or auctions. Voucher privatization was to begin April 1994 with personalized vouchers issued which can not be exchanged for cash. Worker buyouts dominated in 1991 and 1992, but with the change in the law in 1993, 68 enterprises were "privatized" by commercialization and 54 by worker buyouts. This trend accelerated in 1994. Workers waiting to invest in their own place of work would be issued their vouchers at the place of work.

Ukraine

Although the Ukraine passed a law on privatization of SOEs in March 1992, it took until early 1993 before the first medium-sized enterprise was privatized. Under the law a privatization commission decides the method and carries out the privatization. An effort is being made to commercialize enterprises that had been put out under leasing under the former Soviet system. In May 1994 a decree provided for the sale of shares of joint-stock companies. Also, a decree entitles citizens to free shares of state property either through privatization accounts in banks or vouchers.

Kazakhstan

A May 1994 report described private enterprise in Kazakhstan as "relatively small and feeble". A mass privatization program which was planned in 1993 has been recently (spring 1994) launched. Vouchers, which are already distributed to all citizens, can be invested in privatization investment funds (some 140 exist) and the investment funds, in turn, will use them in auctions for state enterprises.

Issues and Possible Explanations of the Comparative Record

We now turn to the question: what factors account for the comparative records of privatization that we have seen? At this point we do not have a unifying theory and will simply try to review some of the evident issues. From the start it is probably helpful to distinguish at least two different issues and factors.

Political Factors

Privatization programs are the result of political processes in the first instance. Different political groups associate privatization in general as well as different means to privatize with different objectives and different impacts on various interest groups. Thus, program choices reflect the weights of these groups and the persuasiveness of their leaders in the political process. We have seen both the opinions of groups and their relative influence change since the launching of privatization.

Among the broader social objectives that privatization in general can contribute to are: justice in the distribution of wealth, the creation of a middle class or other valued political structures, the generation of income for the state, improving the efficiency of enterprises directly by improving internal incentives and indirectly by promoting efficient market allocation mechanisms. Of course, in the political process it must be assumed that individual agents attempt to cover their private interests in broader social and ideological terms.

Economic Factors

By economic factors is meant the incentive and information effects associated with a given program structure. With proper incentives and information, for example, people can be encouraged to participate in privatization projects. Investors and voucher holders need information on the supply of assets for privatization. Bureaucrats, consultants, and employees should "supply" more assets for privatization if they benefit from privatization.

In terms of incentives, for example, there is a tendency for people to see privatization as a zero sum game having a payoff as "either I get richer and you get poorer or you get richer and I get poorer". One way to have privatization be seen as a positive sum game, is to link incentives for privatization to gains from more efficient operation of enterprises, especially dynamic efficiency gains from innovation of new technologies and of new means of organization. Gains (and losses) obviously include social and political benefits, as well as economic ones. Another way to avoid zero-sum mentality is to issue vouchers that permit the general public to share in any gains generated by private agents.

The potential of gains from increased static and dynamic efficiency to provide major incentives for privatization means that it is ultimately difficult to separate an effort to account for the privatization record from the likely behavior of the post-privatization enterprise and the overall effect of privatization on each economy's efficiency. Most of all, because we are discussing the incentives for privatization, it is expectations that matter. Hence, it is what people believe are the effects of privatization rather than the real effects of privatization that initially affect their program choices.

Selected Issues

What are the forms of interaction between the privatization of former SOEs and the overall share of the private sector?

What does this suggest about the two forms of privatization - small privatization and new start-ups versus privatization of former SOEs?

Our table showing the comparative levels of privatization of former SOEs suggests little correlation between the overall share of the private sector and the share of former SOEs privatized. We believe that the overall share of the private sector depends on the extent of small privatization and new start-ups. Are the two processes - small and large privatization - complements or substitutes (competitive)? Or what are the conditions that might make their relationship one way or the other?

Is there a trade-off between the speed and other qualities of privatization? Is it the "quantity" or the "quality" of privatization that counts most?

Mass privatization with vouchers seems to speed privatization. Yet voucher programs have been criticized in the West as well as in the transition countries on the grounds that the resulting ownership forms are weak in enterprise governance as a result of having a large number of small shareholders. This in turn is predicted to result in poor performance of post-privatization enterprises. Good governance and good performance is said to require owner-managers (usually restricted to SMEs), a major (strategic) investor, a developed German-type banking system, or a developed US-type stock market system. Because both the latter are still lacking in transition countries, it is suggested that privatization in Central and Eastern Europe should be restricted to cases where there are owner-managers, or there is a major investor. From this point of view, the approaches used in Hungary and Estonia would be considered more sound than those used in Romania and Lithuania.

Empirically the issues are rather complicated. There is no good evidence of performance differences in enterprises privatized one way or another, except possibly those sold to major foreign investors. In Poland's case the dominant form of liquidation to employee-owned enterprises also results in a theoretically weak governance form.

Centralized privatization, as illustrated by the cases of Poland and Hungary, has not achieved expected targets in terms of numbers of enterprises or assets privatized, although this is the way that the largest enterprises in the region are privatized. Moreover, as in Poland's recent case, political dissatisfaction has been mostly aimed at this form of privatization.

On the supply side, one problem is that project preparation is very demanding in terms of skills and is politically very sensitive. Typically privatization agencies face personnel constraints and often have to make use of expensive consultants. They are often dependent on the management of enterprises being privatized for needed information and cooperation in other ways. This opens the way for accusations of conflicts of interest.

It is also possible, of course, that "regulatory capture" takes place in the forms of interest coalitions between managers and the personnel of privatization agencies. In Hungary, for example, the SPA has been accused of delaying privatization in order to benefit managers. Also, the SPA is said to be a good training ground for new managers when former SPA employees join the management of enterprises that they have just privatized.

The main problem on the demand side has been considered to be the low level of domestic savings compared to the book values of assets to be privatized. However, the problem of the demand for privatized assets is often as much that of attracting available funds as it is in having funds available. Large savings are diverted into government securities with high yields or into foreign currency accounts.

One of the benefits of mass privatization like the Czech one is to increase the supply and diversity of assets offered to savers. It also increases possibilities for portfolio diversification and tends to raise expectations on future yields by decreasing chances of reversible reforms.

While centralized privatization is probably not capable of privatizing the very large numbers needed or of providing what some authors have called the critical minimum levels of privatization, it remains a necessary technique for many cases. It is important, for example, to continue to prepare some enterprises for privatization through public offerings as a way of developing depth in securities markets and financial institutions. Major problem enterprises will have to be considered in special ways, often because they also require restructuring along with privatization. Even though not many enterprises can be handled this way, the accumulated numbers of such special cases will be an important contribution to privatization.

In Poland's case workers were given a general right to buy up to 20% of the shares in their company at a discount of 50%. Szomburg calls this "a necessary price to remove workers' influences on company management". Until commercialization or liquidation the workers' council had the right to block a privatization action and could only be overridden by a proposal by the Ministry of Ownership Transformation (MOT) to the Prime Minister.

There is, of course, a certain political appeal to giving workers a share in the companies where they are going to work. On the other hand, this may also be a way of getting them to accept what eventually turns into a management takeover. Workers are usually in a weak bargaining position, have little interest in normal management problems, and often have high liquidity needs.

In the west, for example, employee ownership is usually unstable. Risk diversification usually calls for separation of employment and saving risks. Often, two classes of employees arise, those who are owners and those who are not. As owner-employees retire, the enterprise becomes a normal management or investor owned firm.

With Romania as an obvious exception, the countries with early mass privatization programs with vouchers have moved faster in the formal privatization of former SOEs than those that have not. For example, the Czech Republic is ahead of Hungary and Poland, Lithuania is ahead of Estonia and Latvia, Russia is ahead of the Ukraine, Belarus, and Kazakhstan. Even Romania is ahead of Bulgaria.

Why is it that some countries chose mass privatization with vouchers and others did not? Does this depend only on ad hoc factors peculiar to each country or are there more general explanations? Estonia and Latvia, for example, may have avoided mass voucher-based programs for a special reason: either it would have risked putting too much economic power in the hands of their Russian minorities or it would have required a discriminatory program that might have risked international approbation.

Estonia, like Hungary, succeeded in significant privatization through foreign sales. Their privatization authorities have been similarly against give-away schemes on grounds of both losing revenues and creating disinterested owners - i.e., on technical and economic grounds.

Even though Poland, like Hungary, still has no mass voucher-based system, unlike Hungary with its seemingly widespread disinterest in voucher schemes, Poland has shown widespread interest. Its problem seems to have been an inability to agree on any practical scheme of mass privatization.

Looking at the Czech Republic and Russia might inform us of factors that favor adoption of mass voucher-based systems. It has been said of both that vouchers were used to incite widespread public interest and support of mass privatization schemes. Still, vouchers were not at first accepted publicly in either country. In the Czech Republic they only became popular, it seems, after the investment funds began competitive advertisements.

Perhaps other common factors should be considered. In both countries, the idea of mass voucher-based privatization was launched early in transition before a political consensus diminished. They had backing at the highest political level and were promoted by rather dedicated persons at the technical level. Finally, both programs found advocacy groups with strong motivations for personal gain. In Russia it is "the industrialists" or managerial group, while in the Czech Republic it is both the investment funds and the managerial group. In both countries, for example, managers have largely decided the privatization projects, while vouchers provided a convenient way to attract outside support - roughly about 50% of total funds in both cases.

All of these similarities should not lead us to forget significant differences in the Czech and Russian programs. By setting up competition among private investment funds and competition in the submission of alternative privatization project for each enterprise, the Czech system created strong incentives to provide information. It also has provided some strong limits on managers. First, there was more transparency concerning privatization programs and enterprise financial conditions available to the public and the investment funds. Second, the public have used the investment funds extensively for risk immunization. Third, the investment funds should be able to eventually be in a position to exert strong governance forces over the managers. None of these factors seem available in the Russian system.

As the Russian program has been carried out under Chubais, its main immediate appeal is to managers and its main political effect may be the breaking of connections between the central bureaucracy and the managerial group, thus leading to a more decentralized Russian economy and polity. In the near future, governance will have to come primarily from market forces and where markets are weak, managers will have considerable room for opportunistic behavior.

A key difference in the Romanian program was that public voucher holders had no choices in either the investment funds used or the enterprises that would be privatized. At the same time, managers and employees have had a diminished role in choosing how their enterprise would be privatized. The Romanian system seems to have maximized the role of the central bureaucracy and so enhanced its ability to benefit materially from privatization. Possibly this is part of Iliescu's "social contract". In any case, neither the public as a whole nor generally the employees of privatized enterprises see future benefits from privatization in the Romanian system.

Not all the countries in the region announced their intention to adopt some sort of mass privatization program. There are at least two reasons. One is simply the strong examples of success. Another is the possibility in Hungary and Poland that the good projects have now been privatized and that remaining projects have real values far below their book values or the amounts that would be politically acceptable to sell them for. Giving vouchers or providing other subsidies to citizen acquisition can be a politically acceptable solution.

Strictly speaking, mass privatization in the Czech Republic and the Russian Federation resulted from a state act that compelled enterprises en masse to privatize. Vouchers enabled the process politically and economically by increasing the demand for privatized assets. In the Russian case, demand was also enhanced by selling shares at discounted prices to workers' collectives. A Hungarian scheme would use subsidized credits in place of vouchers. But all of the forms of asset demand subsidization could be undertaken without a state act to compel privatization en masse.

Any country contemplating a mass privatization scheme needs to decide certain key components, among which we find the following to be critical:
- What is the role of the privatization authority - regulative or directive?
- What form of asset demand subsidy, if any, should be used: vouchers, price discounted shares, or subsidized credits?
- If vouchers are used, should they be issued in name or to the bearer, should they be used only for share purchases or should other forms of assets be available? How much choice in share purchases should be available?
- Should investment funds be predesignated by the state or open to entry competition? Should they be managed by state bureaucrats or by outside consultants? What forms of incentives should be offered, if any?

Concluding Comments

There is not an appropriate way to conclude a paper whose main purpose is to survey information and issues concerning that information. The main contribution of our paper is to estimate the relative extent of privatization of former SOEs in Central and Eastern Europe. We have not seen that done elsewhere.

We have also acquired a relatively good sense of the extent to which three general alternative methods of privatization have contributed. In terms of numbers of enterprises, mass privatization and decentralized privatization have been important. Now, it seems, with one or two exceptions, all countries will institute some form of mass privatization.

Given the rates of privatization that we have seen, what is likely to be the future ownership structures of former SOEs in the region? This question would be better answered on the basis of a more detailed study that considers sector differences. Also, political issues loom rather large outside of Central Europe and the Baltic States.

Bibliography

Bilsen, V., "Privatization, company management and performance: a comparative study of privatization methods in the Czech Republic, Hungary, Poland and Slovakia" in Company Management and Capital Market Development in the Transition. Edited by M. Jackson and V. Bilsen. LICOS Studies on the Transitions in Central and Eastern Europe, Volume 2. Aldershot-Hants: Avebury, 1994.

Boycko, M., Shleifer, A., and Vishny, R., "The Progress of Russian Privatization", in Economic Transformation in Russia, edited by A. Aslund. London: Pinter, 1994.

Carlin, W., Enterprise restructuring in the transition: an analytical survey of the case study evidence from Central and Eastern Europe. Working paper No. 14. European Bank for Reconstruction and Development. July 1994.

Estonian Privatization Agency, Privatization in Estonia 1994. Tallin, May 1994.

Frydman, R. and Rapaczynski, A., Privatization in Eastern Europe: Is the State Withering Away?. Budapest: Central European University Press, 1994.

Galgoczi, B., "Strategies of Privatization in Hungary", Research Institute for Social Studies, Budapest, April 1994.

Jackson, M., (1994a) "Property rights, company organization and governance in the transition" in Company Management and Capital Market Development in the Transition. Edited by M. Jackson and V. Bilsen. LICOS Studies on the Transitions in Central and Eastern Europe, Volume 2. Aldershot-Hants: Avebury, 1994.

Jackson, M., (1994b) "Political Incredibility and Weak Transformation in Romania", East-Central European Economies in Transition. Papers submitted to the Joint Economic Committee, Congress of the United States. U.S. Government Printing Office: Washington, DC, 1994 forthcoming.

Jackson, M., and Bilsen, V., "A Comparative Record of Privatization in Central and Eastern Europe: The Situation in 1994", Discussion Papers on the Economic Transformation: Policy, Institutions and Structure. Leuven Institute for Central and East European Studies (LICOS), Katholieke Universiteit Leuven, Belgium. No. 32/1994.

Kell, K., "Foreign investment and privatisation in Estonia" NATO Economics Colloquium 1994. Brussels, 29-30 June 1994.

Kotrba, J. and Svejnar, J., "Rapid and Multifaceted Privatization: Experience of Czech and Slovak Republics", Research Paper Series Enterprise Behavior and Economic Reforms, Eastern Europe and FSU. Number EE-RPS #19, World Bank, 1993.

Linz, S., "The Privatization of Russian Industry", RFE/RL Research Report, 3:10, 11 March 1994.

Loginov, A., "Privatization in Russia: Results and Prospects" NATO Economics Colloquium 1994. Brussels, 29-30 June 1994.

Major, Ivan, Privatization in Eastern Europe, London: Elgar, 1933.

Mujzel, J., "State-owned enterprises in transition: prospects amidst crisis", in Company Management and Capital Market Development in the Transition. Edited by M. Jackson and V. Bilsen. LICOS Studies on the Transitions in Central and Eastern Europe, Volume 2. Aldershot-Hants: Avebury, 1994.

OECD, Economic Surveys: Hungary. Paris, 1993.

Rainys, G., "Privatization and Conversion of Military Industries in Lithuania". NATO Economics Colloquium 1994. Brussels, 29-30 June 1994.

Sabela, R., "Conversion and Privatisation Issues", NATO Economics Colloquium 1994. Brussels, 29-30 June 1994.

Sutela, P., "Insider Privatization in Russia: Speculations on System Change", Europe-Asia Studies, 46:3, 1994.

Szomburg, J., "Poland: Country Study", Methods of Privatizing Large Enterprises, OECD: Paris, 1993.

Voszka, E., "Variation on the Theme of Self-Privatization", Acta Oeconomica, 45 (3-4), 1993.

PRIVATE SECTOR AND PRIVATIZATION IN SOME CENTRAL AND EAST EUROPEAN COUNTRIES: PECULIARITIES IN HUNGARY

Éva Ehrlich

Hungary, Poland, and the Czech Republic have all made good progress in bringing business and commercial activities back into the private sector. But Slovakia has a long way to go, and large-scale privatization in the three other countries may take at least ten years, says Éva Ehrlich. The pace is slowing now that all the best companies have been sold off. Those in charge of the sell-off - the managers and directors from the old regime - are also holding things up. They're nervous. It will take an economic recovery to calm them down.

Éva Ehrlich is Research Director of the World Economic Institute of the Hungarian Academy of Sciences and professor of economics at Budapest University.

Czech and Slovak Republic, Hungary and Poland: Visegrad Four *(hereafter V4).*

First of all let me emphasize that by now there exists an abundant Eastern and Western literature on the spreading of the private sector in the East Central European countries and on various issues related to the privatisation of state property. Given the limited scope of the present paper, it can only touch upon rather than elaborate and discuss in detail, with references, the most important aspects of these far-reaching and rather complex topics.

In the V4 countries, as in all the former socialist countries, one of the basic issues of social and economic transformation, the change of regime, is the dissolution of state property and gradual establishment of the primacy of private property. Irrespective of party affiliation, the political elites and economic experts of the countries in question share the general view that only the predominance of private property, the personal interest of the proprietor to multiply his/her capital and the personal financial liability involved can put an end to economic squandering, improve the efficiency, competitivity and productivity of the economy and lead to a rational reform of its structure, that is, help overcome the economic crisis and launch modernisation. All V4 countries emphasize that, apart from its strictly economic consequences, privatisation alone can broaden the stratum (class) of property owners, an essential prerequisite of the long-term viability of democracy.

What were the main difficulties the V4 countries had to face in the course of privatisation? How did the private sector extend and how much progress did privatisation make in the countries under scrutiny? What are the characteristic forms of privatisation and the main advantages and drawbacks of the forms implemented so far? In what follows, we shall make an attempt to answer the above questions.

Difficulties of Privatization

At the time of the change of regime, politicians and economic experts alike expected that three to four years would suffice to break the dominance of state property in Central and Eastern Europe. This illusion was shattered by the very first privatisation measures. It became obvious that the decomposition of state property involved problems of an unprecedented order of magnitude.

Unlike the partial privatisation in the market economies and the developing countries, which involves no more than a few big state-owned enterprises in one or another branch of the national economy, the decisive majority, 60 to 70 percent, of all business assets had to change owners, i.e., undergo privatisation.

The scarcity of domestic investment capital, the lack of a property-owning class and lack of experience made the commonplace market economy practice of "first improve, then sell" applicable to a very limited extent only.

On the supply side, the most serious problem was the inadequacy of the inherited economic structure adapted to the needs of COMECON cooperation in every country and rendered totally inadequate by the collapse of the COMECON market and the Soviet one within it. Other onerous aspects of the heritage were the many wasted big investments, the accumulated debts of the big state companies, over-manning (latent unemployment), a centralised administration and the high level of income withdrawal. The situation was further aggravated by the first market economy measures, namely the liberalisation of foreign trade, the cut-back on allocations and severe financial policy measures producing higher interest rates. In the short run, these factors decreased the competitivity and profitability of enterprises and, consequently, the value of state assets awaiting privatisation and valued (devalued) according to their income - generating potential as well.

Demand was hit by the continued shrinking of the national economies, and the ensuing decline of the standards of living and of domestic demand, as well as by the recession in the developed market economies and keen international competition for investments.

Moreover, there were no methods to coordinate supply and demand, that had been tested under similar circumstances. The institutions necessary for the adaptation of procedures - the legal system, Stock Exchange, investment funds, venture capital societies, social security and pension funds - were underdeveloped or non-existent.[1]

As a result of the above-mentioned primary difficulties, the prevailing unfavourable global economic climate and various political considerations, the governments in office since 1989-1990 experimented with the most various forms of privatisation and applied highly different methods and technique.

Extension of the Private Sector [2]

The most significant measure of the spread of the private sector is the growth of the number of private businesses that has taken place in recent years (in Hungary and Poland already from the second half of the 1980s on).

Some private businesses are extremely successful and increase their staff and capital fast. There are already some in every V4 country that had started out as small businesses, grew to medium-sized ones and are now expanding abroad with the assistance of foreign partners (or co-owners). Some joint-venture and foreign companies are even capable of capital exports. The number of joint-venture (foreign- and national-owned) businesses is quite significant and on the rise in every country under scrutiny, especially in Hungary.

In spite of this, however, the spread of private businesses in the V4 countries is still rather limited, albeit now for economic rather than political reasons. These reasons are: the tightness of national investment funds, the embryonic state of the capital market, an atmosphere of overall economic uncertainty, inflation, a lack of the necessary market experience required for successful operation and depression of solvent demand.

For the same reasons, private business is often and to a growing extent a secondary activity in every one of the V4 countries; primary jobs offering greater financial and social security are retained wherever possible.

Dummy small businesses established to evade taxation, conceal revenue or stow away property are on the rise in all V4 countries and especially in Hungary and Poland. In Hungary, for instance, 40 percent of the 850 thousand small businesses registered at end-1993 are "dummies, paper organisations" or "phantom firms". The registered small enterprises often never start operation or suspend it for a shorter or longer period to postpone payment obligations.[4] This means that a significant proportion of the newly founded private businesses - some foreign but mostly national ones - are only testing the water.

The Hidden Economy

From the 1980s on, the non-official (i.e., non-registered) economic sector appeared and began spreading (in different degrees) in the V4 countries as well. Various estimates suggest that the proportion of the non-official, or hidden, economy kept growing in the countries under scrutiny (especially in Poland, Hungary and Slovakia). Unfortunately, relevant official data are available for

Hungary only.[4] It seemed logical to expect that once the constraints imposed on the private sector were abolished, the non-official sector would die out or at least retreat considerably. This tendency, however, has asserted itself but partially: the hidden, grey and black economy beyond the reach of taxation and income declaration is flourishing and spreading.

Tourism concentrating on buying and selling, that is, profiting from the discrepancies of prices and the exchange rates has proved a most profitable business (impossible to tax). With the opening of the borders, smuggling, the dodging of tax and tariff regulations, became much more frequent. With the contribution of various international mafias operating in the European, Arab and Asian market economies, it covers goods originating not only from the V4 countries but from other developed and developing countries all over the world, including drugs and weapons.

The syphoning-off of goods originating in the state sector and the organised theft, robbery and looting of individual property (valuable goods kept at home, motor cars etc.) to resell them is also on the rise.

It should be noted, however, that the existence of "dummy" organisations and small businesses at the periphery of the economy is also motivated by the wish to be ready to grasp any business opportunity that may arise.

In the production sector, especially in agriculture, construction and personal services, it is general practice to leave a considerable proportion of the activities of the registered organisation out of the books, to operate unregistered private organisations and employ unregistered workers, often foreigners looking for casual work.

The anomalies of small businesses and the extent of the hidden (grey and black) economy induce uncertainty, disorganisation and legal chaos in the economies in question. Moreover, the illegal units often operate in the most dynamic sectors of the economy, thereby depriving the state of considerable tax revenue and aggravating the already acute problems of the state and budgetary financing of public expenses caused by the shrinking of the economy.

Despite significant endeavours to cut back the unofficial economy, to stop its spreading and integrate it into the legal economy, no breakthrough has occurred in this field so far.

Proportions of the Private Sector in the V4 Economies

The current private sector/GDP ratios are shown in Tables 1, 2 and 3, respectively, for Poland, Hungary and the Czech Republic. As for Slovakia, a single datum is available: in 1992, the private sector contributed 4.7 percent only of the total industrial output.[5] This minuscule share suggests that the privatisation of state property has hardly begun as yet in Slovakia. In Poland, on the other hand, in 1992 the private sector contributed as much as 47.2 percent of the official GDP, while in the Czech Republic (first half of 1993) the corresponding figure was 44%. In Hungary in 1992 the combined contribution of the domestic and foreign private sector made up 44 percent of the official GDP, not including the production of the hidden economy, while their share in the so-called "extended GDP" including the production of the hidden economy as well amounted to as much as 50 percent.

With the strengthening of private property, the unit size structure of the economies in question is being transformed. The "inverted pyramid"[6] that used to characterise it (few small- and medium-size economic units, many large ones) is being demolished, although so far mainly by the rapid growth of small (and to a lesser extent medium-size) business entities, especially in the services sector. Recently, the "inverted pyramid" of the manufacturing industry,[7] too, has begun to turn the right way up.[8]

As for the contribution of foreign capital in the privatisation process, no data are available except for Hungary. Given the fact that half of the total amount of foreign capital entering the East Central European countries so far went to investments or the purchase of state-owned companies in Hungary, it seems reasonable enough to assume that, of all the V4 countries, it played a significant role in the privatisation processes of Hungary only. However, big transnational firms with widespread international networks are already present in practically every V4 country, and the number of small and large joint-ventures (foreign and national) companies is rising fast everywhere.

In 1988-1993, the amount of foreign functioning capital investments totalled USD 6 billion.[9] Estimates suggest that approximately one third of that amount was spent buying state-owned companies and on restructuring, developing and modernising of companies or parts of them.[10] In Hungary, in the period 1990-1993, the privatisation of state-owned property to foreigners brought in $1.8 billion revenue,[11] 56% of which was paid in cash (60% in foreign currencies, 40% in HUF).[12] Although at the time of its inauguration, the present Hungarian government promised to channel the total privatisation revenue to investment and development projects, budgetary constraints obliged it to use a considerable amount on financing the budget deficit.

Information suggests that the privatisation of state property (with the assistance of foreign capital in Hungary) has made good progress in all the East Central European countries except Slovakia. All three countries are close to the point where state property will no longer dominate the economy.

The following paragraphs survey the main types of the privatisation of state property.

Privatization Forms: Advantages and Drawbacks

The transformation of state-owned companies is a precondition of privatisation. The legal frameworks of the transformation of state companies into joint-stock and limited liability companies have been established in all three countries (in Poland and Hungary already in 1987-88, before the change of regime). This has made it possible to attract both domestic and foreign capital to buy the transformed state companies.

So far the V4 countries have adopted two main forms of privatisation:
• Privatisation by sale: state-owned companies are offered for sale to domestic and foreign investors.
• Privatisation by distribution or allocation of assets: parts of the state assets are distributed among the population free of charge or at a favourable, price in the form of property vouchers.

So far the first form prevailed in Hungary and the second in the Czech and Slovak Republics. Poland has already tried out both. Both forms and many combinations of the two exist not only in Poland, but in the rest of the East Central European countries as well. In the Czech and Slovak Republics, for instance, where so far distribution was the order of the day,[13] the various forms of sale at market price are also present.

Both basic forms of privatisation have their specific advantages and drawbacks.[14]

Firstly, experts think that privatisation by sale is the most promising alternative from the point of view of the restructuring and modernisation of the economy. It adapts best to the demands of the market mechanism, and the impoverished Central and East European states giving significant revenue to cover

Finally, privatization creates true owners - whose own capital is at stake. The main drawback of this form is its slowness due partly to the difficulties of property assessment and partly to the problems of selecting the right buyer. It favours those groups, rather small in the countries under scrutiny (and those entrepreneurs) who already own some property (house, flat, resort house, car, jewellery etc.) or money (foreign currency, cash etc.) to invest, or who have a certain amount of capital as well, accumulated in the old regime.

Secondly, the majority of the Central and Eastern European countries have so far preferred the distribution/allocation form of privatisation. Distribution, free or preferential allocation are "justified" by the fact that state property or a significant part of it was produced by the citizens in the past 40 years who are, therefore, entitled to their share. This method does not require a large amount of capital at a time when domestic savings are scarce. It also ensures that the whole population gets involved in the privatisation process, and brings quick formal ownership transition, stimulates the extension of the developing capital market and further accelerates the growth of the relative weight of private property. Its essential drawback is that "passive property"[15] acquired for free or at a preferential price (including employee buy-out at preferential prices or with credits) is something formal in the sense that the new owner does not take a risk, his/her interest lies in maintaining and preserving the existing company (organisation). This is a more comfortable and favourable alternative than restructuring and modernisation involving much greater risks, but it hinders the assertion of economic rationale. Another drawback is that it provides the state struggling with budgetary problems, created by a shrinking economy, no new resources for help and no revenue to promote modernisation. Also, this method is said to be expensive to administer.

The above advantages and drawbacks of the two forms of privatisation explain why the V4 countries attempt to apply them simultaneously: they try to diminish the inevitable drawbacks associated with one by combining it with the other. Although competent professional circles are of the opinion that real ownership transition, privatisation, economic restructuring and modernisation are realised best via the market form, providing the state with a certain revenue as well, its slowness makes it useful to supplement it with distribution/allocation (including employee buyout).

The combination of the two forms is warranted by political and social considerations as well. In every country under scrutiny, privatisation by sale is entrusted to state agencies, i.e., the process is governed from above to a smaller or greater extent.[16]

It is no wonder that privatisation, the transformation of the economic ownership relations at the basis of political power, is often considered a political issue (a battleground for party interests). The public mostly ignores the sales terms or cannot see through them. Evaluation of assets is done by foreign companies and specialist organisations. The criteria for setting the sale price, and most terms and stipulations included in the final contracts, are usually confidential and themselves suspicious to the public. Sale inevitably means circumventing the new laws, working with the managerial level, operating the assets in question and the spreading of corruption at all levels.

Distribution is more transparent for the public. Ownership transition immediately imposes severe new burdens (e.g., decline of the standards of living, unemployment, professional reorientation etc.) and problems practically unknown before (e.g devaluation of assets, renovation, modernisation etc.) on the whole population. New costs, a new system of values and attitudes and other consequences of transition appear at a time when the economic advantages of modernisation are not obvious as yet. Distribution, as a supplementary form, is helpful in providing political stability and social support in the long period of ownership transition not only for privatisation, but also for the whole process of transformation.

Privatisation is carried out by the Ministry for Privatisation and Administration of National Property in Czech and Slovak Republic, the State Property Agency and the State Holding Company in Hungary and the Ministry of Ownership Transition in Poland.

Types and Methods of Privatization

In general, two types of privatisation are distinguished: small- and large-scale privatisation.

Small privatisation occurs in the domains of retail trade, catering, tourism, the building industry and other spheres of public and industrial services. It aims at the liquidation of state (council) monopolies in the above fields consisting of relatively small entities (e.g., shops) centralised by administrative measures on the one hand and the ownership transfer or lease of small units (e.g., small plants or shop premises) capable of independent functioning on the other. In all V4 countries, small privatisation characteristically broke up networks (e.g., retail networks) and sold their units (shops, workshops) via open bidding.

In Czechoslovakia, compensation by distribution was integrated into small privatisation. In this framework, former owners or their direct relatives could reclaim properties nationalised after February 1948 [17] if the latter still existed physically.

In Hungary, small privatisation by bidding did not take former ownership into account. Former owners or their direct relatives received compensation vouchers for property nationalised or forcibly collectivised after 1948. A rather strict limit was applied: the maximum value of the compensation vouchers allocated for a single property or to a single person was set at HUF 5 million (c. USD 55 thousand). Vouchers can be used to purchase state or co-operative assets through bidding (the claims of former landowners or their descendants are to be met by state farm or cooperative holdings in the given area), to guarantee start-up credits allocated for new businesses, for the preferential purchase of council flats, or to round off the pension of those over 70 years old, etc. [18] A secondary trade in compensation vouchers has evolved: the market price is well below par. The partial restitution of church property (certain schools, convents etc.) is also in progress.

As for Poland, to the best of our knowledge, no restitution or a solution similar to the Hungarian compensation vouchers is being considered there.

Small privatisation has - for the most part - ended (with the exception of Slovakia). Privatisation has obviously improved the quality, management and variety of trade and of services. This significant improvement, however, is not only due to the privatisation of state property, but to a considerable extent also to the fact that new business ventures in these fields yield high profit practically at once.

The main problem of small privatisation was and still is that most of the premises suitable for small businesses still belong to the state (or the municipality) and, therefore, "privatisation" is restricted to their lease. The terms of lease, however, are rather unstable: they may change year in, year out, often quite drastically. This is why private enterprises operating on such rights are often short-term, temporary ventures — an unfavourable phenomenon from the point of view of market development.

The true difficulties of privatisation, however, are encountered in large-scale privatisation. This latter is to transform mammoth companies, break their monopoly, divide them into smaller units and transfer them to private (local, foreign or joint) owners. Large-scale privatisation has just begun in the countries under scrutiny. The growing share of the private sector in the industrial output (cf. Tables I and III) has so far resulted mainly from the rapid growth of the number of small and to some extent also medium-size companies operating in the industrial domain and not the privatisation of big companies.

Methods and Techniques of Large-scale Privatization

As early as 1989 and especially 1990, the management of many state-owned big companies with relatively good business results took the first steps, helped by their former business contacts, either to sell the company or part of it, or attract foreign capital. Such actions (the so-called spontaneous or nomenklatura privatisation) were, of course, in the best interest of the old management wishing to preserve their positions (maybe at a somewhat lower level and with more limited authority) and to acquire property. However, in the majority of the cases, this coincided with a restructuring process. Production units were improved and modernised. Business policy was adapted to market demand and a significant number of jobs were preserved. Government agencies established to control privatisation, however, first halted this process and later on took full control of it for political and power considerations (first in Poland but later on in Hungary as well).[19]

At the same time, they slow down the progress of privatisation initiated from below.

In the framework of "nationalised privatisation", the responsible government agency usually invites closed or, in some cases open, tenders to privatise big state companies, in accordance with the programme adopted by the government. The participants and winners of such tenders represent, for the most, capital, although some capital-strong domestic buyers capable of mobilising significant bank credits have also appeared on the scene. The foreign buyout of national assets provokes some anxiety in the Czech Republic, Poland and Slovakia, not shared, officially, by Hungary. However, there are some very definite signs (in Hungary, too) that foreign buyers often want to conquer new markets rather than boost the activity of the purchased company.

The aim of the already mentioned distribution or preferential sale of state property form of property vouchers is to accelerate privatisation and produce share-owning citizens. "Voucher privatisation" began in Czechoslovakia in Autumn 1991. Every citizen was entitled to purchase state property coupons (vouchers) at a fraction of the real price. This programme became a success after the establishment of investment funds on state initiative to take over citizens' vouchers and purchase shares of state-owned companies with them, especially when the funds in question also guaranteed to pay, on demand, after having exchanged the vouchers for shares, the market price which was at least ten times the original purchase value of the vouchers. The exchange of vouchers for company shares is making good progress in Czechoslovakia (Their exchange for cash, on the other hand, was postponed). In the meanwhile, the assets of the state-owned companies are devalued, and part of the companies in question try to survive by consuming their own assets.

Poland adopted a special scheme to distribute state property that was approved by the Seym [Polish Parliament] in April 1993. More than half the shares of the state enterprises taking part in the action, the majority of all state enterprises, are distributed among some 20 state holdings established for this purpose. Some 10 percent of the shares will be given to their respective employees (the rest goes to the Treasury first). According to this scheme, holding shares will also be distributed to all citizens as a right. This way they will own a share of both their company and the total enterprise assets of the national economy.

The idea of free property-share distribution is fairly unpopular among experts, who emphasize that small share packages owned by small investors will not inspire a genuine feeling of ownership, nor will they lead to strong ownership control. In addition, this creates inflationary expectations - that the preferentially bought shares are guaranteed to be bought in the future. According to common Hungarian views the state-run investment funds will become such huge concentrated economic powers, which - especially if they become involved in political decision-making - will generate state interventions time and again - instead of market impetus. It would be right to refrain from this practice especially as recent history makes former socialist countries specially susceptible.[20]

Competent experts in Hungary propose another form of property distribution. Part of the share block representing profitable state property should be allocated to budgetary public services institutions and societies on the model of the historical public services funds. (Parliament has already passed a bill according to which Social Security should be allocated HUF 300 billion worth of business property.) This is expected to alleviate the burdens of public finances and strengthen the economic autonomy and discipline of the beneficiaries (e.g. old-age-pension funds, big universities and hospitals, municipalities etc.). The problem of implementing this concept is that Hungarian economy suffers from a shortage of profitable state property. This makes the options of establishing profitable public services funds rather limited.

The method of employee buyout is discussed separately, despite its being a special case of "nationalised privatisation", carried out with the approval and under the control of state agencies of privatisation. Its treatment as a separate category is justified by the fact that, as a result, self-managing (or co-operative) economic units may be established. Employee buy-out is most popular in Poland, but it is an existing, though minor, form of privatisation in Hungary and Czechoslovakia as well. It can be efficient and give a competitive edge in cases where the activity to be continued is transparent for the employee, and the operation of the company in question requires special skills and a special know-how. Results obtained so far are positive in those instances where transition led to the profit-oriented performance of workers' self-management or cooperatives adapted to the market conditions.

Current Problems and Dilemmas

It seems that large-scale privatisation will take at least another decade in the V4 countries.

The first great wave of privatisation whether by sale or distribution affected the relatively prosperous big companies that were sold to domestic or foreign buyers quickly. Selling the remaining companies, still state-owned for the most, is a much more difficult task. Given their obsolete structure, low adaptation and income-generating potential, accumulated debts, the uncertainty of the crisis management staff — the result of several factors —, and general decline, it is very difficult to find prospective, local or foreign, buyers. Meanwhile, the assets in question are depreciating month by month.

With the exception of Poland, large-scale privatisation is inevitably slowed down by the continuing shrinking of the economies in question, the further decrease of solvent demand, the uncertain profit prospects of V4 big companies offered for sale and the uncertain return on invested capital.

The fusion of economy and politics was one of the most important attributes of state socialism — if not the most essential one. The objective of privatisation, on the other hand, is to restore the independence of the economy by liberating it from political influence. At the same time, the transfer of state assets (that have, for the most, been the property of the state from the very start) to private owners exerts a fundamental influence on the political and economic structure of society. Privatisation obviously affects the power-political dimension of society, whether by its objectives, its agents or its implementation. Given the inevitable role of the state or rather the government in "denationalization", the process inevitably bears the traits of power (party) policy considerations rather than the marks of economic rationality. Economically "perfect" processes have little chance to be introduced in practice.[21]

Privatisation practice brought to the surface many difficulties unforeseen or underestimated by the experts previously. The most essential of these was the unexpected struggle of the various social strata provoked by the implementation of "nationalised privatisation". No one realised that the clashes of political forces (especially in Hungary) would deprive enterprise management staffs of their self-assurance and turn them into arch-impeders of the privatisation process. Large-scale privatisation requires the active contribution of experts with a thorough knowledge of the given field and the potential markets and good personal contacts, but these people were not considered reliable enough by the newly elected governments (either in Hungary or in Poland).

The above overview of the methods of privatisation was an attempt to present the most common forms of privatisation in the countries under scrutiny and the philosophy behind them. The future alone will tell what other methods and combinations will be required to pursue the ever more difficult process.

One thing, however, seems certain: if economic growth begins and proves lasting and if internal demand starts expanding, the privatisation of the remaining big state companies[22] may well accelerate under the impact of favourable economic and profit prospects.

It seems most likely, however, that the state sector of the national economy will remain higher, in the future, too, than the standard of the developed market economies of our days formed by a historical process of organic development.

As a result of the early illusions concerning the deadline of the privatisation process, experts did not pay much attention to the problem of the management of state-owned enterprises until a domestic or foreign buyer is found. How can big state-owned be managed successfully, in a market-conforming way, throughout the long period of the development of market economy? In our opinion, the operation and privatisation of the economic assets of the state should be supervised and controlled by private business companies.

The share of private sector in the GDP, different branches of economy and employment

Year	Poland[1] in					
	GDP	Industrial Output	Construction	Transport	Trade	Employment (excl. agr.)
	Total = 100					
1990	30,9	18,2	39,7	20,1	51,3	33,6
1992	47,2	35,5	76,5	34,9	85,4	42,2
1993	-	-	-	-	-	46,2

Source: Bogdan (1994)

The property structure of official GDP

Year	Hungary		
	Public	Private	Foreign
		property	
1980	90	10	0
1985	85	15	0
1989	80	20	0
1990	76	23	1
1991	70	27	3
1992	56	36	8
The property structure of the Extended GDP[1]			
1980	83	17	0
1985	79	21	0
1989	74	26	0
1990	70	29	1
1991	63	34	3
1992	50	42	8

Note: 1 incl. hidden economy
Source: Arvay-Vértes (1994)
I

The share of private sector in the GDP, different branches of economy

Year	Czech Republic[1] in		
	GDP	Industrial Output	Construction
	Total = 100		
1990	4,0	-	-
1991	10,62	-	-
1992	20,0	-	-
1993 (6 months)	44,0	18,0	18,0

Source: 1 Kouba (1993)
2 Hunya (1993)

Notes

1. The ideas listed under points 3, 4 and 5 are borrowed from a study by Voszka (1994).
2. In discussing this issue, the author relies on papers by Ehrlich-Révész (1993), (1994).
3. Vértes Cs. (1944).
4. Share of the hidden economy in % of the Hungarian GDP:
   1980   13 %
   1985   14 %
   1989   16 %
   1990   20 %
   1991   25 %
   1992   30 %
   Source: Arvay-Vértes (1994).
5. Kouba (1993).
6. Schweitzer (1982).
7. The favourable alteration of the size structure of the manufacturing industry producing smaller units is the result of a triple process. First of all, the gradual separation of services from manufacturing (and agriculture as well) and their reorganisation in an independent framework suitable for their quick adaptation to demand, a process of long international standing, began in the V4 countries as well. Second, as monopolies are becoming a thing of the past in practically every sphere, the former large manufacturing and services entities are cut down to smaller units. Finally, the independent operation of their smaller competitive sub-units figures in the survival and property salvaging strategies of all the former highly subsidised large or mammoth production companies.
8. Ehrlich (1985), (1993).
9. In the first half of 1993, per capita foreign capital investment was c. USD 600 in Hungary, as opposed to USD 300 in Slovenia, USD 180 in the Czech Republic, USD 100 in Slovakia and USD 50 in Poland.
   The breakdown by countries of foreign capital investments in Hungary was as follows: USA 29%; Germany 20%; Austria 14%; France 7%, Italy 6%; Japan 5%; The Netherlands and the UK 4% each. The remaining 11% was provided by various other countries. (Csáki (1993), p.20).
10. Foreign capital investments in Hungarian privatisation originated from the following countries: Austria 23%; Germany 19%; USA and The Netherlands 10-10%; the UK 8%; Sweden 5%; Switzerland 5%. Belgium 3%; CIS countries 3%; Italy 2%. The remaining 12% originated from various other countries. Source: State Property Agency Privatisation Monitor, March 1994, quoted in Novák (1994).
11. *Source:* State Property Agency Privatisation Monitor, March 1994, quoted in Novák (1994).
12. Szanyi (1994).
13. Estimations suggest that one third of the state-owned business assets was privatised this way [Kouba (1993)].
14. See among others the study by Chin (1993) providing a near-complete content analysis of the most essential, mainly Western, privatisation literature.at least some of the costs of modernisation.
15. The term originates from Ellerman-Vachcic-Petrin (1991).
16. The agencies in question were formed between 1989 and 1991. Their task was to elaborate privatisation measures under the supervision of the state, to design companies remaining in state hands, to supervise the assessment of the assets of state companies or have it done by (local or foreign) firms designated or approved by the agency, to control and even manage, if this is deemed necessary, the whole privatisation process (including the choice of potential domestic and/or foreign buyers) of certain companies and, finally, to supervise in retrospect and occasionally even to cancel privatisations (involving foreign partners as well) sanctified by contract on the initiative of the company in question or the firm assessing its assets.
17. Large factories, estates and banks had been nationalised before 1948.
18. The total value of the allocated compensation vouchers equals approximately 10 percent of the total annual labour income.
19. The majority of the decisions relating to large privatisation is taken by the government agencies (ministries) responsible for this task. As a result of their direction and control (in Slovakia, for instance, Prime Minister Meciar used to be Minister of Privatisation), bureaucrats (not

businessmen) with no special knowledge of the field spend long months or even years looking for prospective buyers (mainly foreign ones) offering "the best potential conditions".

20. Inspite of several experts' view, in the very last month of being in office (just before the parliamentary elections) the Government launched a so-called "Small Investors' Share Programme" which means in fact an almost free asset distribution among citizens (the programme is based upon a preferential credit facility).

21. In formulating the ideas expressed under this point the author relied on the study by Voszka (1994).

22. In Hungary, in 1989-1993, one third of the state-owned big manufacturing companies went bankrupt and await liquidation now. [Ehrlich-Révész, (1994)].

PRIVATIZATION AND CONVERSION OF MILITARY INDUSTRIES IN LITHUANIA

Gediminas Rainys

In the Baltic countries, the business of government is to get the government to mind its own business. That means selling off state enterprises as rapidly as possible. But how? Vouchers give more people a stake in the system; shares bring more money in as a stock market develops. Lithuania has gone for the voucher method, while neighbours Latvia and Estonia prefer the more commercial option. But they all have two problems in common, according to Gediminas Rainys: they need new markets for their goods that former Soviet customers aren't buying; and they need foreign know-how and investment.

Gediminas Rainys is a Senior Economist at the Economic Research Centre in Vilnius.

Privatization and Conversion of Military Industries in Lithuania

The main goal of ownership transformation in Lithuania is to restore private property rights as quickly as possible, to reduce state property to its minimum and thereby to create one of the most important preconditions for the development of an efficient market economy.

During the Soviet period, property was nationalised. Now the government of Lithuania is carrying out the restitution of the nationalised property and paying off compensation. This is causing trouble in the privatization process.

During the period of preparation of the privatization scheme there was heated debate in Lithuania on some fundamental dilemmas. The major dispute was on the issue of whether to implement commercial or distributional privatization. The main argument of the supporters of commercial privatization was that it is the only scheme which can provide efficient private owners.

The supporters of voucher privatization criticised this position, maintaining that in view of the purchasing power of potential investors, privatization could take a very long time and the inefficiency of the remaining state-owned entities would not be compensated by the efficiency of the small number of privatized enterprises. Commercial privatization would create a situation in which ownership could be concentrated in the hands of the former nomenklatura, and the State must compensate its citizens for the low wages which they were paid by the former Soviet regime.

The distributional approach had wide support in the public and Parliament adopted it as the main principle of the privatization scheme.

The privatization of state-owned property is implemented by the Central Privatization Commission (CPC) and by privatization commissions of towns and districts subordinate to it. The CPC adopts privatization programmes for enterprises. It also controls the implementation of these programmes. Drafts of privatization programmes are prepared by Ministries - the founders of enterprises under Republic regulation - and by local privatization committees where an enterprise is in the regulation sphere of local governments. Ministries and local authorities are also responsible for breaking up monopoly enterprises into smaller units.

Mass Privatization Programme in Lithuania

From the very beginning of the process of economic reform, Lithuania decided to speed up privatization by the use of a voucher system. Voucher privatization guarantees that a maximum number of citizens will be able to participate in the privatization process, and that a large volume of state property will pass into private ownership very quickly. The main method of privatizing large scale enterprises including military industries was through public subscription of shares.

Vouchers can be used for privatization of industrial enterprises, housing, agricultural enterprises and land. This is the main difference from the Czech and Polish models, where vouchers can be used for the purchase of shares in selected enterprises. In addition to vouchers, citizens have the right to acquire entities under privatization with a certain quota of cash. This quota is equivalent to the sum of the vouchers granted by the State. No other cash can be used for enterprises privatization unless the limitations have been lifted for the purchase of enterprises not sold in the first round of privatization. The cash quota is not binding when enterprises are sold for hard currency.

Under the mass privatization scheme industrial state property is privatized as follows through auction sales of entities under privatization for relatively small entities, and through public subscription of shares.

Investment Funds

An environment for investment funds was created by giving people the option of purchasing shares in these funds with vouchers. There are 393 investment funds, which control 29% of privatized state capital. The roles of the funds are not distinguished between holding or investment companies.

Investment funds serve an important function within the privatization process. They allow the small investor to invest with a knowledgeable investment manager, and they allow small investors to invest in a diversified fund rather than have to acquire shares in specific enterprises. They can also act as a catalyst for capital development by serving as an instrument to mobilize savings of small investors and eventually to attract large investors.

Commercial Privatization

Commercial privatization in Lithuania is going on according to the privatization programme of state-owned enterprises for hard currency. The Lithuanian national currency, Litas, was introduced in June, 1993. Lithuanian citizens participating in the commercial privatization have to pay for privatized businesses in Litas only. Nevertheless, the CPC amended the list of enterprises to be privatized for hard currency so that large enterprises only were on it so that foreign investments would be attracted. Now there are 45 enterprises to be privatized for hard currency on the list. Portions of shareholdings in medium- and large-scale enterprises included in the privatization programme for hard currency are sold by tender. According to the legislation up to 70 per cent of shares of enterprises to be privatized for hard currency may be sold. The employees in the enterprises can acquire up to 30 per cent of these enterprises.

Foreign Technical Assistance

One of the international donor organizations which that provided technical assistance for privatization is the USA Agency of International Development. KPMG Peat Marwick (Washington) is a foreign consultancy firm involved in the privatization process. Another international donor organization is the Roland Berger consortium. This organization works under the European Community's PHARE Privatization Assistance Project.

Results

Summary data regarding the privatization process during the September 1, 1991 - May 15, 1994 period

	To be privatized	Privatized total	% from enterp. to be privatized
Total in republic:			
number of objects	6897	4594	67
state capital (th.Lt.)	1068879	51670	5
Industry:			
number of objects	862	611	71
state capital (th.Lt.)	645213	311778	48

Military industries are partly or fully privatized by public subscription and by investments funds.

Other Baltic States

Latvia and Estonia started privatization later. Both countries use commercial methods of privatization (sale at open auction or by tender, transformation into joint stock-companies and then sale of shares, lease with option to buy), rather than the distributional method used in Lithuania.

The Estonian programme has two primary objectives: to maintain employment; and to bring about the rapid privatization of state-owned assets and enterprises. Other goals exist, but are secondary to the quick transfer of ownership to private hands. As a result, enterprises are tendered in large (25-30) company groupings. Minimal preparation time is allowed and little information is provided to potential investors. The Estonian Privatization Agency acts as a conduit for all bids and attempts to sign contracts rapidly. Bids can be for 100% of the shares, parts of the business, or for specific assets of the enterprise.

Estonia's privatization programme is comparable with the Lithuanian commercial privatization programme (for hard currency). Lithuania's tender targets the highest value (cash proceeds plus investment commitments) for each individual enterprise tendered. The results are good transaction values when a company is sold. The programme, however, does not address many enterprises and the process is lengthy and resource-intensive. Estonia, on the other hand, addresses a large number of enterprises quickly and concurrently, but may not maximize transactions value.

Neither the Estonian nor the Lithuanian programme specifically addresses the question of restructuring.

The Military Complex

The military complex in the Baltics mainly consists of electronics in Lithuania. The electronics industry is involved in dual-use production. Global markets for industries in Lithuania's sphere of activity are increasingly competitive. Global competitors are seeking to expand their presence in the traditional Baltic States market. Enterprises neglect market-oriented elements of the production value chain (marketing & sales, distribution, customer service).

The scale of enterprises is much greater than that of Western counterparts. Electronics and machine-building enterprises were focused on former Soviet republics and now face overcapacity due to the drop in markets. Many enterprises are built to meet regional, rather than local market demand. Regional markets are in depression, and industrial output is declining. In accordance with Government decrees, military enterprises can delay payments to the state budget and social security fund. The "Vilma" enterprise has started bankruptcy proceedings.

Even more important than privatization is the need for foreign investment and Western technology which would make it possible to restructure the large state enterprises and ensure the production of goods which can compete in the East European area as well as in some Third World countries. A combinate was a multifunctional unit that operated in a non-monetary environment. Combinates cannot be viable in a monetary framework, so they need not only transfer of ownership, but also restructuring, involving the separation of social functions and non-viable productive functions. Retraining programmes for staff and workers are also urgently needed.

Conclusions

Immediate privatization methods (distributional privatization) may be fast, but may leave enterprises in a difficult competitive positions. In many cases, a commercial partnership with a foreign investor will be required to ensure long-term success. Commercial privatization in many cases signifies conversion. Western partners may contribute to the know-how of operations, performed by a typical Western firm. Distributional privatization does not lead to the inclusion of shareholders who can offer additional skills in the running of the business as well as new investments.

Lithuania's preferred option is for employee ownership (with or without vouchers), public subscription (with or without vouchers) and partly hard currency privatization. Other Baltic States prefer more commercial approaches - management business plans, or business plans involving investors.

In accordance with Lithuania government plans, on January 1, 1995 the second stage of will commence, privatization process (the end of distributional privatization with vouchers).

Distributional privatization has one great advantage - after privatization the overflow of capital will be made through the established Stock Exchange. The first Stock Exchange in the Baltics was established on 14 September 1993 in Lithuania. Lithuania has had an advantage in developing secondary financial markets institutes. It gives good possibilities to attract foreign capital through enterprises shares sales.

PRIVATIZATION GERMAN STYLE
A look inside the practices and policies of the Treuhandanstalt

Wolfgang Vehse

Privatization is much more than selling companies to the highest bidder, says Wolfgang Vehse. Before choosing the ideal buyers for former-East German state-owned companies, Germany's Treuhandanstalt evaluates potential buyers following several criteria: the amount and targets of planned investment; ability to provide job guarantees; environmental clean-up policy; market analysis; turnaround strategy; future product strategy, and purchase price. After three years of existence and some 35,000 privatizations, the Treuhand's objectives are nearing completion.

Dr. Wolfgang Vehse is Director of the Treuhandanstalt, the German organisation responsible for the privatization of East Germany's state-owned enterprises.

The economic - and of course political - changes in central and eastern Europe present a new challenge to all of us and will form the central focus of our future work.

In pursuing this task, I would like to contribute my experiences with the political and economic transformations in East Germany that I have gained during the past three years.

We have noticed in Berlin that the work of the Treuhandanstalt is receiving increasing international recognition. Interest in how the Treuhand operates, what it has achieved so far and whether its experience can be applied to the reform process in Eastern Europe is growing.

With this in mind, here are some basic comments about the objectives and the experiences of the Treuhand.

The Treuhandanstalt's Legal Mandate

* Transform the command economy of the former German Democratic Republic into a private market economy based on private enterprise in harmony with the tenets of a socially - oriented free market economy.
* Refashion - through privatization - former state-owned enterprises into companies competitive on the international market.
* Remove such companies that could not make the transition from

command to private economy from the market.
* Ensure that as many jobs as possible were preserved and/or
 created.
These tasks cannot be approached without the appropriate preparation. The foundations must first be laid. The Parliament and the Government of the Federal Republic of Germany needed to create the necessary preconditions to tackle a task of which the scope and inherent problems could not be preconceived and had never before been confronted.
* The Treuhand was made the sole owner of all former state-owned
 companies which were transformed into joint-stock companies.
 The Treuhand holds all shares of these companies. It is
 important to note that the firms are not yet privatized. This
 helped us avoid an ideological conflict by ensuring that the
 Treuhand was selling property that it owned and NOT selling the
 "property of the people" (Volksvermögen).
* The Treuhandanstalt as a more or less independent agency - and
 not the political system - was given by legal mandate the
 responsibility for the privatization, restructuring and
 turnaround of the East German economy.
The agency functions like a private enterprise - for most decisions, business considerations take precedence. Political compromises, which can be meaningful in many cases but were not desirable in the Treuhand's work, took a back seat in decisions.
* Governmental credits and guarantees totalling 30 Billion DM a
 year provide a comprehensive basis for financing the
 privatization, restructuring, and turn-around as well as the
 closure of companies.
* The decision to improve the transportation and communication
 networks was made early in the process and is well underway.
* The Western German legal system was applied to the new German
 states. Administrative organs and the justice system of East
 Germany received a face-lift. They were improved step-by-step
 with the help of West German personnel.
* Macro-economic issues (regional and structural policies, for
 example are decided by the federal and state governments.
 Issues that overlap with the work of the Treuhand are discussed
 in joint committees. The political responsibilities between the
 Treuhand and the government are not allowed to become blurred.
* The responsibilities in the area of social policy resulting
 from the privatization process were settled as early as Spring
 1991 in an agreement reached among the federal government,
 state governments, employer associations, trade unions, and the
 Treuhand. The Solidarity Pact of 1993 confirms this commitment.

* The personnel necessary to tackle the tasks of the Treuhand
  came from both the political and economic sectors. Four
  thousand specialists with experience in business, law,
  technical matters and administration work in the central
  Treuhand agency as well as fifteen decentralized offices.
  Eastern Germans comprise two-thirds of the agency's workforce.
  Employees from many different countries provide international
  expertise. Members of the executive boards and the supervisory
  boards as well as the managers of Treuhand companies provide
  additional management experience in both national and
  international business.

Independent but Controlled Operation

The Treuhand may operate independently but it does not operate without
controls:
  * The Treuhand's Supervisory Board- which has more
    representatives of the national and international business
    communities than politicians - oversees general operations.
  * Germany's Minister of Finance oversees the legal and
    substantive work of the agency.
  * The parliament's "Treuhand Committee" is the control instrument
    of the Parliament.
  * The Federal Audit Office oversees the budget.
  * The Federal Cartel Office as well as the European Community
    keep track of merger and competition issues.
The parliament (and not the federal government or the Treuhand)
has determined that the economic perspectives of the company
and the financial and social security of the employees of the
company should be the deciding factors in the privatization of
a company. The fulfilment of these conditions cannot be
determined merely from the (possibly highest) purchase price.
A reliable prognosis is possible only with a detailed
privatization and turnaround concept which potential investors
must present at the beginning of the negotiations with the
Treuhand. In that concept, investors must deal with planned
investment, job guarantees, a future product line, market
analysis, cost and revenue calculations, and the financing of
environmental clean-up, among other things.
These considerations are the main reason why the purchase price is only one
of many deciding factors. Investment and job guarantees are as important - and

sometimes even more important. We aim for a complete privatization and turn-around of a company by the investor. We do not deal in coupons or vouchers.

The Treuhand After Three Years of Operation

The Treuhand is now approaching the end of its operational work. We assume that - as long as the economy does not decline any further - our operations will cease at the end of 1994. By that time we will have found solutions for all companies owned by the Treuhand.

In October 1990 the Treuhand began with 22,000 companies in the service sector (retail, wholesale, restaurants, hotels, travel agencies, pharmacies, bookstores, movie theaters, etc.) and approximately 8,500 industrial companies (often in the form of conglomerates). We knew nothing about these companies.

After three years our results are:

* All service sector industries have been privatized. More than
  70% of these companies went into the hands of eastern Germans.
* By breaking up the industrial conglomerates, the original 8,500
  industries became 13,640 companies. Of those 13,640 we have
  privatized 14,079 companies and/or divisions. The majority of
  these were sold to small and medium-sized investors as small
  and medium-sized companies. The Treuhand has realised over
  2,65,200 Management-Buy-Outs/Management Buy-Ins.
* In 1992 the Treuhand privatized 500 to 600 companies or company
  divisions a month at a rate of 25 to 30 privatizations a day.
* 43,200 Hectares of farmland, 6,660 Hectares of forest, 31,800
  real estate properties.
* 198.2 Billion DM in investment guarantees from investors, 1.5
  Million guaranteed jobs, 52.7 Billion DM in privatization
  revenues.
* 190 companies are still available for privatization.

But we have not had only positive experiences. The Treuhandanstalt, politicians, West German industry, economics institutes as well as intelligence agencies had overestimated the value, the productivity and the efficiency of the East German economy and, as a result, underestimated the task lying before us.

Some typical estimates :

Modrow - the last communist Minister President of the former GDR - in February 1990:

1.3 trillion DM

Rohwedder - the first President of the THA - at the end of October 1990 in Vienna:

600 billion DM

The total opening balance of Treuhand companies on July 1, 1990 - from the standpoint of January 1993 - was minus 270 billion DM.

The result of this experience is the recognition that the process of transformation from a decimated command economy to a free market economy with the privatization, turn-around and closure of companies is a time-consuming and very expensive undertaking. We have spent 150 billion DM alone on turning-around companies. At this point we foresee a final balance of minus 275 billion DM.

Specific Aspects of Germany Privatization

There are special aspects to the lengthy and expensive transformation of the economic system in Germany. Namely, that the Treuhand must privatize in a competitive, open, international market.

On the one hand, this presents the eastern German economy with a large drawback in comparison to other Eastern European economies. On the other hand, it is also an advantage because of the resultant pressure to modernize and to increase productivity.

As a result of economic and monetary union on July 1, 1990, East German companies were confronted with international competition from one day to the next. The companies were not prepared for such a change in terms of their operational and cost structure or their products.

They no longer received any price subsidies, any help from advantageous exchange rates, nor benefits from artificially low wages; they received no protection from imports and no special export promotion; and for political reasons were not granted any structural adjustment measures in order to ease the transition into the Common Market, as Great Britain, Denmark, Spain, Greece and Portugal had previously received. The East German economy was left without any markets. Even its domestic market had disappeared. Eastern European markets provided no hope and western markets were beyond reach.

Even though it recognized the problem, the Treuhand could not and cannot help. We cannot provide our companies with markets. We can only - at great expense - help them develop new products and raise productivity in order to improve their chances of privatization. The quickest route to markets is through a private investor. This is an additional reason for rapid privatization.

The transformation of an unproductive centrally-planned economy to an economy based on private enterprise and determined by the laws of the free market unavoidably results in temporary upheavals in the workforce structure.

Many people have lost jobs they held for years for several reasons:

* Unprofitable companies not capable of being turned-around had
  to be closed (we have had to shut down 3,270 companies up to
  now, while managing to preserve some parts of the companies

through creative solutions).
* Companies received better technical equipment, a more efficient
  infrastructure and a better trained workforce. Some workers became
  "redundant employees" and were no longer needed.
* It will take some time before new business structures
  (industries, services handicraft) can absorb the temporarily
  unemployed workers. This has deeply affected the well-trained,
  highly involved and motivated worker in eastern German and has
  produced some sceptics of the free market.

We had to recognize that our success was more dependent on "management-transfer than we had first realized. It is easier to get financial assistance than to find internationally recognized managers experienced in turning around companies to work for a short while in eastern Germany.

Privatization in eastern Germany cannot be a solely German endeavor. We are interested in international investors, because we believe that they bring not only know-how and good-will-transfer but also lead to a more rapid integration of our companies into the world market.

One must make an effort to attract international investors. There can be no categorical reservations against foreign investment. Foreigners need and expect equal opportunities in relation to domestic investors. This means receiving comprehensive information, attentive care at home as well as in Germany, attractive incentives and our willingness to allow them 100%-ownership in the company and permanent ownership of land. The high level of participation by international investors in the restructuring process has validated our efforts.

We have sold 840 companies to international investors, who have, for their part, provided over 10% of all investment and job guarantees.

The Treuhand intends to share its impressions and experiences

We know that because of structural differences the privatization of the East German economy cannot be directly compared with the privatization efforts of the central and eastern European states. Our privatization philosophy cannot be simply transferred; our "management-transfer" and transfer of capital cannot be repeatedly copied. But the problems that we were, and still are, confronted with also exist in these countries. When our expertise is requested, we are prepared to share it.

A successful transformation of a command economy into a market economy based on private enterprises cannot, however, be forced. Such a transformation necessitates the same basic conditions in every country:
* A stable political system.
* A common fundamental acceptance of the economic policy to be
  followed.
* A proven and uncomplicated legal system.
* Competent and loyal administrations in the states and
  communities.

* An efficient and flexible social welfare system that - within
  a free market system - can absorb and moderate structural
  unemployment.
* A well-organized and trustworthy financial system and currency.

This framework and these conditions, which exist in Germany today, were a major reason for our successes in the privatization process. We must work together in Central and Eastern Europe to ensure that these conditions are established as soon as possible.

PRIVATIZATION IN POST-COMMUNIST ECONOMIES: A THEORETICAL ANALYSIS

Bülent Gültekin[2] and Michael Goldstein[1]

Each post-communist country is finding a different road to the free market - and so should the different companies, says Bülent Gültekin. Small firms should be sold off or given away as quickly as possible. Large companies are more tricky. They must be large enough to achieve economies of scale, but without becoming unwieldy. Professor Gültekin adds a warning to large enterprise analysis: the most important question is not "how", but "why". Privatisation is a means, not an end. This debate is really about boosting efficiency and output, and raising living standards.

Bülent Gültekin is a visiting Professor at Koç University in Istanbul, and an Associate Professor of Finance at the Wharton School of the University of Pennsylvania. He is the former Governor of the Central Bank of Turkey, and former principal privatization advisor to the Polish government. Michael Goldstein is Professor at the University of Colorado at Boulder.

Privatizing Central Europe is a daunting challenge for financial theorists and practitioners alike. Perhaps no other change in economic philosophy has occurred in such a short period of time. These changes are massive, both in absolute and relative terms. Unlike prior privatizations in countries with developed or semi-developed capital markets, there is no capital market infrastructure, no market-oriented accounting or reporting systems, and a dearth of technologically advanced fixed assets such as computers. The very size and nature of such a change, the vast number of people and economic resources affected, the need to develop market structures, and the need to reach a new equilibrium as rapidly and efficiently as possible seem to demand new approaches and ideas.

To fill this demand, many proposals for privatization programs have been supplied by economists and practitioners to speed the privatization process. The proponents each claim that their proposal "solves" the privatization problem in a superior manner with a maximum of efficiency and a minimum of cost. These proposals fall into various categories. The general fund scheme calls for the creation of a single, large mutual fund containing all of the shares of the privatized companies, with the public holding the mutual fund shares.

Other proposals call for the distribution of vouchers to be used to bid for the shares, or even direct distribution of shares to the public. Some limited forms of financing have also been suggested, such as debt financing of shares similar to the LBO concept or ESOP financing. Some others recommend privatizing the pension fund system in conjunction with other measures, such as increasing the role of the banking system.[3]

Other authors have focused on specific privatizations or general caveats as to the process of privatization.[4] To date, however, there has not been a theoretical analysis of the privatization process. This paper fills this gap by applying the rich body of knowledge contained in over fifty years of finance literature to the issues raised in the privatization process. More specifically, we reduce three generalized privatization schemes to their fundamental values and apply modern finance theory under a variety of assumptions. We then compare the results as predicted by finance theory with those claimed by the proponents of these schemes. Unlike much of the literature that proceeds it, this paper is predictive, as opposed to descriptive.

To this end, we have organized the paper as follows. Section I contains a brief description of the current state of affairs in post-communist countries. Section II contains a brief discussion of the definitions of, and goals for privatization. Section III provides familiar theoretical underpinnings for why these goals will be achieved through privatization. The bulk of the paper is in Section IV, which contains the discussion of three privatization proposals reduced to their purest form: free distribution of actual shares, free distribution of vouchers with no nominal value that will be used to bid for shares, and distributing the primary securities to listed closed-end mutual funds. Section V discusses preliminary issues related to the market for control. Finally, Section VI contains the conclusion and some policy recommendations for the privatization process.

The Setting in Post-Communist Countries

Privatization consists of a complex interlocking set of operations which depend on the state of the economy. In a developed market economy such as the U.S. or the U.K., the emphasis is on the transfer of state assets into private hands to remove politics from business decisions, thereby making a more efficient use of assets. In developing market economies such as Chile or Latin America, this objective for privatization is still present, but the need to develop capital markets is also an important objective, as well as a constraint on the process. Although there are substantial differences in the privatization experiences of developed and developing countries, the private sector has typically been at least a modest component of the economy.

In contrast, the privatization process in post-communist countries takes a different definition. Here, privatization plays an integral role in the transformation of the entire current economy into one that is market driven. Privatization, therefore, as used to describe the process elsewhere, does not adequately describe the enormity of its role in post-communist countries, where it involves a total restructuring of the economy into an entirely different form with new institutions and management skills. It requires the processing of a large stock of enterprises from state-owned to privately-owned, the development of the necessary elements and institutions of a market economy (including the human skills needed in this new structure), and the commercialization of companies before and after ownership changes.

Substantial difficulties inhibit the rapid implementation of privatization programs, such as:

- The generally inefficient deployment of assets.
- An insubstantial private sector.
- A shortage of market-oriented professional managers.
- An inadequate financial structure.
- Inappropriate corporate governance practices.
- A monopolistic market structure.
- The large number of enterprises to be privatized.

Capital markets are not fully developed. Moreover, the banking system does not have experience in operating under market discipline, nor does it have experience in developing or exercising market discipline on its borrowers.

These institutions therefore cannot be relied upon for governance, monitoring and capital allocation. Furthermore, most private individuals have very limited accumulated wealth and therefore face severely limited capital constraints due to the poor state of the capital market and banking sectors. Privatization, therefore, needs to be considered in the context of a society and economy undergoing massive changes.

In addition, almost all participants have almost no information. The government (the current official owner of the assets) does not know the underlying value of the assets, and citizens have even less knowledge, having never seen an income statement or balance sheet. While the managers may have more information regarding the assets they control, even their information is not of very high quality as they have not been operating under market conditions.[5] Even relative prices are uninformative, as they are not market-driven.[6]

Due to the practically nonexistent level of information on individual firms, extensive research will be necessary merely to determine what firms own and what they have earned, let alone determine what they are worth as an ongoing concern. In addition, the high level of uncertainty as to the eventual equilibrium make long-term analysis near impossible. All of this must take place in an environment with limited technological abilities, so that even the computers to undertake the analysis are not available.[7]

This research will be extensive and costly, especially relative to the level of wealth in the society.[8] Until privatization occurs, information will not be produced because there is no ability to realize private returns on investment in information. With so little information available, information asymmetry will be low and almost all investors will be similarly uninformed.[9] Therefore, extensive and expensive information searches need to be undertaken for reasoned and accurate information to be included in market decisions and transactions. Due to the high costs involved, this might not occur.

Privatization: Definitions and Goals

Definition

Before embarking on a discussion of privatization, it is useful to examine what the term means. It is apparent that privatization means different things to different people. To some, it is the reestablishing the links from companies and factors of production to the capital markets. To others, it is a change in the corporate governance structure.

In fact, privatization is all of these and more. Privatization is a variety of measures and steps to change the way raw materials are converted into consumption goods. This process entails removing government control and interaction and replacing it with private actors. Merely changing one of the variables might not be sufficient. For example, if prices are still determined by government fiat, it will not matter if corporate governance is switched from public to private hands. Alternatively, if everything is owned by the government, it may not matter if prices are allowed to fluctuate.

Therefore, privatization is a process, a method of changing production and pricing from public to private hands. To accomplish this result, many steps need to be taken in an orderly and systematic fashion. For example, a significant number of financial and governmental institutions need to be in place to insure optimal results. Stock exchanges do not occur overnight: laws need to be written; security and exchange commissions need to be established; accounting procedures need to be developed; clearing methods, brokerage houses and investment banks need to be created; and exchanges, physical or electronic, need to be arranged all before trading can take place. Many players in the privatization arena fail to recognize this necessity, offering privatization proposals or procedures, instead of detailed privatization plans.

Goals

An understanding of the goals of privatization is necessary before evaluating the merits of any particular privatization scheme. Unfortunately, there has been some confusion in the literature as to the goals of privatization. Some have seen privatization as an end itself, not as the means to an end. If this were so, then privatizing would simply be a matter of changing the ownership of the company from the state to private hands. Instead, privatization is undertaken to achieve a more important objective: the improvement of enterprise efficiency and a change in ownership sufficient to alter corporate governance.

Hence, privatization is of primary interest due to the implicit assumption that private control increases efficiency.[10] Thus, privatization has the ultimate goal of increasing societal consumption by increasing the output of vastly under-utilized assets and by a more appropriate allocation of resources across these assets. Restated, privatization wants to change the control of the factors of production to increase output, and reallocate resources across assets to maximize the value of the output.

These two changes occur in different markets. The first change, changing the control of the factors of production, occurs in the labor markets. The second change, the reallocation of resources across assets, occurs in the capital markets. This paper primarily focuses on the second issue, that of reallocation of resources through the capital markets. If trading is allowed to occur, then the capital market may both help reallocate resources across assets by indicating relative pricing and also provide a market for ownership rights, thereby allowing a market for control to be created as well. Since the markets of control and ownership of income streams are linked by the same instrument, i.e., shares, some attention is also placed on the ability of shareholders under the different scenarios to affect a change in the control of the factors of production. Liquidity for individuals is also an important concern.

Meeting these Goals in a Competitive Market

Before we analyze how well the proposals meet the goals of privatization, a reasonable question to consider is how these goals are met in a competitive market. The theoretical answer has been given by the First Welfare Theorem and the Second Welfare Theorem of Economics, which relate a competitive allocation with pareto optimality.

From the First Welfare Theorem, we can see that an allocation that is the result of a competitive equilibrium (in which firms maximize profits, households maximize utility subject to a budget constraint, and markets clear) will result in a Pareto optimal allocation.[11] The Second Welfare Theorem indicates that any Pareto optimal allocation can be achieved through the competitive process by the appropriate assignment of property ownership rights or redistribution schemes.[12]

The underlying tenet of modern-day privatization is the Second Welfare Theorem. It indicates that by changing the endowment structure, any parieto optimal allocation may be achieved through competitive markets. Privatization in post-communist countries may be viewed as the redistribution of endowments across a populace such that, given the developments of markets and corporate structure, a desired parieto optimal solution will be achieved as the result of the competitive process. Since different privatization proposals will result in different distributions of wealth across the populace, different competitive equilibria will be achieved depending on which proposal is implemented.

Each of these results will have strong implications on social welfare. Since the Second Welfare Theorem implies that any competitive equilibrium may be reached if endowments are properly redistributed initially, and since privatization proposals seem to imply different initial distributions and different resulting competitive equilibria, the implementation of these proposals may result in significantly different levels of social welfare. As this aspect of privatization is quite important, this paper will develop the different distributional structures that will result from the implementation of these proposals. The implications for social welfare, however, are left up to the reader.

Privatization Proposals

While there are many variations of the privatization scheme, we will analyze only three schemes which are the base cases underlying most privatization schemes that rely on capital markets for ownership changes and corporate governance: free distribution of shares directly to the people, the creation of mutual funds, and the distribution of vouchers. These analyses provide insight into results for combination of these schemes.[13] Therefore, the analysis has been limited to these three extreme cases.

Privatization proposals may be analyzed on a myriad of levels and the criteria for their evaluation also depend on the objectives of the government. In this paper, privatization is assumed to have two essential goals: increasing the value of the output and reallocating resources across factors of production. This paper primarily looks at the latter of these two goals. It does so by analyzing the resulting distribution of shares and wealth and determining if trading in the underlying shares will occur.

While trading of securities is not essential for all forms of privatization, it is crucial to the success of the privatization process that rely on capital markets for efficiency gains and changes of control. If trading occurs, then relative pricing across firms will be established and thus capital may be allocated more efficiently. In addition, the presence of trading will allow changes in corporate control. However, if in these schemes there is no trading, then there will be no price discovery and no valuation of assets, nor will external changes in control take place. Finally, we predict and describe the most likely market and ownership structure and the competitive equilibria that will result from these basic proposals using the existing financial theory.

To develop this analysis, it is important to follow the historical train of thought through which these privatization proposals evolved. Each proposal builds upon and is intertwined and interlinked with its intellectual predecessors as each tries to address some of the problems in these mass privatization schemes. Therefore, we begin in the next with a discussion of the most basic form of privatization, the free distribution of shares, and examines the benefits and pitfalls of this type of proposal. This proposal is then used as the base case against which other proposals are evaluated. We then proceed to look at free distribution of shares through mutual funds, which was the next step in the development of privatization proposals. After demonstrating the inconsistencies in this type of proposal, we examine the currently popular voucher scheme proposals, and demonstrate some of the pitfalls and difficulties inherent in these voucher schemes. While each section may be read independently, the ideas build upon each other and are best understood in sequence. For this reason, it is to the base case of free distribution of shares that we now turn.

Free Distribution of Shares Directly to Citizens

Some form of free distribution is a part of almost every large privatization plan. The most basic form of privatization is to distribute actual shares in each company to each citizen as a form of an initial endowment without the provision of any additional information. It is viewed as one of the fairest ways to distribute initial endowments. The underlying assumption is that the population, on their own, will exercise the rights contained within these shares to control the underlying assets and increase the productivity of the nation. In addition, it is assumed that market participants will trade such shares with each other on the market in such a way that prices are established and that the underlying value of such firms may be revealed. Implicit in this assumption is that the market, on its own, will engage in information-gathering and attempt to price the securities on a semi-informed basis. At the same time, it will exercise its rights of ownership to increase the earnings and dividend stream potential of the underlying assets by exerting control over management. The proposal assumes that the market would act on its own to establish valuation and price discovery.

Trading in this setting will be necessary for control changes, information accumulation and intertemporal transfers of wealth. However, high brokerage, information, and organizational costs will hinder trading.[14]

Transaction Costs and Trading

Each individual will receive a collection of shares that may be a large proportion of his/her overall wealth. The value of the endowment the individual receives in any one firm will be very small. This level of smallness, as we shall see, may result in a no trade situation, and therefore inhibit price discovery and/or changes in control.

Organized Markets: High Brokerage Costs Prevent Trading

Trading would involve incurring brokerage and transaction costs. These brokerage and transaction costs are likely to be large compared with the underlying value of the shares to be traded.[15] In fact, depending on the eventual market structure that evolves, it is likely that the brokerage and transaction costs would exceed the value of the shares themselves. No trading will occur as a result. Even if the agent wished to intertemporally transfer any wealth from the future to the present, the costs of transacting will prevent this from occurring.

For trade to occur, the value of a share must be at least twice the cost of brokerage.[16] The cost of transacting has some minimum fixed costs that must be met, regardless of volume. These costs are large, relatively speaking, even on modernized U.S. exchanges. Presumably, they would be prohibitively expensive in underdeveloped exchanges. Therefore, it is likely that we get no trading in individual securities due to high brokerage costs.

These size problems do not occur only on the first day of trading. In fact, after the initial round of trading, it will be necessary that the expected return from trading - and not merely the expected value of the share - will exceed the transaction costs. By similar mathematics, it can be shown that the difference in the expectation of the value of the share between the buyer and the seller must exceed twice the transaction cost per trade for trade to occur.[17] If transaction costs are high, such a discrepancy in beliefs will occur only infrequently, inhibiting the development of a secondary market and resulting in thin capital markets.

Disorganized, Non-Centralized Market: Price Discovery Breakdown

Of course, it is possible that exchange could occur if transactions costs were reduced. One way that this could occur is by informal, non-centralized trading. However, this would lead to the result of wide and dispersed trading, which would result in non-effective price discovery. Without centralized reporting of transactions, prices would vary from location to location and participants would be unable to learn from each other's trades. Centralized, liquid capital markets will not occur, preventing price discovery and thus proper resource allocation. Therefore, informal, non-centralized trading will develop to reduce transactions costs, resulting in ineffective price discovery.

Demands for current consumption are likely to cause unorganized selling of shares across the countryside without any form of publicly disclosed price information. Given the strong desire for current consumption by the average citizen, a few capital rich individuals will travel the countryside purchasing shares from citizens anxious to convert their shareholdings into cash. With the lack of information as to fair competitive prices, it is likely that many of these sales will take place at prices significantly below those that would occur on more organized markets. In these countries, there is a social and political concern that this would result in the nomenklatura owning the majority of the shares at bargain prices.[18]

If follows that if no trading occurs due to excessive brokerage costs, there will not be any incentive to accumulate information, as the cost of acting on that information would exceed the value of that information itself due to brokerage costs alone.[19] Therefore, another implication is that information accumulation will not occur if high brokerage costs prevent trading or cause non-centralized trading. Such uninformed disperse trading may lead to speculative behavior, resulting in high uncertainty and volatility, and ultimately undermine investor confidence in the system itself.

Information Costs Inhibit Information Accumulation

In Grossman and Stiglitz (1980), the number of informed traders is endogenously determined based on the cost of acquiring such information. The cost of information could be very high and its quality low. Therefore, with the possible exception of management, it is likely that there will be few, if any, informed traders in the market. More accurately, the relative asymmetry in information between market participants will be low since the quality of information is so poor and the cost of accumulating information is so high. Thus, there will be little information accumulation, the price system will not be informative and the markets will be very thin due to high information costs.

A key assumption in this and many other privatization proposals is that the market, on its own, will accumulate information and value the securities, thereby relieving the government of its responsibility to do so during the privatization process. As is noted above, such a reliance on the market could hinder the development of capital markets and the privatization process itself.

Information is, in many ways, a public good. As such, economic theory predicts it will be underproduced in a competitive economy. Therefore, reliance on the market for the production of information seems shortsighted. In addition, if one assumes risk averse investors, firms will be valued below their true value if there is an underproduction of information. Many schemes purport to "solving" the privatization problem by leaving information accumulation to the private sector. As has been shown, this more likely exacerbates the problem.[20]

Control Changes Blocked

An investor would also want to increase the value of his/her holdings by increasing the value of the underlying assets. In this case, it will be necessary to remove or change management, or at least management controls and incentives.

Wide Dispersion of Owners Prevents Control Changes

Changing managements require the collective action of individual investors, who must be united and organized. If organizational costs are so large that they exceed the expected return the investor will receive as a result of the organization, then no one will undertake such an organization as the costs outweigh the benefits. With a diverse shareholder base, it is likely that the costs of organization will be very large. In addition, no one shareholder has any incentive to incur such costs, since, as Grossman and Hart (1980) note: "The proper management of a common property is a public good to all owners of the property... If one small shareholder devotes resources to improving management, then all shareholders benefit." (p. 59)

Since each investor was give such a small endowment of each firm initially, the relative benefit of organization for any particular individual will be small. Given shareholders that are widely dispersed and the difficulty of collective action, it is unlikely that the relative benefit of organization for any particular individual will exceed the cost, and thus, wide dispersion of shareholders results in no organizational activity or control.

"No Trading" Prevents Control Changes

It will not be in any individual's interest to initiate or complete any organizational activity unless he/she can accumulate enough shares to do overcome organizational costs. However, as Grossman and Hart (1980) point out, it will also be necessary that the investor receive some form of extra compensation or private benefit to induce the investor to incur such costs.

If, due to capital constraints or brokerage costs, the individual cannot accumulate sufficient shares or if a market does not exist for trading, then no such action will take place. However, this in turn prevents the accumulation of shares and thereby external changes in control. If so, there will neither be trading nor will there be an increase in efficiency in the use of the underlying assets, and thus both of the aims of privatization will have been thwarted. Thus, if there is no trading of individual securities, then external changes in control are blocked.

Implications

Infinite divisibility of a firm is not necessarily a good thing. The unbundling of the economy into such small pieces will cause transaction costs to take on unusual significance. Transactions costs will prevent trading, information accumulation and control changes. Organizational costs are always high with an atomized shareholder base. Information accumulation costs will also take on new importance as they will be quite high due to the poor level of information available.[21] Lack of liquidity in the marketplace will hurt many investors looking for intertemporal transfers and hurt the economy in preventing price discovery and control changes.

It appears important that trading be allowed and that control not be dispersed too widely. There is probably an optimal level of concentration of ownership which is likely to be dictated by the eventual brokerage costs of trading. These costs are likely to be such that they imply that one share per firm per person is not a tenable solution. One instinctive alternative to this vast dispersion of shares is the distribution of shares via a small number of mutual funds.

Free Distribution of Shares Through Mutual Funds

Perhaps in recognition of the problems associated with a wide dispersion of shares, others such as Sachs et al. (1990) have proposed creating a small number of mutual funds, which will each be given shares in a large number of state-owned enterprises (which have been converted into joint-stock company form). It is assumed that these funds will invest resources in information accumulation and trade these underlying securities among themselves so as to enhance the performance of their fund. Shares of these mutual funds will be distributed to the citizenry and can be traded. Each citizen will receive an equal endowment of shares in each mutual fund, thereby maintaining a sense of overall fairness. This proposal assumes that the mutual funds will price the underlying securities and trade among themselves so that citizens will be able to determine the value of their mutual fund shares by noting market value of the fund's portfolio. Furthermore, the plan assumes that capital market discipline will force the mutual funds to be effective managers of the firms in their portfolios.[22]

No Trading in Underlying Securities

There will be no trading of shares of the underlying firms among a few large mutual funds with identical endowments if the underlying securities themselves are not traded among small investors. This result occurs because the small investors, who, because of their intertemporal consumption preferences, differing utility functions, or other reasons, may act like the liquidity traders. Without liquidity traders there will be no trading.

Grossman and Stiglitz (1980) noted that there will be no trading if agents have homogeneous beliefs and endowments. Each fund manager will have the same belief structure, since no fund manager will invest in information accumulation in these markets due to the high cost of information, the existence of asymmetric information, and the lack of liquidity traders. If fund managers expend resources on information gathering, it will rapidly be known by the other fund managers due to the small number of funds. Since there are no liquidity traders to absorb trading losses, the another fund managers will assume that the first fund manager has superior information and will therefore not trade in that market.

The classic free rider problem described in Grossman and Hart (1980) will also prevent information accumulation. Any increased profits due to better management due to information accumulation will be shared with the other funds as they each own equal endowments. The first manager will be worse off than each of the other funds, as he/she expended resources but will receive the same return. Therefore, fund managers will not expend the resources on information accumulation, resulting in no trading or information accumulation.

If, instead of identical endowments, the funds are given random endowments, the mutual funds will restructure their portfolios in single trades of large blocks of shares so that each fund ends up with majority control in the enterprises in which its endowment is the largest relative to the other funds. Trading will stop once they reach equilibrium optimal portfolio weightings.[23]

Once a fund has majority control in a firm, it will be advantageous for that fund to expend resources on restructuring the firm's underlying assets to improve its efficiency since the fund will receive the benefit of such an investment of resources. It seems possible, therefore, that funds will rapidly strive for control.

The fund that owns a majority of shares will now be an insider, or an "informed" investor, and will have superior information as compared with the other funds, which, comparatively, are "uninformed" investors. At this point, asymmetric information theory indicates that there will no longer be trading in such shares. There have to be two sides to the trade for there to be trading and for prices to be established. Due to the asymmetric nature of the information and the lack of liquidity traders, both sides of the transaction will not wish to trade at the same time. Grossman and Stiglitz (1980) prove that if there is no liquidity traders, there can be no equilibrium.[24]

These funds have no liquidity needs, and therefore will not be liquidity traders. Nor will anyone else. With no liquidity traders, there will be no trading.[25]

Bundling: Mutual Fund Shares Become Primary Securities

Without trade, information about the value of individual firms will not be known. Values of individual assets cannot be determined from the price of a portfolio of assets if the individual assets are not also traded. The value indicated by the market for the mutual fund shares will be for the assets as a group, and it will be impossible to separate out the value of the individual non-traded units. The problem is that the mutual funds are not redundant securities. Markets are not complete; the trading of each firm's share would expand the market and provide new information.

So, if financial markets are to provide signals, or information about individual stocks, the securities themselves must first be traded among a large number of investors. Otherwise, trading shares of closed end mutual funds when the underlying securities are not traded does not complete the markets. In this case, funds themselves become primary securities rather than redundant securities and cannot be easily priced.

In addition, due to the wide dispersion of ownership of mutual fund shares and the extraordinarily high information costs in evaluating the value of the mutual fund share (since, to value a mutual fund share one would have to determine the value of each underlying asset and determine how its value compares with the entire portfolio), trading in the mutual fund shares would be merely speculative, and not information-driven.

Implications

It seems that care needs to be taken to insure that exogenously imposed structures not only do not inhibit capital market development but more seriously do not hinder the development of a market economy overall and the ability to change the corporate governance structure. This scheme, if implemented as offered, would hinder the development of capital markets and might result in even more serious consequences.

While mutual funds seem to reduce the dimensionality of the problems associated with the direct free distribution of shares noted earlier, they create worse problems of their own. The lack of liquidity traders rapidly produces the result of no trading which has undesirable consequences. First, no trading results in no price discovery. Second, the lack of trading prevents the creation of a market for control, which could directly prevent optimal changes in the corporate governance structure. As Grossman and Hart (1980) point out, it is only the threat of removal by an outsider which will force a manager to act on behalf of the shareholders.

If the underlying securities themselves are not traded, trading of the shares in mutual funds does not provide any information about the underlying security valuation. Schemes that only allow trading of closed-end mutual funds that purport to solve the issue of valuation in this fashion are flawed. Furthermore, without trading in the underlying securities, it will be hard to price the assets in the fund, and therefore it will be difficult to value the mutual funds. Given the difficulty in valuing these funds, price discovery will be limited even in the mutual fund shares themselves. The lack of information will result in speculative trading. Speculative trading will distort price formation, undermine financial stability and investor confidence, and could lead to fraud.

The economy will suffer from the random grouping of firms into closed-end funds because these companies will not be grouped optimally to take advantage of natural synergies. Assuming that a market structure exists, societal resources would be used to regroup them if necessary.

Even worse, these groupings cannot be undone easily if the underlying securities are not traded.[26] Not only would optimal groupings be prevented potentially causing large inefficiencies. The inability to undo these groupings make this proposal worse than direct free distribution, as society is at best equally as well of as with free distribution (if groupings are random), and potentially worse off (if unnatural monopolies stifle growth and competition).[27]

These results hold assuming that there is a sufficiently large number of mutual funds to create a competitive market and industrial structure. If only a handful of funds are formed, as proposed by Sachs et. al. (1990), then the mutual fund scheme creates an economy with five giant holding companies, either conglomerates if companies are distributed randomly or giant structural monopolies if the groupings are specialized. Those who advised the use of five mutual funds unknowingly recommended an economy that will be more centralized than under communist rule. While these authors seem to imply that distributing shares through five mutual funds would instantly create a market system, actually such a scheme would have been an excellent mechanism to nationalize a market economy.

It is apparent that artificially grouping firms into funds may cause significant problems. Neither extreme dispersion nor extreme concentration of shares seems appealing. As an alternative to the two previous free distribution of shares proposals, some have proposed auction processes using vouchers. It is to one such proposal that we now turn.

Distribution of Shares Using Vouchers

In both of the previous proposals, actual shares were initially distributed to citizens. Under voucher schemes, however, vouchers instead of shares are distributed and are used in auctions for shares of state-owned enterprises to determine the initial distribution of shares. Therefore, while in the previous proposals each citizen received the same endowment in shares, in this proposal they will receive the same value of endowment in vouchers. However, by using the vouchers in auctions, the actual composition of their ultimate initial endowment of shares will differ based on their bids during these auctions.

Auctions, of course, do not require vouchers for their operation.[28] Shares of state-owned enterprises could be sold in auctions where cash is used for payment. However, voucher auctions are frequently proposed in lieu of cash auctions due to the perceived fairness of voucher auctions. In voucher auctions, every citizen receives the same initial endowment of vouchers and therefore everyone starts off equally. However, the few individuals which currently have sufficient capital to participate in cash auctions are viewed suspiciously by the remainder of the public as it is perceived that this capital was accumulated illegally and unfairly under the previous regime. In addition, there is also concern that foreign investors will purchase the nation's assets at bargain prices if cash auctions are used. As voucher schemes allow for the exclusion of these groups, many feel that the *ex-post* results from voucher auctions are likely to be more politically acceptable than those of cash auctions.

We will therefore analyze voucher schemes in which auctions will take place where only vouchers may be bid.[29] The results of these auctions are not dependent on whether these vouchers are sold or given away freely.[30] The general example of voucher auction schemes calls for the distribution or sale of books of vouchers, with no nominal value. Auctions of state-owned enterprises will take place, with only vouchers accepted as payment. Prior to the auction, vouchers can be traded for money. After the auction, a secondary market for shares will develop.[31]

On the surface, the voucher and auction mechanisms of this scheme appear to create a vastly different proposal than the previous schemes such as the free distribution of shares. However, as we shall see, this method brings us to the same results as previous methods, differing only in the path taken and the cost of getting there.

Free Distribution vs. Voucher Systems

The privatization proposals discussed in this paper are actually different distribution mechanisms implying different methods and forms for distributing endowment initially. However, it is not the initial endowment which is of concern, but the competitive equilibrium that results. While different initial endowments appear to imply different resulting competitive equilibria and different distributions of wealth across the populace, this is not always the case.

Many believe that the use of vouchers result in superior and different competitive equilibria than the free distribution of shares. While it is true that voucher systems will likely result in a different initial endowment of shares immediately after the auction takes place, it is not necessarily true that the resulting competitive equilibria will be any different than the one which results from the free distribution of shares. After the auction of shares for vouchers, a normal trading market for shares will be in place, which is simply an auction market denominated in cash. While voucher auctions are competitive markets, so too are equity markets.

To see this, assume a frictionless world with perfect information and no brokerage or transaction costs in either the voucher auction market or in the equity market that follows. As the auction allowed investors to adjust their portfolio holdings costlessly, at the end of the auction they will hold their optimal portfolio. Now consider the first day of trading. While it is true that before the opening of the equity market on the first day the portfolio holdings of a investor in the voucher scheme will be different than the holdings of the same investor who received a free distribution of shares, at the end of the day both will have the same holdings. This analogous result occurs because both may costlessly readjust their portfolio holdings in the equity market during the day. The only difference is that under the voucher scheme the investor is initially able to adjust his portfolio in the voucher auction market, while under the other scenario, the readjustment takes place in the equity market. In either case, both investors end up with the same portfolio holdings (subject to some constraints on the form of the auction described below). The only difference is how the ultimate endowments are achieved.

Of course, in the real world, transaction costs are a significant issue. However, since both markets can get investors to the same result, the only relevant question is which can achieve the result at the lowest cost to society. While both schemes require the development of equity markets, the voucher scheme also requires the creation of an entirely new additional market, the voucher auction bidding market, which is a sunk cost and is worthless as soon as the auction process ends. Even if both systems had no brokerage costs, there is an expensive additional fixed cost under voucher schemes. The variable transaction costs to the investor under a voucher scheme will have to be significantly less than under a free distribution scheme for the voucher scheme to be optimal.[32]

Vouchers and Auction Design

The design of the auction greatly affects the results of the voucher auction. Perhaps the most disruptive auction would be a one-time single auction in which all state-owned enterprises are auctioned simultaneously. In such a system, the relative prices in vouchers are not relevant for pricing securities in currency. Instead of imparting information as to the relative value of the underlying good, the voucher prices merely impart the relative expectations of what others will bid.[33] The information useful in such an auction is how many vouchers are other investors expected to bid which requires an investment in information to determine how much to bid. Therefore, the relative prices of shares in vouchers will provide little information as to the relative value of these shares in money. This information is necessary for proper capital allocation in the future. Any investment in information used to determine the value of shares in vouchers would be an investment in information on how much others are going to bid and not the relative value of the shares. Since such information will not impart useful information for society, it would be a deadweight loss.

Another problem with one-time auctions is that it is possible that an investor will consistently bid too low and thereby be closed out of the bidding process. For example, imagine everyone has 10 points and there are 10 firms. Individuals 1 to 9 bid eight points on firms 1 through 9, respectively, and two points on firms 2 through 10. Individual 10 bids one point per firm. In the end, individual 10 receives nothing. He has been effectively closed out of the bidding process. Therefore, demand and supply are not matched.[34]

An iterative process can be used to solve the mismatching of demand and supply, but this will still not solve the problem of the lack of relative pricing. In an iterative process, the vouchers are returned and the process is begun anew. Therefore, even though the market may eventually clear and demand may equal the outstanding stock, relative prices do not emerge as there is no penalty for overbidding or future benefit from underbidding. This occurs because vouchers are not the numerary for consumption. If the outstanding capital stock is subdivided into manageable units and the auction process is repeated with different voucher books so that again a certain voucher book is only valid for a certain auction, then the above results still hold because the above scenario has merely been repeated multiple times.

A necessary condition for vouchers to reveal relative prices is the same book of vouchers be valid for more than one auction in the series. These relative prices will impart some information, as the expected value of a voucher should be worth its proportion of the overall market value of the firms in the auction. [35] Unlike the previous example, over-bidding in early auctions will cause under-bidding later and under-bidding earlier will force over-bidding later, encouraging bidding as accurately as possible. [36]

The Emergence of Financial Intermediaries

An interesting feature of the voucher systems is the possibility of endogenously created mutual funds. One can consider the endowment of vouchers as an initial endowment of one unit of capital. While we can also consider the endowment of shares received under the free distribution of shares scheme as a unit of capital, transactions costs of handling so many shares are mitigated if single voucher packets can be tendered as they are smaller in unit size and are more fungible. Mor importantly, as vouchers are used before the auctions, they allow for the *ex ante* investment decision as well as *ex post* monitoring which is present in both cases. (The financial intermediary will need to undertake similar monitoring functions on its ultimate endowment of shares, whether this endowment is the result of the deposit of shares under the free distribution scheme or the results of auctions under voucher schemes.)

Research on financial intermediation, such as *Leland and Pyle* (1977) and *Boyd and Prescott* (1986) discuss the creation of mutual funds under this scenario. *Campbell and Kracaw* (1980) extend this work to argue that these funds would also need to provide other services as well for their existence to occur.

Perhaps the most applicable work is by *Diamond* (1984), which points out that a financial intermediary will minimize the cost of monitoring information (or, in this case, gathering information or exercising control). Diversification within the intermediary helps lower these costs. He also notes the optimality of debt contracts within his model and that the intermediary will hold illiquid assets. He notes "The centralization of monitoring each loan by a single intermediary will mean that there are not active markets for these assets" (p. 410).

The benefit to vouchers, therefore, is the ease with which financial intermediaries may be created to mitigate the cost of transacting and monitoring. While mutual funds may also be endogenously created if shares are freely distributed to citizens directly, the transaction costs of handling so many shares may inhibit their growth. Thus, while the creation of a voucher auction market creates additional fixed costs, it may reduce the cost of financial intermediation sufficiently to make voucher schemes less costly than other methods.[37]

However, the ease with which financial institutions can be created may also be a potential source of trouble for voucher schemes. The key to Leyland and Pyle (1977), Campbell and Kracaw, and Boyd and Prescott (1986) is that the monitor must invest his own capital, and will suffer losses for non-compliance.[38] Likewise, the key to Diamond (1984), is the non-pecuniary penalties incurred by the monitor, such as jail or having his legs broken, if he fails to honor his obligations to his investors. Fund managers will over-promise if they suffer no losses for non-performance.

Diamond (1984) predicts that a single intermediary will prevail, owning the entire share of assets. If a single fund owns all the assets, the value of the fund will approximate the wealth of the society. The results implied by Diamond (1984) are extreme, but it demonstrates that when there are no penalties for non-performance, funds will compete for size, inducing fund managers to make promises that may only be fulfilled by achieving size alone. There is no disincentive to make such promises as there are no penalties for non-performance. Only a few funds, however, will achieve sufficient mass to fulfil their promises. The rest will default. Apart from the political problems that may result, we have replaced state-ownership with a most a handful of funds. The same problems with over-concentration still apply.

Implications

Auctions with voucher systems is essentially a different mechanism to redistribute the endowment of shares. Equivalent results under voucher auctions occur in the cash-for-share auctions inherent in equity markets. The only differences will be due to brokerage and set-up costs.

One-time auctions do not allow price discovery or relative pricing. Citizens should receive a one-time allocation of vouchers which can be used in sequential offerings. This enables vouchers to have money-like qualities, and the resulting prices will be close to relative prices because over- and underbidding will be penalized. Designing such schemes is theoretically difficult and operationally expensive. While voucher auctions may be intuitively appealing because the process seems competitive, the emerging results are not necessarily relative prices. Establishing relative prices still requires an investment in information and creating ingenious auction schemes that mimic the role of money. Short of this, voucher auctions become an arbitrary allocation scheme. The problems associated with a low level of information continue to apply to voucher auctions as they do to any other distribution mechanisms. Unless there is substantial investment in information, auctions do not solve the problem of valuation.

Vouchers may lead to the endogenous creation of financial intermediaries due to lower transaction costs. On the other hand, enforcement mechanism are also required for financial intermediaries to function appropriately. No losses for non-performance encourages an inherent tendency to compete for size by over-promising, possible defaults by small funds, and concentration of ownership by a few large funds.

The experience with the voucher system in Czechoslovakia proves enlightening. As predicted, many mutual funds have been created. These mutual funds have not been required to invest their own capital, nor are they being monitored effectively by the government of Czechoslovakia. Most appear like the Diamond model, offering guarantees of fixed returns as high as 1000% for the deposit of vouchers, and only a handful of funds attracted a large portion of the outstanding vouchers. Given the lack of infrastructure and regulations, many mutual funds do not fear legal redress for non-performance of their contracts. This structure is prone to investor disappointment. After two years of preparation, the process has only just begun. The eventual outcome of this process remains to be seen.

The Market for Control: One Final Concern

In developed markets, shares of a firm are the instrument through which a variety of investment, ownership and control issues are determined. Shares give the shareholder specific rights and claims in the financial world that are unique and are tied together as a bundle in the typical common share. A typical common share gives the holder the following:

- The ownership right to the underlying physical and intangible assets of the firm.
- A residual claim on the future earnings that result from the use of these assets.
- The right to control the underlying physical and intangible assets.

Although obvious, these items are important in the study of privatization methods, as they each indicate different areas of concern. Most, if not all, privatization methods incorporate the use of shares in their proposals. However, many of the concerns that privatization proposals wish to address deal with only a subset of the three areas that a typical share encapsulates. For example, the primary goal of privatization is the increase in societal output. Therefore, it is the control feature of the share with which most privatization plans are concerned, as it is hoped that changing the control of the asset will result in a change in the use of the assets in such a way that an increase in the quantity and quality of goods will be realized. The other features of a share are there to provide the proper incentives for the use of such control, although in actuality these incentives may not result in the desired outcome.

The market for corporate control may also be affected by the voting structure of securities.[39] Grossman and Hart (1988) note the free rider problem inherent with an atomized shareholder base. If shares are widely held such that the holdings of any individual agent are small, individual shareholders will not have the proper incentives to exercise their control and remove inefficient incumbent management. Within their model, the authors show that the allocation of ownership and control across securities helps determine the cost and success of removing incumbent management.

Their model is highly dependant on the distribution of private benefits of management across various management teams. Within their model, allocation of control is unimportant if private benefits to both parties are small, and so separate securities for ownership and control may exist, or they may be contained in the same security with one vote per share. If both parties value control because both parties will receive private benefits, then one vote per share is not optimal as there will be differing markets for ownership and control. Finally, if one party has private benefits, the optimal mix of ownership and control are different, depending on who receives the private benefits.

It is in the development of the capital market structure that these issues are of most concern. Trading of shares is desired as it will impart information to the market which will increase efficiency by improving the allocation of resources from one area to another. The goal of privatization is not the creation of a stock market but the increase in efficiency and output. Thus, the creation of a stock market is a means to a desired outcome, and not an end in of itself. Note, however, that the price of a share and the volume of trading will be a function of the four aspects of the share listed above. There will be a market for control, as well as a market for the residual claim on the earnings, as well as a market for the underlying value of the assets. Unfortunately, there will only be one instrument, the common share, for each of these markets. Therefore, certain desired outcomes, such as an effective change in the control of the firm, may not result if the market for trading shares is blocked.

For example, Grossman and Hart (1980) argue that the possibility of takeover bids will encourage existing management to realize higher values of the firm. If a takeover is impossible, however, due to the lack of trading, such an increase in the realization of the firm's value may not take place.

Bagwell and Judd (1989) consider control issues relating to payout and investment decisions. They note that transactions costs of rebalancing portfolios are an important factor in the optimal decision rule. If transaction costs are small, than majority rule is optimal. If, however, trading is blocked due to high transaction costs, than a different rule is optimal. Their model indicates both that blocked trading affects the market for control and that control is important for issues beyond takeover situations.

Conversely, if the market for control reaches equilibrium, it is possible that trading will cease and therefore although optimal control may have resulted information as to the allocation of resources may not result as there may not be revealing prices. This is the case when there is a complete merger or takeover or buyout. At this point, the shares of the initial firm are no longer available on the market, and therefore the resource allocation information contained in the price of these shares will not be made available to the general market.

Conclusion

As is often the case, reality meshes with theory imperfectly. Individuals in Central Europe are certainly more varied in beliefs, information levels, endowments, wealth, risk parameters, and preferences than most theories allow. However, a reasonable case can be made for many of the simplifying assumptions made above.

Most likely, any of the privatization proposals will, over time, result in the development of capital markets. The key question, however, is how long and at what cost, and who will profit along the way. The search for the optimal privatization program is a search to find the most rapid, least costly method of fully transforming an economy to maximize its output efficiently, but at the same time to find a method that is equitable, fair, and politically acceptable to an estranged populace.

It appears that, like it or not, there is no getting around the process of information - gathering and price - discovery when offering securities in such undeveloped capital markets as exist in Central Europe. To rely on the market system to invest on its own in such information gathering is unrealistic and wasteful of societal assets. First, the cost of acquiring information makes such investment unlikely in a competitive market. Second, to the extent that this process is undertaken by more than one firm, it is an expensive waste of societal resources. Basic information on a company, such as assets, revenues, etc., is and should be a public good. As it is a public good, such tasks should be undertaken by the government on behalf of the entire citizenry.

In addition, to the extent investors are risk averse, they will value assets at lower than their expected value. To the extent that investors are very unsure about the quality of their information, all assets in the economy will be valued at lower than their worth on an expected value basis. At an extreme case, the relative values that arise may be more of an indication of the relative certainty of information provided than an accurate assessment of the relative productive capacity of these assets. As a result, efficient allocation of capital and resources across assets might not occur.

To avoid such problems, the government should invest in the costs of an IPO process for each large firm in order to establish some benchmark from which investors, acting competitively, can use as a starting point for their own analyses. Information accumulation will take time and money, but having a credible, public starting point will both reduce price uncertainty and prevent a redundant waste of resources.

As a result, vouchers with no nominal value do not seem to provide much additional information to a privatization process, but do significantly increase the cost and difficulty. Therefore, such a process does not seem optimal. Likewise, the creation of a limited number of mutual funds is not a good idea as it is difficult to see why trading will occur and it subverts the market's natural tendency to create such funds. In fact, it may prevent the optimal grouping of assets. Given the implicit assumption inherent in the privatization process that the market can allocate resources better than the government, it does not seem optimal for the government to attempt to replicate the market's actions. Unfortunately, solely relying on the free distribution of the physical securities may not be much better due to the high transaction costs involved. In addition, it does not provide for the opportunity for citizens to opt to purchase small companies in their entirety instead of purchasing shares in large corporations. As Winton (1990) and others have shown that at times such a structure might be optimal, it seems optimal to insure that this possibility exists.

It seems obvious, therefore, that different privatization methods should be used for different companies with different needs. Most agree that the smaller sized companies be given or sold to individuals or small groups as rapidly as possible. The trick is what to do with the larger concerns. As we have seen, there is an inherent tension between too much concentration and too little. Free distribution of shares will inhibit price discovery due to transaction considerations and will have control problems. Oddly enough, the same problems exist for too much concentration; control problems also result from trying to manage a company that is one-fifth the entire economy and simply is too big.

The solution seems to be in the appropriate bundling of securities. The package should be valued highly enough that it will overcome transaction cost problems, yet small enough to allow for effective control. These packages should be sufficiently specialized that it makes economic and managerial sense for the pieces to be together. Intelligent bundling of companies to achieve vertical integration or economies of scale will also allow for managerial economies, thereby spreading a scarce human resource in those markets more efficiently and will create value. The result is that fewer shares will be distributed with greater per unit share value, enabling trading to occur. At the same time, these companies will be sufficiently small that they may be unbundled later, by external forces if necessary. Great care needs to be taken in creating the market structure to avoid setting up industry monopolies to ensure competition. However, it seems likely that such a bundling can occur without necessarily creating undesirable monopolies so that optimal trading structures, corporate governance and economic efficiency will result. While these efforts will take time and energy, the results will surely be worth it.

Footnotes

1. University of Colorado at Boulder. I gratefully acknowledge generous financial support from the Geewax-Terker Foundation and the Rodney L. White Center for Financial Research, the Wharton School, University of Pennsylvania.
2. The Wharton School, University of Pennsylvania and Koç University, Istanbul, Turkey.
   This research was funded by Weiss Center for International Research, the Wharton School. The authors would like to acknowledge extensive discussion on the matter of privatization and privatization processes with Gavin Wilson of the International Finance Corporation during the Summer of 1990 in Washington and Warsaw. Additional research help was provided by Sondra Baron, Ian Murray and Elizabeth Palmer. In addition, we would like to thank Anthony Santomero, Christopher Leach, Andrew Winton, Greg Van Igwen, James Mahoney, Michel Habib, Ananth Madhavan and Franklin Allen for their helpful comments and suggestions. All remaining errors are, of course, ours.
3. For example, Sachs (1990) proposed creating five closed-end mutual funds. See Frydman and Rapaczynski (1990) or Nellis (1990) for voucher and direct distribution systems. LBO-style debt financing can be found in Jedrzejczak (1990) or see Gates (1990) for ESOP financing. Mendelson (1990) suggests a variety of methods including using pension funds and the banking system.
4. Luders (1990) contains a detailed description of the Chilean privatization experience, along with an analysis of the consequences of privatization and the lessons learned. Hinds (1990) considers various problems in privatizing Central European economies and recommends that a mixed strategy of a variety of privatization processes be pursued. Vuylsteke (1990) also notes the various procedural changes needed for privatization in Central Europe and recommends a multi-faceted strategy.
5. One concern that arises due to the low level of information available to outsiders, including the government, is that managers, who currently have control of the assets, may misuse such control for their own profit. As a result, the government will need to protect against fraud. Indications of this situation may be shown by the recent rescinding of a sale organized by the managers of a large hotel chain due to the huge underpricing of the sale.
6. This lack of accurate information is the result of two factors. First, accounting standards and reporting systems over the past 45 years were not designed for a market system, leading to a lack of accurate market-oriented historical information on which to base investment decisions. Even if this information were available, the prevalence of government subsidies, control and intervention limit the relevance of such data for imparting market information. Finally, the system, as it changes from a communist to market controlled economy, will be undergoing a change in fundamental values and prices as it adjusts to reach a new equilibrium. It is uncertain what future cash flows and interest rates be, especially in the near term. These factors combined veiled a situation in which there is little information provided to the decision makers in the marketplace, and the value and reliability of existing information is low.
   (Mathematically, one can model the problem as follows. The investor is interested in determining the value of a firm V. However, he/she can only observe X_i, where $X_i = V + e_i$ where e_i is a noise term distributed normally with mean 0 and variance S. The investor gets to observe N realizations of X, so $E[X] = E[V] + E[e] = V + O = V$, but the variance of this estimate will be S/N. Therefore, the situation the investor in Eastern Europe is facing is one in which there are few observations (i.e., N is small) and in which the reliability of these observations

is small (i.e., S is large). Therefore, the reliability of his estimate of V is very low since S/N, the variance of that estimate, is very large.)

7. Our teams' personal Toshiba laptops were the most powerful personal computers in the entire Ministry of Finance in Poland.

8. For example, the typical cost of privatizing one company is approximately $500,000.

9. Managers, who might have more information overall, may not have useful information regarding the actual market value or potential for their firms as their external environment is changing rapidly and it is uncertain how they will adapt. In any case, due to concerns about fraud, insider trading, and political unrest, it will be likely that managers will be barred legally from acting upon their information. Even if they could do so, wealth and borrowing constraints may prevent them from being able to use their information in the marketplace.

10. The underpinnings of this assumption begin by assuming that private ownership of the factors of production results in more effective control of these assets. More effective control in turn implies more efficient use, which in turn increases the overall net production of society. If ownership of the factors of production can also be traded, then relative prices may be established which will allow for more efficient allocation of resources across assets, increasing the overall net production of society yet again. These increases in production enable a society to increase consumption.

11. A competitive allocation is an allocation a and a price system p such that:
Firms maximize profits, i.e., yf is the optimal solution to:
$Cf(p) = max\ p * yf$ s.t. yf is an element of Yf for firms f = 1..N
Households maximize utility, i.e., given initial shareholdings snf and Cf(p) and endowments en, consumption xn is the optimal solution to:
max uh (Xh) s.t. $p*xn = p*eh$ + sum {snf*Cf(p) from f = 1..N}for households h = 1..M and markets clear, i.e., for goods i = 1..L, sum over h {xhi} < = sum over h {ehi} + sum over f {yfi}

12. One implication of these theorems is that it is necessary to have a full price system such that markets clear. This requires that the markets be complete, so that all items may be priced. Therefore, capital markets are necessary to indicate the price, or value, of a factor of production.

13. The authors prepared an extensive set of summaries and evaluations of a wide variety of privatization schemes for the Minister of Privatization of the Republic of Poland in 1990. These summaries may be available from the authors upon request.

14. We should note a number of corner solutions to start which relate to intertemporal consumption. First, if the communist regimes were completely successful in their experiment in that all individuals have the same wealth, information and utility functions, then we get that no trading will occur as everyone will value everything equally, as noted in Grossman and Stiglitz (1980). If, however, they have different intertemporal demands for consumption, they will trade with each other to meet their intertemporal demands, as per Hirshleifer (1970) or Barro (1974). But what will they trade intertemporally? If they are in the CAPM world of Sharpe (1963, 1964), they will hold the market portfolio, which was their initial endowment.
Therefore, there once again will not be any trading across securities but trading of the entire market portfolio across individuals depending on their intertemporal marginal rates of substitution of consumption differ.
Another area to note is the limitations on foreign ownership that many countries have imposed as part of their privatization plan. These limitations follow naturally from the above theory in that foreigners are likely to have more wealth than the indigenous population. Barring any legal constraints, it is likely that there would be a massive intertemporal transfer of wealth and consumption from the local population to the foreign population, resulting in foreign ownership of the majority of assets in the country. While there are many potential benefits of such a structure (due to more effective management techniques, industry expertise, information acquisition abilities, and optimal intertemporal transfer opportunities), the political cost of such a transfer is deemed to outweigh such benefits.

15. For example, Poland has 38 million citizens. Using annualized earnings for the first quarter of 1990 and a estimated price/earnings ratio of 4, collective market value of the 484 largest firms is $24.6 billion at a translation rate of 9,500 zloty/$. Assuming that every Pole gets one share of every firm, we get an average value per share of only $1.34 per share. It is important to note that this number is likely to be artificially high as it is based upon estimated earnings

which are to a large degree fictitious because of the hyper-inflation toward the end of 1989. See Gultekin and Wilson (1990) for further estimates. The transactions costs of trading a single share would be higher than that, given the cost structure in the U.S., which is more advanced and should have some scale economies.

16. To see this, assume that the value of the shares are known with certainty. To save time and notation, let us look at a representative agent's endowment. His/her endowment will be a collection of shares, one from each firm in the nation. Therefore, the agent's endowment is worth $e = \sum_{i=1}^{N} v(i)$ where e is the value of the endowment to each individual, v (i) is the value of one share in the with firm, and N is the total number of firms in the economy. Note also that v(i) = V(i)/P, where V(i) is the value of firm is as a whole, and P is the population of the entire country. Therefore, for P large, v(i) is small unless V(i) is very large, although e could be large if N is large.

Assume now that trading is not costless, but incurs a cost b. Surely for all v(i) < b, no trading will occur since the profits from even initiating the transaction are negative, i.e., v(i) - b < 0. Of course, if no one will sell, than no one can buy, unless they are willing to pay p such that p - b > = 0. However, if v(i) < b, then this means a buyer will have to pay p > v(i), which isn't rational since his return will be negative since v(i) - p < 0. In fact, the buyer would not even pay p = v(i), since the buyer will also incur transaction costs of b. Therefore, the most the buyer is willing to pay is p = v(i) - b. For the seller to agree to transact at all, he must receive at least p = b to recoup the transaction costs of trading. To have trading, the price must clear between the buyer and the seller. Therefore, at the minimum, the price must be b = p = v(i) - b, so for trading to occur, a necessary condition is v(i) > 2b.

17. If the value of the firm is not known with certainty, then a slightly different scenario results. In this case, it is necessary that the expected return from trading at least has to exceed the cost of completing a trade for trading to occur. Therefore, it is now true that for the buyer that E[v(i) - p] > = b, or equivalently, E[v(i)] - b > = p. Since the seller faces the same minimum constraint that p > = b, we get at least E[v(i)] = 2b.

18. We hasten to point out that such an equilibrium, although perhaps not desirable, will be parieto optimal once achieved. As Varian (1984) points out in illustrating the First Welfare Theorem in the Edgeworth Box, if there is $100 to be distributed, one solution is to give me all of it and you none of it. While this result may be parieto optimal (in that we cannot make one person better off without making the other worse off), you may not like it very much. 19 In fact, as Grossman and Stiglitz (1980) point out, the very existence of brokerage costs will prevent trade if traders have the same endowments and beliefs since they would end up with their original endowments in a competitive equilibrium but will still incur trading costs if they trade hat if beliefs are different? Grossman and Stiglitz (1980) note that: "... when initial endowments are the same and peoples' beliefs differ slightly, then the competitive equilibrium allocation that an individual gets will be only slightly different from his initial endowment. Hence, there will only be a slight benefit to entering the competitive market. This could, for sufficiently high operating costs, be outweighed by the cost of entering the market." (p. 402)

20. Furthermore, if leaving initial information production up to the market was such a good idea, then we would see more of it in developed capital markets. Instead, even in developed markets, we see new firms go through an expensive IPO process to provide information to potential investors at the expense of the firm as a whole. Surely if it were cheaper and better to leave such information accumulation up to the market firms would do so as they would achieve a competitive advantage. Instead, firms produce information once for all investors to see as it is surely cheaper for the firm to do it once than for each investor to undertake these costs on their own. As the government is the current owner of the firm in post-communist countries, the analogy still applies.

21. The creation of financial intermediaries, however, would be helpful in mitigating high transaction and information costs. One can consider the endowment of shares as an initial endowment of one unit of capital. Leland and Pyle (1977), Boyd and Prescott (1986), Campbell and Kracaw (1980), and Diamond (1984) address the creation of financial intermediaries. A discussion of these papers and the issue of financial intermediaries is taken up in the following section on voucher schemes.

22. The description here is only a general outline of the intent of the proposal. More detailed information relating to the operational aspects of this plan may be found in Sachs et. al. (1990) as appraised in Gultekin and Wilson (1990). Operational problems with this scheme as in all others are ignored here. For example, finding and appointing board members to a very large number of companies is non-trivial, assuming sufficient skill exist.

23. There may be a very short period of trading initially as the funds restructure their portfolios. Grossman and Stiglitz (1980) and Grossman and Hart (1980, 1988) provide some indication that this result will occur. One could, for example, assume that the cost of obtaining information in the Grossman and Stiglitz (1980) model is the cost of gaining control. Due to the problems noted earlier regarding the lack of market-oriented accounting standards or financial reporting mechanisms, etc., it may be impossible for outsiders to acquire information effectively. Insiders, however, may have access to information due to the very nature that makes one an insider. The only way to become an insider in this case is to gain control.

These trades would be undertaken without information as no fund would find it advantageous to complete extensive research on a company prior to obtaining control. The high information costs involved in such research would not necessarily be offset by potential gains since the cost of attaining such information is fixed regardless of the number of shares owned. In addition, the sheer magnitude of the number of firms to be analyzed would likely inhibit such research until a fund has a majority share. Furthermore, the cost of information acquisition in an economy where there is no tradition of external reporting is more costly than many people realize. More important, this cost is invariant, whether the acquisition of information is done by merchant bankers or mutual funds. In addition, the worldwide supply of individuals or firms capable of completing such research is sufficiently small that the task could not be completed without the other funds knowing which funds have evaluated which enterprises. A fund will not wish to trade with a fund that has superior information; therefore, the potential gains of getting such information will not be realized. As each fund is rational and assumes all other funds are also rational, no fund will expend significant resources on analyses which require expensive information gathering. Therefore, initial trading prices will not reflect information, but merely preferences for a redistribution of endowments.

24. This result occurs because the expected value of the returns achieved by an uninformed investor when trading with an informed investor is negative. To see this, note that the informed investor knows how much the firm is worth and will not overpay when buying or underprice when selling so his expected value of trading will always be positive. The expected values of returns on trading between uninformed investors is zero, since neither party has better information so neither party will do better on average.

Since the uninformed investor has a positive probability of trading with an informed investor on any given trade (since he does not know the identity of the counterpart to the trade), the expected value of trading for the uninformed investor is negative, as shown below. The uninformed investor, on average, loses when trading in a market with informed investors, and so will not trade with them, unless there are the presence of liquidity traders who will trade in sufficient quantity to subsidize the losses of the uninformed investors. Since there will be no liquidity traders, there will be no trading, and, as a result, information will not be reflected in the prices.

The lack of trading occurs because of the lack of liquidity traders present to compensate the uninformed investor for trading in a market with asymmetric information.

The liquidity traders trade not for informational reasons, but for exogenous ones, such as intertemporal switching from investment to consumption, due to unexpected sudden needs for cash (such as medical emergencies, car troubles, etc.). Since these liquidity traders no longer want to hold the securities, they will trade regardless of price. As a result, the expected value for an uninformed trader of trading with a liquidity trader is positive. The liquidity traders, therefore, subsidize the uninformed traders for trading in a market which also includes informed traders. Without them, no trading will exist.

To see this, assume that in the absence of informed traders the price for the kth trade on the ith stock is given by $pk(i) = v \bullet (i) + ek$, where $ek - N(0,1)$. Then the profit or loss from the kth trade if it is a purchase is $tk = Pk(i) - v \bullet (i) = ek$, and the reverse ($-ek$) if it is a sale. Therefore, the expected value of trading in a market with only uninformed traders is $E[tk] = E[ek] = 0$. If we assume that there are q informed traders in the market, the expected value of a purchase for an uninformed investor is:

E[trading/presence of informed investors]

= q * E[return/informed investor] + (1-q) * E[return/uninformed investor]

= q * {[v•(i) - p(i)] * I[v•(i) < p(i)] + [p(i)] - v•(i)] * I[v•(i) > p(i)]} + (1-q) * 0 < 0 here I[]
is the indicator function, taking a value of one if the statement inside the brackets is true, and
zero otherwise.

25. Even if we relax the lack of liquidity traders somewhat, we do not improve the situation significantly. For example, assume that a small proportion of the shares of the underlying securities are distributed directly to the populace, for example, to the workers of each firm. In this case, the workers may act as liquidity traders, should they choose to trade their shares (which may be unlikely due to control considerations and high brokerage costs). However, Grossman and Stiglitz (1980) show that the percentage of trades undertaken by liquidity traders directly, affects the level of prices, because it induces trading by the uninformed traders. If there are very few trades by liquidity traders, it becomes increasingly likely that an uninformed trader will be trading with an informed trader, and so the uninformed trader will be less likely to trade. Uninformed traders will also require substantial inducements to trade in such an environment, which will cause large spreads to occur, as shown in Glosten and Milgrom (1985). Grossman and Stiglitz (1980) also show that the level of trading and the information content of prices depends on the number of liquidity traders. Thus there will be very few liquidity traders and extremely thin trading.

26. While the entire mutual fund could be taken over, sheer size would prohibit such a massive undertaking without governmental assistance, which is exactly the opposite of what privatization is attempting to achieve.

27. In fact, as there is always the possibility to mimic the groupings that result in this scheme if free distribution is used, a degree of freedom is lost and society is surely net worse off, as under the free distribution scheme it could always mimic any grouping occurring in this instance.

28. Likewise, voucher schemes do not require auctions. For example, distributing vouchers which can only be tendered one-for-one for specific shares is identical to simply distributing the shares themselves with one additional step in the process. If vouchers with a nominal value are distributed which may be tendered for a variety of shares which will be offered without an auction process, the government is actually attempting a typical initial public offering (IPO) process. Such IPO processes may accept either both cash and vouchers or just vouchers alone. In either case, the government will need to price the shares prior to the IPO and over- and under-subscriptions may result from under- or over-pricing. For this reason, distribution methods using auctions have been suggested in order to avoid the necessity of developing a mechanism to determine share allocation.

29. There are a variety of permutations of voucher schemes. One option is to give the vouchers nominal value and both cash and vouchers to be used to purchase shares during the auctions. If the vouchers are sold to the public for their exact face value, it is difficult to see why vouchers would be purchased. Cash can be used to purchase many goods, while vouchers can only be used for privatization auctions. Since cash can also be used for privatization auctions and the price of a share in cash is the same as it is in vouchers, cash would dominate vouchers and no one would hold vouchers. As a result, proposals with vouchers with a nominal value that are to be used in auctions along with cash often suggest that the vouchers are to be sold for less than the face value or even given away freely. Such vouchers include the "privatization bonds" in Poland or convertible bonds which may be exchanged for shares in other countries. However, the sale of these vouchers at a discount create interesting arbitrage opportunities, the outcome of which depend on the ability to trade the vouchers on secondary markets prior to the auction.

30. Before beginning, it is important to note that any nominal value on the voucher is irrelevant as it merely determines the number of "points" the voucher is worth. Unlike money, vouchers have no intrinsic value and cannot be converted into consumption. Therefore, the price rationing system is not functioning as it would be in typical financial markets. In financial markets, the price of the share and the return on the share are in the same units, i.e., money or a direct substitute. However, in a voucher bidding process, the cost of the share is a unitless voucher, while the return is in money. Vouchers, since they cannot be converted into consumption with

certainty, have an indeterminate value. Their value is dependant in many ways on the eventual prices of the securities in terms of vouchers, which is unknown prior to the auctions.

31. Such a scheme is presented in Frydman and Rapaczynski (1990). The basic premise of this proposal is that ownership of industry will be transferred to the masses of the population, but at the same time, control of industry will be vested in highly efficient institutions (investment funds) that will bring modern knowledge, skills and technology to the industry. This supporters of this plan have assumed that the individual investor will not make their own decision regarding the use of vouchers, but instead will delegate that decision to large, competitive mutual funds, which will be managed initially by foreign banks and investment houses. This plan assumes that the funds themselves should have different general strategies in terms of risk profile or industry weightings.

They will charge management fees, which will be determined by the level of competition among the funds. Fund performance will be monitored by the investors' movement assets among the funds. The funds should be sufficiently large so that there is incentive for them to do research and perform well; also, they will have an incentive to acquire large blocks of shares, in order to exercise control over management and implement appropriate changes in the enterprise. An inherent assumption in this plan is that the market will monitor the funds, and the funds will monitor the privatized enterprises. The funds could develop similar to the German system in which the banking sector plays an important role in the monitoring of the productive sector.

32. The high fixed costs included in the voucher system - including the cost of designing such a system, educating the populace, creating the proper infrastructure for the bidding process, etc. - could make it likely that the total societal costs will be greater under a voucher scheme. In addition, society members unused to capital markets will have to learn one system only to discard it and learn another

33. For example, many business school MBA programs in the United States have installed elaborate auction systems for students to select courses or interview slots. Their admissions offices assures us that these students are talented and highly educated. Therefore, these students should act as good proxies for the actions of others in what essentially is a voucher scheme. Each student is endowed with the same number of points, and the interview slots surely have value, albeit an uncertain one (especially in a declining economy), as they are a necessary but not sufficient condition for an eventual job.

It almost always turns out that, out of 100 points, certain courses or interview slots tend to cost approximately 96 points, with the remainder going for one point or less.

According to participants, they bid this number of points because they expected that others would as well and they knew that if they bet less, they definitely would not receive the course or interview. They also noted that over the years, the number of points bid converged, as they had access to the cost in points of last year's winning bid. Finally, they noted that it was certainly not true that those jobs were 96 times more valuable than the other jobs. (This was even more true for the courses.)

Instead, it was simply that they felt that the cost in points for certain jobs would be around 96 and for others around one or two and so they bid accordingly. In other words, they bid points not on the relative value of the interviews themselves, but on what they believed others would be bidding. Schools which prevent disclosure of previous results of auctions show very high variability in the price in points for the same course with the same professor from one semester to the next, indicating such structures do not lead to price discovery.

34. In general, voucher systems encourage specialization, since, as shown above, those who concentrate their bidding will be more likely to receive the shares, or, in fact, any shares at all. This will increase investors idiosyncratic risk. On the other hand, voucher schemes may be appropriate for privatizations which include all state-owned assets, and not just the largest of the state-owned enterprises, as some individuals may use their vouchers to purchase a small store or enterprise in its entirety. This action may be privately optimal for the individual involved if he/she receives some additional benefit, as in Grossman and Hart (1980), as it is, in effect, a takeover of the small enterprise. Recent work by Winton (1990) indicates that for certain firms large investor claims will provide optimal monitoring and control, resulting in optimal managerial effort. In fact, Winton (1990) shows that under certain conditions, unlimited liability ownership forms, such as a sole proprietorship or a partnership, are more optimal than

limited liability forms, such as a corporate form with limited liability.

While one benefit of this method of privatization is that it will allow optimal ownership of small businesses, and will allow governments to structure such ownership in an optimal manner, other methods of privatization do this as well. In particular, privatization schemes which use vouchers with a fixed nominal value would also work, as well as schemes which incorporate ESOPs or LBOs. As noted by Vuylsteke (1990) and Hinds (1990), a mixed strategy calls for separate privatization forms for large and small companies are optimal as they would also achieve this result. The auction process itself is not a necessary component of deriving the benefit noted in Winton (1990).

35. For example, if there are 100 vouchers in existence and the total value of the firms to be auctioned in this sequential auction is $500, then the expected value of each voucher is worth $5.

36. The final auction in a sequential auction will resemble a one-time auction. Overbidding will no longer be penalized and underbidding will not reap future benefits.

37. A problem with arguments for the development of financial intermediaries is that non-tendering shareholders will also benefit from any steps that the financial intermediary might take to improve the earning potential of the firm, as noted in Grossman and Hart (1980). As the investors already own shares in the firm at no cost to themselves, they can "mimic" the holdings of the financial intermediary in the sense of Campbell and Kracaw (1980) merely by following a buy-and-hold strategy. Therefore, as noted by Grossman and Hart (1980) or Campbell and Kracaw (1980), it is necessary that financial intermediary owners receive some private benefit from owning the financial intermediary, either due to management contracts of the financial intermediary with the firm or due to other services the financial intermediary can provide.

Otherwise, no one will tender their shares to a financial intermediary and will instead simply hold their portfolio, partially because brokerage costs prohibit them from selling their shares. However, the use of vouchers should allow the low cost development of financial intermediaries if one can assign them before the auction takes place.

38. In the event that financial intermediaries are capitalized in hard currency, the may purchase vouchers and bundle securities so as to avoid transaction costs problems may arise and will allow investors that prefer immediate consumption to liquidate their holdings, as discussed previously in the section on the free distribution of shares. The same results apply.

39. See Allen (1989) for an excellent survey.

PANEL II

Privatization of Defence Industries in the Framework of Privatization at Large: Commonalities and Specifics

Chair: Reiner Weichhardt, Deputy Director,
NATO Economics Directorate

Panelists: Keith Bush
Radomir Sabela
Fredrik Behrens
Thierry Baumgart
Alexander Kennaway

CONVERSION AND PRIVATIZATION OF DEFENCE ENTERPRISES IN RUSSIA

Keith Bush

Conversion is hard in the West. In Russia, the problems are even more formidable. The tradition of creating state monopolies in defence production goes back to Tsarist days. Now the hothouse doors are open, and Russia's cosseted defence plants are having to pay market prices for raw materials and market wages for skilled workers. And with no more Warsaw Pact partners, she also has to make all her own weapons. Small wonder that there has been little enthusiasm to date for conversion, says Keith Bush. Things are moving - but a change in the political climate could uproot the whole process.

Keith Bush is a Senior Associate at the Centre for Strategic Studies in Washington. During his professional career, he has acquired wide-ranging experience as an analyst of the Soviet economy.

The conversion/ diversification of defense industries in the West will be difficult enough, but the problems facing the former Soviet Union and Eastern Europe in this area look even more formidable. In Russia the thrust of conversion will be via privatization. Formal voucher privatization has proceeded rapidly throughout the economy, but questions remain for privatized defense plants in respect of the remaining degree of state control and the amount of operational autonomy left with the enterprises.

The conversion/diversification of defense industries to the production of civilian goods and services presents appreciable problems in any developed society, but the challenge to the military-industrial complexes of the former Soviet Union and in Eastern Europe appears to be even more formidable than in the West.

The American experience has been typical of the starting point of most Western attempts to retool their military-industrial complexes. Defense firms have traditionally been geared toward working for one single customer, in the shape of the Department of Defense, that sets the price, pays much or most of the bill upfront, and then provides new infusions of cash as each specified phase of the project is completed. The factories have been accustomed to long production runs and lengthy lead times. In many instances they have been the sole suppliers of a given piece of military hardware or have been able to arrive at comfortable market-sharing arrangements. For reasons of national security, they have generally been sheltered from foreign competition. The prices paid for their products have often been a secondary consideration, provided that they meet stringent quality and performance standards.[1]

Defense plants in Russia, in other former Soviet republics, and in Eastern Europe start from much the same kind of operational environment, but are confronted by additional obstacles. Traditionally, the defense industry in prerevolutionary Russia and in the former USSR was a state monopoly, though with some competition organized among design bureaus to stimulate alternative designs of new systems.

The prices of their material inputs were kept artificially low, but now they must reckon with inputs priced at or near world levels. They rarely had to meet the full burden of depreciation, premises, and research and development costs out of their operating budgets. They have lost their privileged status that guaranteed them access to the highest available levels of personnel and technology and priority in respect of supplies. To a much greater extent than in the West, many of them are located in one-company towns and cities, where virtually the entire population is dependent on the plant, and no alternative employment is within commuting distance.

Unemployment exchanges are nonexistent or function poorly. The housing market is in its infancy, and much of the available living space is in fact company housing. For the above reasons, labour mobility has tended to be much lower than in the West. Nevertheless, there has been a considerable outflow of skilled workers from the military-industrial complex during the past few years, owing in large part to the prolongation of wage controls in the complex after such controls had broken down in most other sectors, starting in 1989, combined with sharp cuts in state defense procurements. Most of those who voted with their feet were presumably the younger workers residing in large cities.

Factories have typically provided a whole range of infrastructural services - such as clinics, kindergartens, creches, vacation resorts, canteens, and even farms - for which local authorities are reluctant or unable to assume responsibility. Unlike their Western counterparts, most of them have no marketing experience or expertise. And the defense industries in these countries have been isolated to a far greater degree from manufacturers of civilian products and lacked feedback in both directions.

The Progress of Privatization Throughout the Economy

After the launch of the conversion program in December 1988, in the USSR and then in Russia, several blueprints were drawn up and much debate ensued over how to proceed with the conversion of the military-industrial complex, but little progress on the ground was evident until 1993. In the wake of such traumatic events as a prolonged economic recession, savage cuts in state procurements of military hardware, a sharp fall in arms exports for convertible currencies, and tardiness in accepting the precept of Charles Dickens's Mr. Micawber that budgetary outgoings should approximately match budgetary income, defense manufacturers were finally persuaded that conversion must proceed in earnest and that the process would not be financed primarily by outright grants or soft credits out of the federal budget. Instead, plants would have to generate the necessary capital themselves after privatization[2].

Since the freeing of most wholesale and retail prices in January 1992, the privatization program in Russia has been the most important facet of President Boris Yeltsin's economic reform. In its pace and scope, it has far exceeded comparable processes in both West and East. Although formal voucher privatization started only in October 1992, by the end of March 1994 most of the economy had been formally destatized. Anatolii Chubais, the deputy prime minister in charge of privatization and the chairman of the State Committee for the Management of State Property (GKI), was able to present an impressive balance sheet at a news conference on 23 March.

Some 15,000 large industrial enterprises and more than 80,000 small enterprises -70% of the total- had been turned into joint-stock companies. Chubais declared that more than half of the gross domestic product was now being produced outside the state sector[3]. It is probably true to say that privatization in Russia is now irreversible. Opinion polls regularly show a majority of the population in favour of the program, and even its most outspoken opponents do not advocate its cancellation or any attempt at renationalization.

Yet what we have seen during the past eighteen months has been the formal destatization of much of the economy. There is much to the charge put forward by the reform economist and current presidential hopeful Grigorii Yavlinsky: "What has happened so far is not privatization, it is collectivization, which puts the workers and managers in charge of enterprises. Their interest is in increasing wages, not investment. This is a new problem created by this style of management"[4]. His point is taken by some of Chubais's advisers, who concede that "workers and managers often end up with more than 70% of the shares of the privatized companies" and that concessions to the managers of privatized plants have been "simply enormous"[5].

The criteria for the success or failure of the program must surely be whether privatization has changed the way in which the plants operate and are managed. Maksim Boycko, the head of the Privatization Center, claimed that more than half of the privatized firms had already altered their product mix -although he did not spell out to what degree- and had introduced incentive-based wages. At the first 215 meetings of shareholders, according to Boycko, the incumbent managers were removed from twenty-nine factories[6]. Critics are less sanguine and claim that little has changed, apart from the formal deeds of ownership. Most managers remain in place, little headway has been made in reducing widespread overmanning, and many plants appear to survive on soft credits. But it is early days yet, and major shifts in direction can hardly be expected only a few months after the outset of formal privatization; especially as many facets of the operational environment remain untouched.

It is probably true to say that the command economy in Russia has been dismantled but has yet to be replaced by the mechanisms, the nuts and bolts, of the market. As Chubais himself admitted, the whole concept of privatization could come to nought without the implementation of broader macroeconomic reforms and the establishment of a reliable financial system with a functioning capital market[7]. At the time of writing, despite the best of intentions and a multitude of promises, no really hard budget constraints have been introduced for plants in the state sector or for most, if not all, of those that have been formally corporatized or even privatized.

Only a handful of enterprises have been declared bankrupt, and it was not until March 1994 that the government started listing candidates for bankruptcy proceedings[8]. And to judge from a recent interview with the head of the Federal Administration for Insolvency Cases[9], prompt action in this regard should not be expected. The official rate of unemployment is still about 1%, and even the true unemployment ratio of, say, 6-8% by no means corresponds with a drop of over 40% in gross domestic product since 1990. The establishment of functioning anti-monopoly legislation is a lengthy business in any economy, and it has hardly got off the ground in Russia.

Import competition is unknown in many sectors, and protectionism has been heightened by the raising of import tariffs as of 15 March 1994. The level of foreign investment in the Russian economy remains low -a total of perhaps $7-8 billion at the end of 1993[10] - which is understandable, given the maze of conflicting legislation and the lack of property rights and stable institutions guaranteeing contracts, not to mention the wholly unpredictable system and punitive levels of taxation. Indeed, what Seagram's manager in Kiev said of Ukraine is true of most, if not all, of the former Soviet republics: "It is now impossible to do business in Ukraine legally and make a profit"[11].

Conversion via Privatization

By the end of 1994 about 1,500 of the roughly 2,000 major defense plants in Russia are due to have been formally privatized[12]. How will they fare in comparison with the other privatized factories in the remaining sectors of Russian industry? What are their strengths and weaknesses?

The good news is that the products of defense enterprises in the former Soviet Union have long been virtually the only fabricated goods that have been able -nay, obliged- to compete on the world market. These enterprises' workforces and technologies were selected from the best available in the country. Many of them should presumably therefore represent an attractive prospect for domestic and foreign investment funds. Their premises and equipment are, generally speaking, superior to those found in civilian industry. Their social infrastructural amenities tend also to be better than those at their civilian industrial counterparts. Until fairly recently, the level of work discipline was also higher: in mid-1993 their representatives could claim that "compared with the overall chaos in the country, order, organization, and discipline have been preserved at defense industry enterprises"[13]. This may no longer be the case. By March 1994 mutterings of discontent were getting louder, after months in which the economy-wide payments arrears crisis had affected defense plants also, and many employees had been working part-time or had been obliged to take unpaid leave.

During the phase following voucher privatization, however, the defense plants in these countries will face some obstacles in common with all other factories. One troublesome issue is the legacy of decades of integration with other former Soviet republics and, to a lesser extent, with East European members of the now defunct Warsaw Pact. Thus, according to a deputy chairman of Roskomoboronprom, the umbrella organization in charge of Russia's defense industries, without inputs from other former Soviet republics Russia can produce only 17% of the military hardware it requires. It will therefore need to collaborate on defense output with them for at least another five to seven years[14]. But this cooperation is imperilled by payments problems, breakdowns in supplies, and stoppages caused by fuel shortages.

To date, the conversion effort in Russia has been propelled largely from the top down. And yet the political leadership, in the shape of Roskomoboronprom, has shown little enthusiasm for the privatization process[15]. A similar distaste has been shown by the key defense official concerned with conversion, Deputy Defense Minister Andrei Kokoshin[16].

The main problem for all these privatized companies -defense and civilian alike- will be to find independent sources of capital[17]. The problem may be more acute in the case of defense plants, though, in that clarity has yet to be established on the degree of independence of these plants and how much of a controlling influence will be retained by the government. As Chubais put it: "Real sources of finance that could rescue enterprises exist, but will never agree to invest resources in state [defense] enterprises, because they do not know how such an enterprise will be managed, what belongs to them and what does not, to whom state property belongs - to the director, to the work force, to the State Committee for the Management of State property, or to the government"[18].

Under the provisions of the presidential decree on the privatization and state regulation of the defense industry, which modified the terms for its privatization, in the case of those enterprises in which the state retains an ownership share, the government will retain a role in the appointment of executives. Moreover, the mechanism for floating the shares of defense enterprises will make it difficult for outsiders to gain a sizable ownership share[19]. In a recent pronouncement, the deputy chairman of GKI in charge of privatizing defense plants said that, of the 850 eligible factories that had not been privatized by the end of February

1994, the state would retain a majority share in 150 of them for three years and would exercise veto powers over managerial decisions at 600 plants[20].

Conclusion

Although the necessity to down size the former Soviet Union's monstrous military-industrial complex has been evident and generally accepted for several years, Russia, which inherited about 80% of that complex, has taken only hesitant steps toward converting its defense industry. Not until 1993 was the decision taken to effect and finance this process by means of privatizing the bulk of the defense plants. Progress in the formal voucher privatization of these plants has been impressive in the past few months. A crucial requirement for the privatization process following the initial voucher phase will be the clarification of their executive autonomy and the demarcation of government control in key aspects of their management. Otherwise formal privatization is unlikely to bring the new and substantial investment that is necessary for effective conversion.

The complete transition to some variant of a market economy in Russia, the other former Soviet republics, and Eastern Europe will take generations. Likewise, the conversion/diversification of their large military-industrial complexes -a vital component of the transition process- will require decades, even if reform elements survive in top government positions to maintain the momentum. A shift in regime in favour of a figure such as Russia's Liberal Democratic party leader Vladimir Zhirinovsky or former Vice President Aleksandr Rutskoi could stall or delay this forward movement; all bets would then be off.

FOOTNOTES

1 See The Economist, 2 April 1994.
2 Keith   Bush,   "Aspects   of   Military   Conversion   in   Russia", RFE/RL Research Report, no. 14, 8 April 1994.
3 Ostankino Television, 23 March 1994.
4 Cited in The Economist, 12 March 1994.
5 Ibid.
6 The Washington Post, 31 March 1994.
7 The Wall Street Journal, 1 February 1994.
8 ITAR-TASS, 4 April 1994.
9 Novoye vremya, no. 2, January 1994.
10 The Wall Street Journal, 26 January 1994.
11 International Herald Tribune, 29-30 January 1994.
12 Interfax, 7 April 1994.
13 Delovye lyudi, August 1993, p. 26.
14 Interfax, 8 December 1993.
15 See Bush, "Aspects of Military Conversion....".
16 This was demonstrated most clearly in his interview with Rossiiskie vesti, 22 July 1993, but also in subsequent pronouncements.
17 Anatolii Chubais in The Wall Street Journal, 1 February 1994.
18 Ostankino Television, 3 February 1994.
19 Julian Cooper, "Transforming Russia's Defence Industrial Base", Survival, Winter 1993, p. 157.
20 Interfax, 28 February 1994.

CONVERSION AND PRIVATIZATION IN THE CZECH REPUBLIC

Radomir Sabela

The political changes in Europe have led to substantial cutbacks in arms production. In the Czech Republic, the sheer size of the defence sector meant that the government had to run a massive conversion programme alongside its privatisation programme. The government set up a special fund in 1991 to make this conversion as painless as possible. Some companies quietly ceased their activities; others were retooled to produce consumer goods. Radomir Sabela reports on how his country has gone about transforming its swords into ploughshares.

Radomir Sabela is the Deputy Minister for Industry and Construction in the Ministry of Industry and Trade of the Czech Republic.

With the changes in the internal situation of Central and East European States and the reduction in European conventional weapons, a significant cut in military production, development and deliveries has occurred, even in the Czech republic. As a consequence of this process, conversion has become a crucial issue.

The decline in armament production within the Czech republic industries profile, during the years of 1987 - 1992, is documented by the following table (billions of Czech crowns, in current prices):

	1987	1988	1989	1990	1991	1992
Czech republic arms production	- 11.5	- 12.3	- 10.5	- 7.5	- 4.5	- 2.4

Between 1989 and 1990 the problems related to unused armament capacities were solved by Federation State Budget allocations:
- in 1989 - 68 millions of Kf, on the stocks cover,
- in 1990 - 388 millions of Kf, onto 25 organisations profit.

The State's response met the immediate problems, and in certain organisations were possible negative economic consequences prevented. However, this approach has been unsystematic.

1991 was a turning point for the State's role in armament industry conversion. Important measures were enacted to help the most affected organisations.

A "Special Technology Extra Fund" was set up for the year 1991. Organizations with unusable stock or fixed assets were given assistance. And there was State Budget support for new civilian production projects.

The Fund was designed to cover those armament productions with no guaranteed outlet ensured,such as those with a single-purpose nature, the conversion of which has a fixed feature (ammunition plants).

Where this production output has not been exported during the following years it has been, gradually, purchased by the Czech republic Army.

Companies with unusable stocks were allowed to liquidate up to 40 per cent of the price based basic assets. They have been compensated for the remaining 60 per cent from State Financial Assets.

Where there was no investment credit, the unusable fixed assets were liquidated and depreciation was calculated according to the basic assets,

Those with an unpaid credit were liquidated to meet the unsettled credit balance owed to the State, reduced by the liquidation yield.

Support has been provided for 30 per cent of the Project machinery investments, for 100 per cent of interest on the credits for the Project machinery purchase, for a new product licence purchase, or for a new technology.

Between 1991 and 1993, State Budget support amounted to about 510 millions of Kf, disbursed to 35 organisations for 60 projects.

Those Projects may be described as follows:
- Projects towards extending and improving existing Civilian Programs which had been, in addition to the arms manufacturing, part of the organisation's production profile.
- Projects towards implementing new production programs designed for the home market gaps, or for export.
- Projects towards the manufacturing of purchased products for final production assembling purposes.

The above mentioned system of state assistance to the organisations affected by conversion has, without any doubt enabled some of them to launch new production Programs.

Owing to the high number and variety of conversion projects, however, they have not produced marked structural changes in Czech industry.

Conversion has been carried out during the transition towards the market economy and this is of crucial significance.

In this connection an important role has been played by the Economic Reform Macroeconomic Frame set-up, particularly by the policy of currency stabilization and finance restrictions, prices liberalization, but, mainly, by the change in ownership relations - privatization. Privatization has been, of course, dealing even with the arms industry.

Despite some considerations concerning the specific features of the armament industry, no special legal provisions have been made for them. They have been subject to all privatization legislation. Armament enterprises have been included in both privatization waves.

Privatization

In the starting year of 1989, the Net Product Breakdown was as follows:
- Nationalized sector (State enterprises and cooperatives) - 97.4 per cent of Net Product,
- Private sector (approx. 2 per cent of over-all assets) - 3.6 per cent of Net Product.

Most organisations formerly under the authority of the Ministry for Industry and Trade were privatized within the framework of the so called "Big Privatization" during the course of two waves. The First Wave has been concluded, and the Second is still in progress.

The procedure has comprised:
- A privatization project (legal entity or individual) evaluation at the Founding Ministry level (in our case on the Ministry for Industry and Trade level), and
- The decision on the National property and Privatization Ministry level, or by the Government.

The National Property Fund has been established and authorized to administer the assets until the decision on its Privatization.

The principal methods of privatization have been:
- Public tender.
- Direct sale.
- Coupon privatization.
- Assets free transfer on municipalities.
- Auction.

The Ministry for Industry and Trade has played a founding role in case of 1,712 enterprises and limited companies, of which 220 have been proposed for liquidation (as of December 31, 1993, 62 of them have been liquidated). In the privatization First and Second Wave, the assets have been included in the total value of 683.5 billions of Kf, of which 225 billions of Kf went on the coupons (33 per cent); the number of subjects amounted to 1,335 and of Projects to 9,117.

During December, 1993, State ownership still amounted to 32.1 per cent of the assets, while private property represented 67.9 per cent (of which the coupon method represented - 28.8 per cent and others - 39.1 per cent).

The arms industry's key enterprises have been privatized, mostly into limited companies with a certain coupon privatization share (e.g. AERO Prague, Czech Armoury at Cesky Brod, Meopta at Prerov, Engineering works at Policka, Sellier and Bellot at Vlasim, Tesla Prague, Synthesia at Pardubice), one by a direct sale (Vlárské Engineering works at Slavicín), and one by public tender (Tesla at Pardubice).

The State has preserved its influence in some of them by holding a certain share package, or through a "golden share" (e.g. Czech Armoury, Sellier and Bellot, Engineering works at Policka).

Evaluating the privatisation of the arms industry, executed without exemption within the whole Czech Economy Transformation, has been up to now impossible.

Regardless of the privatization method and of the preservation of State influence or not, there remain some organisations within the Czech Republic industrial base with interests in certain armaments production, wich are trying to suceed with their deliveries to the Czech Republic or other armies, even in co-operation with foreign partners.

PRIVATIZING DEFENCE INDUSTRIES: A SHIPPING SECTOR CASE

Fredrik Behrens

When western governments sold off their shipyards in the 1980s, they went into a thriving private sector that could help them diversify by absorbing new products and creating new markets. Even so, the exercise wasn't painless. The yards had to break up to survive, and many of them have only recently become competitive. Russia's shipyards are walking a higher tightrope with no safety net, says Fredrik Behrens. Either the Russian state or foreign investment will have to provide one.

Fredrik Behrens is the Executive Vice-President in charge of International Developments of the Norwegian company, Kvaerner Rosenberg a.s.

The shipyards and their related construction industry play an important role in employment and have a strategic role as an element of the defence industry. This is why many shipyards in western Europe were nationalised and "protected" when shipbuilding in the 1970s experienced a dramatic fall after a rapid rise. Japan and South Korea's present dominant position in shipbuilding is primarily due to this double change in the market and national "protection" of West-European yards. Only lately have some European yards again become competitive.

In Norway, increased investment in offshore oil and gas activities lessened the impact on employment from reduced shipbuilding. In the UK and continental Europe the impact on employment and the costs to society were dramatic.

A Brief History of a Selection of Companies

Kvaerner Govan shipyard, Glasgow, UK

The yard was founded in 1854, and nationalised in the 1970s as part of British Shipbuilders. It was privatised in 1988, becoming part of Kvaerner, and became successful and profitable in 1994.

The privatisation process reduced the number of employees from 2,200 to 1,500. Investments were made in modern hull construction technology as a part of the privatisation agreement with British Shipbuilders. The yard was and is a merchant shipyard, with limited military experience. Today the yard operates in close co-operation with other Kvaerner shipyards. Joint orders on ships series, exchange of personnel and co-operation in productivity measures and supply are important elements of its success. Changing labour relations was a difficult task, which only ended successfully after some turmoil. Absenteeism was reduced from 22% in 1989 to 5% in 1993.

Kvaerner Govan recently won the contract for a new British helicopter carrier through its business relationship with the VSEL (Vickers), which at a time was also a part of British Shipbuilders. After privatisation, it continued as a military specialist, particularly on submarines. VSEL closed their shipyards recently as a private company, when it was made clear that carrying on as a military shipyard was not commercially attractive.

The present collaboration is seen to have a future in cases where the merchant yards maintain their competitiveness and by this give added value for money for the part of the military orders where merchant shipbuilding standards and procedures can be used, and the defence specialists develop and exploit their speciality on the elements of the order where such knowledge is of greatest importance.

Kvaerner Govan are seeing increased subcontracting on steelworks and specialist work on the control area in addition to the traditional subcontracting of insulation, ventilation, carpenters and electrical installation which they share with the local construction projects. They also used to subcontract painting, but have built a department themselves to operate their painting facilities in close co-operation with their modern production line. There is a rather poor infrastructure in terms of unit subcontracting in Glasgow and the company is raising discussions with their regular subcontractors about their willingness to take the peaks and valleys.

Swan Hunter Shipyard, Tyneside, UK

Founded 1842 - Nationalised 1977 - Privatised 1986 (management buy-out) - crises since 1993

At the time of losing the helicopter carrier to Vickers/Kvaerner Govan, 2600 people were employed. Today, one year later, 800-1000 are still working. In 1993 when the contract was awarded, comments in the press referred to differences in quality between the naval yard and the merchant shipyard. It is difficult to have a specific opinion on such matters, but these kind of comments are quite common when industry changes and clients change their priorities. Today, one year later, Swan Hunter is still bidding on smaller naval contracts. There are speculations about a French group being interested in taking over the company, provided contracts to keep it going can be secured. Otherwise, it is expected that the yard will close down in the near future.

Kvaerner Warnow Werft, Warnemünde, Germany

This yard was founded after World War II in East Germany and privatised as a part of the Treuhandanstalt mission to become part of Kvaerner.

This conversion includes privatisation as well as the initial investment to build an entirely new and modern yard, introducing the latest technologies in shipbuilding. The conversion happened soon after the reunion of Germany and therefore in parallel with the conversion of the political system, including the social security system. The reunification of Germany is easing the conversion process for the earlier employees compared to what is expected for industries in the other former socialist countries.

By 1990, the Warnowerft employed 5,700. The conversion will bring this down to 2,400. At Warnow, the yard had started on a program to produce consumer goods, a pattern well known at the larger industries from the later period of the Soviet communist system. They produced things like trailer hitches, refrigerators etc. which in the market-driven West are found as parts of completely by different industry groups than shipbuilding. These activities were lifted out of the new company and privatised separately with other owners. Some continued for a while in the old buildings at the wharf, some moved and some were shut down.

From the remaining workforce it was the administrative personnel more than the skilled labour that faced the most difficulties. Something like 70% of the administrative staff had to be laid off.

Early pension and redundancy were part of the conversion package. Unemployment after the initial period was not. It is therefore not possible to give a comprehensive picture of the cost of conversion, but it is surely beyond the cost for starting up an entirely new yard in any of the western countries. In the case of Warnow, the heavy burdens were laid on German taxpayers, and there were motives and financial capacity to support such a development.

Support of this kind is not available in Russia. Therefore the sufferings will be harder there and the speed with which conversion takes place will be much slower.

Horten Verft, Horten, Norway

(Earlier The Main Naval Yard of Norway)

Horten Verft was founded in 1818 as the main yard of the Norwegian Navy. It was converted to commercial operations in 1948 (together with other Norwegian Defence industries Kongsberg, Raufoss). Still owned by the state, it went bankrupt in 1986 caused by the general collapse in the shipbuilding market. In the 1970s it produced excellent merchant vessels which, combined with naval and other state orders, kept it alive for longer than many of its European competitors. Operations stopped completely after the bankruptcy. The different facilities and departments of the yard were privatised as single companies as an "Industrial park" taking advantage of its location in a more densely populated part of the country than most other yards. The activities are, however, low compared to before the bankruptcy.

Recently, a local entrepreneur with background in the earlier shipbuilding industry in the area has obtained an order for a ship, where the hull is bought cheaply abroad and where the outfitting is going to take place at the facilities in Horten using the small private companies in the "industrial park" as subcontractors on the order. It still remains to be seen if the skills are available, but it could be the start of a trend since there are parallels in the area of ship repairs.

The history of Horten Verft also illustrates other trends. The yard dominated the building of the national Navy up to the mid '60s, although several vessels were imported just after the War. Since then the Royal Norwegian Navy went for small fast vessels made out of thin plate steel. New private yards were engaged for this task. After the initial naval order, the yard(s) obtained a series of contracts for fast vessels that were used for passenger transport. The original navy design was adjusted to accommodate aluminium as material and was also redesigned as catamarans. The first orders were for the Norwegian coastal traffic, and later it became an export success. This developed a cluster of fast vessels producers in the country and although location and ownership shifted over time, the industry is a sizeable supplier of fast vessels on the world market today. The current building program of the Norwegian Navy is dominated by advanced catamarans in GRP material. It remains to be seen if this could be the start of a similar success as the aluminium vessels.

Haugesund Mekaniske Verksted, Norwegian West Coast

This yard has been successfully kept alive by combining construction and installation work for the North Sea oil and gas activities with ship repair, which is a continuation of their long-standing traditions. This is unlike the other Norwegian shipyards, where the way to success seemed to be either to convert completely to offshore fabrication or to specialise within narrow niches of merchant shipbuilding. Those who did not, died. Also unlike the other yards that survived the difficult '70s and '80s in Norway, the Haugesund yard has until lately not become a financial success. Two major events caused the change Major layoffs were made in 1991 and the yard was thereafter sold to an expanding shipowner who obtained the yard for around £5 million. The yard has land and facilities that would cost more than £50 million if they were built and procured today. All costs related to the layoffs and restructuring were met before the sale.

Kvaerner Rosenberg , Stavanger Norway

Founded in 1896 it had a difficult life until it expanded rapidly in the '50s and the '60s under a Norwegian shipowner and became among the world leaders in building the largest crude oil carriers of the time. It lost out to the Japanese when ship sizes exceeded 150,000 DWT. It was taken over by Kvaerner in 1970 pioneering the construction of carriers for Liquefied Natural Gas (LNG). In the shipbuilding crises of the late '70s it was rescued by conversion to an offshore fabrication yard. It benefited by its geographical location and government policies to support national participation in the supplies to the oil and gas investments. Today that market is also declining. It has been opened for international competition following both the national policies and the development of technologies and the industry.

In a study of its further development, the yard found that the conversion from a shipyard to an offshore fabrication yard would require importing labour from Finland and the UK with additional skills in welding and engineering. Just five year later, as a consequence of conscious programmes, the yard had fully developed these skills. The skills had also been spread to local subcontractors so that on later projects, when the yard doubled its activities, most additional labour was taken from the local infrastructure and very few imports were necessary. It was also found that on average, the yard kept busy an equal number of employees at its local subcontractors as it employed itself. Many of the subcontractors' employees were people that earlier were employed by the yard. While the yard trained their young apprentices into the new skills, it was a flow out of the yard, partly by layoffs and partly through the natural turnover of the workforce. This flow ended up in new businesses that were partly engaged by the yard where they came from and partly engaged by other business opportunities in the area.

Later on the yard made a comparison of its activities with similar companies in the UK and the US. It found that the UK yards had simpler facilities and benefited from the larger infrastructure of the area. The UK yards rented equipment and services on a part-time basis which the Norwegian yard owned and kept itself and therefore paid for full-time. In the US, this was almost developed into the extreme where even welders operated as contractors on an individual basis, taking care of their own transport and maintenance of their own equipment.

Coming to Russia we found the extreme opposite situation. The yards are much more vertically integrated and the yard produces a number of parts that its Western colleagues buy on the market. Some examples are furniture, castings, flanges, bolts, etc., etc., which they today also are trying to sell directly on domestic and export markets. Such things were out-sourced by the Norwegian yards in the '60s and '70s, some even earlier. The Russian yards are also trying to increase sales by changing the product range to consumer goods that can be made in their existing facilities.

This difference of structure leads to extremely difficult management tasks for the leaders of the industry that have to cope with a number of markets and technologies while their western colleagues have the luxury of specialising into a few.

Trends in European Yards and Fabrication Industries

From these examples, certain trends appear that are relevant for consideration by those developing conversion programs for Russia.

- Many shipyards and fabrication facilities in western Europe have been privatised in such a way that they bear no or at least very modest financial costs from the investments. Merchant shipbuilding is also subsidised to balance the competition from the Far East, although such subsidies are expected to end.
- Modern shipyards are very automated in constructing the hull. This and their other functions like berths, docks and outfitting facilities favours repetition of similar sizes and designs. To exploit this, they stay within niches in the market, selling their types world-wide.
- There is a trend towards out-sourcing, meaning that functions that earlier were integrated in the organisation of a shipyard or a fabrication facility are more and more taken over by subcontractors in the market. This out sourcing is driven partly by the need for more flexibility, to absorb the peaks and valleys of the activities by sharing the resources with others. It is also driven by the trend towards more sophisticated and more professional ways of operation.
- Military customers accept to an increasing extent standard commercial technology for their new vessels.
- There is a trend towards more and more rapid change of technologies. If the end - user owns the industry supplying him, he tends to adopt more slowly to the new technologies.

Tasks to Consider

The basic question is how the reorganisation of the political system in Russia will take place and how and when new, stable conditions are established to define the split between the private sector and the public sector. This will take some time and the solution will obviously Russian and not a copy of any other nation. But it is critical for the stability of local communities that intermediate solutions are sought that will allow the industry to develop and not just wait.

Russian shipyards hardly can be expected to cover the costs of conversion. Such costs will have to be supported by the state or by other sources outside the yard. This applies both to the cost of preserving the skills of personnel during the conversion process and the investments in the upgrading of the facilities.

In order to become competitive, investments and physical changes of the facilities have to be made. Protecting the industry by giving them certain rights in the national markets only has meaning if there is a relevant national market. Such markets will only follow if there are effective strategies to develop the natural resources in the area, which further requires acceptable conditions for foreign capital to invest. Further, the protection only gives a short-term benefit. The story about British Shipbuilders and its parallels in other countries lasted only ten years and gave no competitive advantage for the future.

An initial out-sourcing could simplify the management task of conversion. If foreign partners are being sought, different partners are relevant to different elements of the existing organisations. The out-sourced elements may contribute to different future activities both within the defence industry and the exploration of natural resources of different kinds more easily than if they remained a part of one comprehensive organisation.

Standard technology for civilian applications often meet the requirements of the military forces, giving less needs to distinguish between defence and civilian sectors (although with some exceptions).

The breaking up of the large complexes are necessary to adapt to technology developments more rapidly.

L'AVENIR DES INDUSTRIES LIÉES À LA DÉFENSE

Thierry Baumgart

Dans un contexte mondial qui a fortement évolué au cours de la dernière décennie, il est nécessaire de repenser l'avenir des industries de défense. En France, le Commissariat général du Plan a créé à cette fin un groupe de stratégie industrielle qui a réuni toutes les parties concernées. Thierry Baumgart nous explique comment les industries françaises, qui ont longtemps contribué à l'équilibre de la balance commerciale du pays, doivent s'adapter à une contraction brutale des marchés. La création de groupes puissants au niveau international par le biais de restructurations, de reconversions et de structures de coopération durables, ainsi qu'une valorisation efficace des technologies et une rationalisation des dépenses budgétaires sont des conditions indispensables à la pérennité d'activités où la France s'est particulièrement distinguée depuis le début des années soixante-dix.

Thierry Baumgart est Chargé de Mission au Commissariat général du Plan à Paris.

Le Cas de la France

Nouvelle donne géopolitique et conséquences sur l'évolution des besoins militaires, désarmement et baisse des budgets de défense, mondialisation de la compétition, évolution des technologies, nécessité, enfin, d'une Europe technologique et industrielle forte et compétitive, tous ces facteurs ont rendu nécessaire une large réflexion sur l'avenir des industries de défense.

C'est pourquoi le Commissariat général du Plan a proposé que cette réflexion ait lieu au sein d'un groupe de stratégie industrielle composé de toutes les parties prenantes : industriels, administrations, partenaires sociaux, représentants locaux concernés, experts, groupe présidé par Marcel Bénichou, président de l'Office National d'Etudes et de Recherches Aérospatiales, qui a travaillé pendant une durée d'un an. C'est la première fois qu'une réflexion sur un tel sujet, traditionnellement considéré comme délicat, était menée au Plan.

Prenant la politique de défense comme une donnée, le groupe s'est fixé pour objectif de proposer, selon différents scénarios d'évolution nationale et internationale, des mesures permettant de valoriser les compétences humaines, industrielles et technologiques dont notre pays a la chance de disposer en la matière.

Les travaux du groupe ont été achevés à temps pour qu'il ait pu apporter sa contribution à la commission chargée d'élaborer le livre blanc sur la Défense qui a servi de base à la loi de programmation militaire 1995-2000.[1]

La Place des Industries de Défense dans l'Économie Nationale

Depuis les années soixante-dix et jusqu'à aujourd'hui, les industries liées à la Défense ont apporté une contribution tout à fait significative à l'équilibre de notre balance commerciale, à l'emploi, ainsi qu'au développement technologique général de la France. Cette contribution a, d'un point de vue historique, d'abord été apportée grâce à leurs composantes militaires, puis par la suite également grâce à leurs composantes civiles dont les précédentes ont permis l'essor.

La France fait partie, comme les Etats-Unis, l'ex-Union Soviétique et le Royaume-Uni, des pays exportant une forte part de leur production. L'existence d'un budget de défense important, quoique bien sûr très inférieur à celui des Etats-Unis et de l'ex-Union Soviétique, la compétitivité de l'industrie française sur les plans de la technologie et des coûts et la politique étrangère de notre pays, lui ont permis de prendre une place dans presque tous les créneaux de matériels.

Poids de l'industrie de défense dans l'économie
- Comparaison Etats-Etats-Unis/Europe/France -
Année 1992 (milliards de francs)

	Etats-Unis	Europe (CEE)	France
Budget de Défense	1 754	972	195
Budget de Défense en % du PIB, y compris les pensions 5,4 %	5,4 %	2,7 %	3,4 %[2]
Chiffre d'affaires de l'industrie de défense	730	338	113
C.A. réalisé à l'export Budget de R & D Défense	75 261	72[3] 81	30 32

Sources : SIPRI, OTAN, DGA.

Les exportations représentent aujourd'hui de l'ordre de 30 milliards de francs par an, soit le quart du chiffre d'affaires du secteur. Déduction faite des importations, qui résultent surtout des programmes en coopération, l'industrie de Défense présente un solde positif d'environ 25 milliards de francs.

Les industries liées à la défense contribuent notablement à un emploi industriel de qualification élevée dans leurs différents domaines d'activité. Grâce à un réseau dense de sous-traitants elles contribuent indirectement à l'emploi dans des secteurs connexes.

Les effectifs employés directement dans l'industrie d'armement ont atteint un maximum de 310000 personnes en 1982. La diminution de ces effectifs a été due jusqu'en 1990 à la baisse des emplois travaillant spécifiquement pour l'exportation qui se situent aujourd'hui aux alentours de 40000 personnes. Les emplois directs pour les besoins nationaux, qui étaient stables aux alentours de 200 000 personnes depuis plusieurs années, sont à leur tour concernés puisqu'ils ont diminué depuis 1991 pour atteindre le chiffre de 190 000 personnes. Les effectifs directs s'élèvent ainsi à 230 000 personnes début 1993, soit 5 % des effectifs de l'industrie et la production de l'industrie d'armement représente 2 % du PIB marchand.

Les sociétés travaillant pour l'armement exercent pour la plupart une activité civile, souvent majoritaire dans leur chiffre d'affaires, mais elles comportent des sites quelquefois entièrement dévolus à l'armement, créant des zones où la sensibilité à cette activité est importante.

Notre industrie d'armement présente un niveau technologique et industriel aujourd'hui très proche de celui des Etats-Unis, lui permettant ainsi de réaliser, certes avec parfois quelques années de décalage, des systèmes militaires équivalents, voire meilleurs. En Europe, l'industrie française se place le plus souvent au premier rang, particulièrement en matière technologique. Cette position a été acquise et maintenue grâce à un effort de recherche et développement très important représentant en moyenne 28 % du chiffre d'affaires.

On constate toutefois quelques facteurs de fragilité dans la maîtrise de certaines technologies de base. Il existe en effet une dépendance partielle de l'industrie française à l'égard des Etats-Unis et du Japon, notamment pour certains nouveaux matériaux et composants électroniques.

L'intérêt attaché à l'existence d'une industrie nationale de défense explique en grande partie l'émergence de nouveaux producteurs. Les pays concernés ont, pour des raisons de souveraineté, de développement technologique, ou d'insertion dans le commerce international, décidé de mobiliser une part des ressources nationales afin de créer et de favoriser le développement d'une activité dans ce secteur.

Les caractéristiques particulières et l'importance des industries d'armement dans l'économie nationale soulèvent cependant certaines controverses et conduisent certains à s'interroger sur leur positionnement au sein du tissu industriel français et plus généralement à renouveler l'analyse des relations entre l'économique et le militaire.

Une Situation de Rupture

Après les bouleversements européens récents, la probabilité d'une menace de type soviétique s'est amoindrie à court et à moyen terme. Mais de nouveaux risques apparaissent : instabilité liée à la disparition de l'URSS, risque de prolifération, situation économique et politique dans le Tiers-Monde. Le contexte actuel est caractérisé par une baisse structurelle du marché de l'armement depuis le milieu des années 1980 et par une diminution des budgets occidentaux de défense en monnaie constante.

L'industrie d'armement doit donc s'adapter à une situation de contraction des marchés qui s'est brusquement accélérée pour des raisons tenant essentiellement à l'affaiblissement de la menace à l'Est. La France a connu cette évolution plus tardivement que les autres pays occidentaux puisque le recul du marché intérieur de l'armement en monnaie constante ne s'est fait sentir qu'à partir de 1991 alors qu'il a été amorcé en 1988 au niveau mondial. De plus, ce recul n'a pas atteint jusqu'à présent en France l'ampleur qu'il a connu aux Etats-Unis ou en Allemagne.

Dans ce contexte se développe, chez certains responsables, la conviction que la France doit pouvoir récolter beaucoup plus largement les dividendes macro-économiques de la fin de la guerre froide par une diminution radicale de son effort financier pour la défense et une affectation des sommes ainsi économisées à d'autres usages.

Toutefois, il faut être conscient que les "dividendes de la paix" pourraient se révéler illusoires aussi bien à court-terme qu'à moyen terme ou même à long terme ; à court terme en raison du coût d'une problématique de reconversion industrielle, à moyen terme à cause du financement des opérations de maintien de la paix et à long terme en raison de la nécessaire modernisation des forces, qui devront plus que jamais être en mesure de faire face à des situations diverses et imprévues.

L'Accroissement de la Concurrence

Outre l'évolution des parités monétaires qui a contribué à la dégradation de la compétitivité, vis-à-vis des Etats-Unis bien sûr, mais aussi vis-à-vis du Royaume-Uni, notre principal concurrent européen, il convient d'apprécier à leur juste mesure les efforts de nouveaux producteurs pour entrer sur le marché de l'exportation d'armement, ainsi que l'agressivité des Américains pour y maintenir leur suprématie.

Le soutien de la parité du franc, qui peut être supportable par certains secteurs industriels principalement en concurrence avec l'Allemagne, a des effets négatifs sur le secteur de l'armement qui se trouve surtout en concurrence avec les Etats-Unis et le Royaume-Uni.

La puissance des Etats-Unis en matière d'armement repose sur un effort budgétaire pour la défense qui reste considérable, ainsi que sur le soutien des secteurs qui ont permis aux Etats-Unis d'acquérir une suprématie, notamment le secteur aérospatial qui bénéficie de très importants crédits publics. Les développements de matériels sont effectués avec le concours de l'Etat qui met en oeuvre tout un ensemble de moyens techniques et financiers.

La politique d'exportation se fait avec le soutien fort du gouvernement américain qui a adopté un certain nombre de mesures pour la faciliter : interventions de haut niveau, démarchage pour les autorités politiques, présence diplomatique sur le terrain, lien entre l'achat de matériels militaires américains et la couverture militaire américaine. Ces aspects confirment que l'exportation d'armes est un des éléments de la politique de défense des Etats-Unis, et de leur politique industrielle en général. Les industriels américains, quant à eux, tiennent le haut du pavé dans les classements mondiaux.

A l'évidence enfin, les Etats-Unis sont conscients que la puissance industrielle qui s'est construite en Europe, dans l'armement comme ailleurs, leur enlève des parts de marché. Les industries européennes de défense — et tout particulièrement les françaises — deviennent leur cible principale.

La faible taille de notre marché national, qui provoque un important effet défavorable sur les coûts de production dû aux volumes et cadences de séries faibles par rapport aux Etats-Unis et à la Russie, est également un facteur important à prendre en compte pour apprécier la compétitivité de notre industrie.

Les Conditions de la Pérennité

Des entreprises restructurées, puissantes et exportatrices

La pérennité des industries liées à la défense ne sera assurée que si tous les acteurs concernés oeuvrent pour créer des entreprises ou des groupes puissants au niveau mondial, car c'est une nécessité technologique, industrielle, financière et commerciale.

Il faut donc que l'industrie française de l'armement s'adapte à la nouvelle donne géopolitique, améliore sa compétitivité et accroisse ses capacités exportatrices. En effet, sa concentration encore insuffisante entraîne des faiblesses et des fragilités qui seraient corrigées par la constitution de groupes plus forts, évitant ainsi les concurrences internes qui peuvent être causes de pertes d'efficacité et accroissant la puissance financière des entreprises face notamment aux firmes américaines.

La nouvelle donne géopolitique pèse sur l'ensemble de l'industrie européenne d'armement, qui se trouve dans une triple situation d'infériorité en raison de sa surcapacité globale, du cloisonnement excessif des marchés nationaux et du trop grand nombre d'entreprises. Les restructurations que connaît actuellement l'industrie américaine d'armement accentuent d'ailleurs cette différence de taille déjà importante aujourd'hui.

Mais la constitution d'entreprises et de groupes puissants et exportateurs ne peut se faire sans le soutien des pouvoirs publics qui interviennent dans la plupart des pays, et notamment aux Etats-Unis, à de nombreux titres dans ce secteur. Les rapprochements industriels à travers les frontières supposent donc une volonté commune des gouvernements concernés.

Une Ouverture Maîtrisée des Marchés en Europe

L'intégration croissante des marchés en Europe concerne aussi le domaine des industries de défense. En premier lieu, la grande majorité des sociétés du secteur n'a pas une activité essentiellement, ni même parfois principalement, militaire. Or ces sociétés font partie de nombreuses coopérations dans des domaines connexes à l'armement. En second lieu, le caractère dual des technologies, notamment dans les secteurs de l'électronique et de l'aéronautique, limite quelque peu la distinction entre applications civiles et militaires des produits.

De même, le mouvement vers une Union de l'Europe Occidentale (UEO) plus présente dans les problèmes de sécurité et vers une Agence européenne de l'armement, irait dans le sens de liens plus étroits entre les industriels des différents pays.

L'impossibilité d'un décloisonnement total des marchés par une déréglementation complète du secteur de l'armement en Europe rend nécessaire, plutôt que l'institution d'une "préférence européenne" généralisée, l'adoption de règles pragmatiques aussi bien pour les échanges internes que pour les exportations.

Il est possible cependant de promouvoir une certaine organisation du marché avec les Etats-Unis, à la double condition d'une véritable réciprocité dans les échanges et de la prise en compte des spécificités du marché de l'armement.

Une Notion Élargie de l'Indépendance

Les restructurations industrielles européennes à venir risquent de conduire à la perte par la France de sa situation d'indépendance quasi totale dans le domaine des armements. Des créneaux seront perdus au profit d'autres pays européens mieux placés; d'autres seront partagés.

Ainsi, la future Europe de l'armement connaîtra sans doute globalement une situation analogue à la situation française actuelle, c'est-à-dire la capacité de produire sur le territoire européen la quasi totalité des armements nécessaires à sa défense.

Les Voies de l'Adaptation

Faute de pouvoir agir efficacement sur les facteurs exogènes qui expliquent les difficultés de l'industrie de défense, les solutions à ses graves difficultés passent sans doute par des décisions relatives aux structures industrielles des industrielles ou des pouvoirs publics.

Restructurations et Reconversions

L'industrie de défense française doit réduire fortement son format et parvenir à un nouvel équilibre, qui parait être inférieur d'un tiers à celui de la fin des années 1980. Le groupe préconise de mettre en oeuvre le resserrement du dispositif des industries de défense par allègement des effectifs affectés aux programmes d'armement en se fondant en particulier sur l'hypothèse défavorable du scénario d'exportation pour dimensionner la fabrication des matériels chez les maîtres d'oeuvre et les équipementiers. En revanche, il estime nécessaire de conserver la pleine capacité de conception et d'assurer la pérennité des bureaux d'études pour les créneaux qui seront conservés.

Les maîtres d'oeuvre devront veiller à conserver un taux de sous-traitance suffisant. Les sous-traitants devront être incités à se diversifier hors des industries liées à la défense. Pour cela, il faudra faire évoluer les relations de maître d'oeuvre à sous-traitants vers des relations de partenariat.

Le défi pour accompagner une nouvelle et sensible réduction des sureffectifs qui apparaît inéluctable est donc considérable. Et ce n'est pas le premier défi, puisque les industries d'armement ont déjà dû supprimer 80000 emplois directs dans les dix dernières années. Cependant, les restructurations à venir devront être mises en oeuvre dans une conjoncture économique générale moins favorable qu'auparavant. Elles demanderont sans doute plus de moyens et plus de temps que les restructurations passées. Une amélioration relative passe par des moyens financiers adaptés, par une approche géographique et d'aménagement du territoire volontariste et par un dialogue social approfondi, nécessaire pour imaginer des mesures efficaces qui impliquent à la fois civils et militaires, administrations, syndicats et élus.

Les nécessaires restructurations de l'industrie française de l'armement supposent aussi un vigoureux effort de reconversion. Toutes les possibilités internes de reconversion doivent être explorées. Elles apparaissent toutefois limitées et ne peuvent en aucun cas concerner des établissements entiers. La diversification des activités rencontre également des limites qui tiennent à la forte surface financière qu'implique une politique de reconversion; en outre, la réutilisation de tout ou partie des moyens humains et matériels existants n'est possible que dans la mesure où les nouvelles activités sont d'un niveau technologique élevé, correspondant à la qualification des personnels et où les techniques mises en oeuvre sont voisines.

En fait, la diversification est déjà largement à l'oeuvre dans les industries d'armement qui se caractérisent par leur dualité technologique : aérospatial, électronique professionnelle; les marges d'extension sont en conséquence limitées. De plus, la crise de l'aéronautique civile et les incertitudes sur l'espace accentuent plutôt ces difficultés.

Un effort particulier d'innovation devra être accompli pour susciter la création de nouveaux emplois dans les sites les plus touchés :

- Mise en place d'un fonds interministériel d'intervention industrielle qui viendrait compléter les actions industrielles trop limitées de l'actuel fonds pour la restructuration de la défense.
- Professionnalisation de la fonction de reconversion dans l'entreprise.
- Mise en place de structures propres à développer les transferts de compétences au profit des PME.
- Définition par les maîtres d'oeuvre et les autorités locales de projets d'actions éligibles au programme européen de reconversion des industries de défense KONVER et élargissement des zones éligibles à ce programme pour y inclure les régions principalement concernées par la réduction des effectifs industriels de défense.

Les principaux pays concernés par la reconversion de leurs industries de défense y consacrent un effort budgétaire important. La France ne doit pas être à la traîne dans ce domaine; elle peut au contraire bénéficier de l'expérience de ceux qui ont dû s'y résoudre avant elle.

Un Cadre Renouvelé pour les Coopérations Internationales

Il convient d'accentuer - en tout état de cause - l'évolution engagée vers des programmes en coopération pour bénéficier de ses avantages économiques face aux coûts croissants des programmes d'armement et aux limitations budgétaires. Mais cette évolution, si l'on veut en tirer tous les fruits, devrait être conduite en surmontant ou en atténuant les effets pervers des coopérations actuelles qui résultent essentiellement du heurt d'intérêts nationaux, divergents au premier abord. Les rapprochements au niveau industriel peuvent avoir un effet d'autant plus bénéfique qu'ils sont intimes et donc pérennes.

Les concentrations nationales ne sont pas un préalable systématique à toute alliance européenne. Elles ne présentent d'intérêt que si de véritables synergies industrielles existent entre les entreprises et si elles permettent la constitution de pôles d'excellence dans des activités susceptibles d'être filialisées avec un partenaire européen. Il convient à cet effet de favoriser des structures industrielles transnationales plus durables que celles adoptées pour la plupart des coopérations existantes.

Face à l'actuelle situation de surcapacité de l'industrie européenne d'armement, et à la nécessité d'étendre la coopération en amont des développements, l'intégration par le biais de groupements d'intérêt économique (GIE) apparaît insuffisante.

Il convient de la faire évoluer, chaque fois que possible vers des rapprochements capitalistiques, notamment sous forme de filiales communes des grands groupes nationaux lorsqu'ils existent.

L'internationalisation des économies, des entreprises et des technologies nécessite moins désormais une coopération qu'une intégration des moyens technologiques, industriels et commerciaux au sein de groupes dont l'efficacité se mesure à la rapidité d'action. Les coopérations traditionnelles, lentes et procédurières, ne résistent plus aujourd'hui aux exigences du marché. Les alliances, participations ou fusion de sociétés autorisent au contraire la constitution de groupes intégrés de dimension européenne ou mondiale.

Sur le plan institutionnel, la création d'une Agence européenne de l'armement permettrait progressivement d'européaniser la recherche, les développements exploratoires, les centres d'essais et les programmes.

Rationalisation des Dépenses Budgétaires

Un grand système de combat moderne nécessite une dizaine d'années d'efforts de développement auxquelles il convient d'ajouter au préalable la durée d'acquisition des technologies correspondantes. Cela nécessite que l'Etat donne un éclairage à suffisamment long terme de ses besoins de défense, sous forme de lois de programmation militaire plus longues et mieux respectées, même si une révision peut être envisagée mi-chemin.

L'allongement excessif de la phase de développement d'un programme est générateur de surcoûts. De plus, cela diffère la capacité de l'industriel à proposer à l'exportation le matériel issu de ce développement. Il convient en conséquence de conduire les programmes d'armement en respectant un rythme de réalisation propre à assurer leur maîtrise. Une telle politique devrait conduire à éviter de lancer simultanément trop de programmes nouveaux, en étalant les lancements dans le temps.

Les industries liées à la défense sont composées en majeure partie d'entreprises ou d'établissements sous contrôle public, qu'il s'agisse de sociétés nationales ou d'arsenaux. Il importe que leur statut, s'il est maintenu, n'entraîne pas de handicap grave en matière de compétitivité, de souplesse de gestion, de dynamisme commercial ou de diversification civile. Il appartient aux pouvoirs publics de continuer à promouvoir les aménagements nécessaires.

Valorisation Efficace des Technologies

Il convient de renforcer et mieux formaliser la concertation dans le domaine de la prospective technologique entre le ministère de la Défense et les industriels de l'armement. En particulier, il y a lieu (pour chacune des 24 technologies critiques inventoriées) de veiller à faire un effort cohérent avec la priorité affichée et à prendre toutes les mesures nécessaires pour conserver en France la maîtrise des technologies pour lesquelles on veut une indépendance totale.

De même, il faut établir avec nos partenaires européens une juste répartition de l'effort dans la quasi totalité des domaines critiques pour lesquels une autonomie de l'Europe paraît indispensable et renforcer la coopération en matière de recherches de défense entre les pays européens.

La grande majorité des domaines technologiques, critiques ou non, intéressant la défense ont un caractère dual et les recherches font de ce fait l'objet d'un double pilotage par le Ministère de la Défense et par un ministère civil (Recherche, Industrie, Transports, Télécommunications...). Dans ces domaines il convient principalement de mettre en place, là où elle n'existe pas encore, une coordination interministérielle efficace qui participe à une bonne analyse des moyens à mettre en oeuvre et à la définition des programmes de recherche qui doivent être conduits en commun pour des raisons d'efficacité.

Si la diminution des budgets d'équipement militaire devait se poursuivre, il conviendrait nécessairement de privilégier, par rapport aux budgets de production à court terme, les financements de l'Etat en matière de recherche, de développements exploratoires et de démonstrateurs. En effet, bien que soutenu, notre effort national dans ce domaine (ainsi d'ailleurs que l'effort global de l'Europe de l'Ouest) demeure à un niveau très inférieur à celui des Etats-Unis, non seulement en valeur absolue, mais aussi en pourcentage du produit intérieur brut (voir tableau ci-dessus).

Une telle orientation au bénéfice de la recherche de défense ne peut être que favorisée par une meilleure diffusion dans le tissu industriel du potentiel scientifique et technologique développé sur crédits militaires dans les centres de recherche et les grandes entreprises. Le partenariat technologique, permettant aux PME de participer au développement des produits en tant que partenaires et non comme simples sous-traitants, doit être encouragé.

Amélioration de l'Action Commerciale Internationale

L'industrie française d'armement estime que sa position commerciale souffre d'une mobilisation relativement limitée du savoir-faire et des moyens des armées pour promouvoir les matériels en usage dans nos forces. Elle déplore également dans certains cas la lenteur de la prise de décision gouvernementale pour la prospection ou la vente à certains pays.

Dans la mesure où le coût d'un réseau d'implantations commerciales est très élevé pour un industriel, et compte tenu du caractère spécifique du marché de l'armement, il est recommandé de mieux utiliser les réseaux de l'Etat à l'étranger. La position commerciale des industries françaises d'armement souffre parfois d'un service après vente insuffisant. Qu'il s'agisse de vente ou d'après-vente, un dispositif étatique ou professionnel assurant une formation approfondie des futurs agents de l'industrie, des offices de vente d'armes ou de l'Etat, serait d'une grande utilité.

Il est enfin recommandé de réexaminer, en vue d'une optimisation de l'ensemble des forces de ventes, les rôles respectifs des offices de vente d'armes et des réseaux commerciaux des industriels.

Les adaptations nécessaires de notre industrie d'armement concernent autant les entreprises que les pouvoirs publics. Elles doivent être conduites aussi bien sur un plan national qu'au niveau européen. Il s'agit, en effet, d'assurer au moindre coût la meilleurs défense pour la France, tout en mettant l'industrie de Défense de notre pays en condition d'affronter les formes futures de la compétition internationale. Plus particulièrement, il s'agit d'oeuvrer à l'édification d'une industrie européenne de l'armement, véritable compétiteur ou partenaire de l'industrie américaine, et fondement d'un pilier européen de Défense.

Notes

1. Rapport publié à la Documentation française: "L'avenir des industries liées à la Défense", décembre 1993.
2. Les notions communément admises en France conduisent à retenir un budget de Défense hors pensions par rapport au produit intérieur brut marchand soit 3,1 %.
3. Y compris les exportations intra-européennes.

PRIVATIZATION OF DEFENCE INDUSTRIES IN THE FRAMEWORK OF PRIVATIZATION AT LARGE

Alexander Kennaway

Perhaps the major barrier to successful defence privatization is one of perspective, says Professor Alexander Kenneway. The west should leave aside its macro-economic models and textbook scenarios, and producers in the east must undo themselves of the illusion that production can stay as it is, or soon "return to normal". Practical solutions are the only way forward: the west should be bringing eastern defense industries advice, lots of training and a focus on practical, small-scale economic victories.

Alexander Kennaway is professor of Conflict Studies at the Research Department of the Royal Military Academy, Sandhurst, UK, and a Foreign Member of the Ukrainian Academy of Transport.

First of all, allow me to state one truism on the subject of privatisation. The ownership of a company cannot be an end in itself, except to dogmatists. The issue is - which structure best assists the firm to flourish and to contribute to the well being of the national economy?

Why Are some Activities in State Ownership?

Some sectors of the national economy of most western industrialised democracies are or have been owned by the State for three basic reasons:-

1- A belief that some essential services would not be sufficiently profitable for private ownership and therefore would not be delivered effectively

2- A belief that elements crucial to the security of the nation should be in state ownership and directly under state control. This has applied especially to defence establishments, in research, manufacture and maintenance for the equipment of the armed forces.

3- A basic political belief, that state ownership is more likely to serve the interests of the nation if the main motive of private profit is absent.

All three motives have, from time to time, operated in western Europe. The second also prevailed in the USA and to some degree still does.

The third governed the policies of those countries under the control of Marxist parties. Marx, who was writing in England during the 1860s on the basis of his researches into the state of English capitalism of the 1830s-50s, was driven by his view that private enterprise exploited the workers and retained too great a share of the proceeds, thus denying them as a source of wealth for the national good. He argued that nothing had intrinsic value, which was created only by labour. The Labour Theory of Value went on to state that the difference between the selling price and the cost of labour was Surplus Value and was appropriated by the capitalists.

If the State took the surplus it could finance everything for the benefit of the Nation. It was a corollary of Marxist socialism that competition was wasteful and that central planning would direct resources more efficiently than a free market could. This view was also shared by many Socialists in western Europe. Their acceptance of the Labour Theory of Value allowed them also to slide into a romantic view of industry, namely that only the factory was a source of wealth, created by the horny-handed proletariat and that everyone else outside it was an unnecessary overhead. Consequently many socialists ignored marketting, product planning and even design for the customer.[1]

The Case Against State Ownership & Control

The reaction against State ownership can be summarised as follows :

1- Centralised planning is more inefficient and less flexible than the sum total of individual business planning carried out by firms concentrating on their own business. Done well, firms will maximise the use of resources; their own business plans must be flexible enough to take account of inadequate assessments of the business environment especially of the competition. This as analogous to Von Moltke the Elder who correctly observed "No (military) plan survives contact with the enemy". Failure, naturally leads to a redistribution of the remaining resources of the firm by one means or another open within a free market economy.

2- State ownership usually requires the firm to come to the Treasury, (the Ministry of Finance) to borrow money for expenditure beyond its immediate ability to finance essential investments from its own retained profits. This places the firm under non-commercial restraints dictated by national policy or by the Government's sense of priorities in allocation of its own funds. This restraint severely limits the business performance of State-owned enterprises.

3- State ownership in many countries, even within a free-market economy, has led to management and workers alike adopting attitudes which ignore all the fundamental tests and criteria of efficient business. They have grown up with the assumption that the Government has a duty to subsidise them and also, often enough, to support unchanged their activities as they have become. As State employees they tend toward the view that change, however inevitable, is a threat to their way of life. Measurement of performance by any test of competitive market economics is also regarded as an unpleasant intrusion.

This has even been true when such enterprises, such as coal mining, although a monopoly supplier of coal, faced technical competition from gas, electricity and other sources of energy.

It is not difficult to see why many, not just on the right wing of politics, have concluded that the State is not competent to direct specialist services delivered to the market, trade and manufacturing industry and furthermore it should seek to interfere as little as possible in directing those sectors.

Some British Experiences

The issue of ownership and control can, however, especially in theory, be separated. In Great Britain the State sometimes held a so-called Golden Share in nationalised firms; this enabled it to veto decisions of the otherwise independent Board which it considered to be against the national interest. One such firm was British Petroleum, now fully privately owned. This form could be regarded as a first, modest step toward privatisation.

My experience as a Director of a British nationalised industry suggests that it is by no means axiomatic that State-owned firms must be directed and managed less well than private firms. The competence to perform in business depends upon the culture of the firm and this in turn depends on the ability and vision of the Board to set the strategy, to motivate and lead the people to perform to ever better standards in serving their market. If the organisation has been run by State employees, the chances are that much will have to be done to change the culture to one that can become excellent in a competitive market. The ability to generate at least as much income as is spent is an indispensable discipline, especially to those who previously regarded the aim of the work to provide a service but one that was never subject to such a criterion of performance.

British experience shows that it is essential to make these changes, to improve the business competence of a firm before it is privatised. One may instance British Airways, British Gas, British Steel. The lesson for Eastern Europe and the former Soviet Union is that this process took years even when it took place within a well established market economy with all the legal, financial and governmental structures in place and when it was possible to invite successful businessmen from the private sector to become directors and managers to run them.

There is no major issue of privatising British defence contractors, which have almost all been in private hands since their inception.[2] The problems that they face are those due to contraction of military orders. Some firms have dual purpose subsidiaries, whereas others are often separately managed. The value of this arrangement is to try to divorce the two cultures - military and civil. Defence contractors rarely understand marketing to civilian customers since their close collaboration with the Military results in the latter performing many of the marketing functions. Secondly, defence contractors are nowhere renowned for cost-effective and competitive products. This is partly due to the need to respond to complex, many would argue, unnecessarily so, specifications and bureaucratic procedures and partly because cost has not traditionally been a high priority in weaponry.

Restructuring the main defence contractors is proving to be very difficult, partly for these reasons. It is also not cost-effective to adapt factories dedicated to things like tanks, submarines and warships to making civilian products. The same is true of dedicated yards for servicing nuclear-powered submarines. The down turn in orders for shipping as well as for other marine structures such as oil well platforms has been accompanied by effective competition from Korea and other countries. Consequently there are bound to be closures in both shipyards and dockyards.

However the resulting social problems are fewer than has been the case with the closure of many "smokestack" industries.

American experience is also somewhat harsh. Major Government-owned naval yards and other facilities, such as aircraft repair bases have been closed and turned over to completely different uses.

Prime defence contractors such as General Dynamics have also closed some of their major plants rather than attempt to convert them to civilian uses. This was in spite of the fact that the plants were of the highest standard; modern, well laid-out, well managed and manned by people living within an entrepreneurial environment.

Sub-contractors were always more diversified, selling into civilian and military markets. In the field of electronics reports suggest that civilian products were superior to those destined for defence purposes in design, advanced technology and in value for money. Consequently firms in this business suffered hardly at all from the contraction in defence orders.

American industry, it would appear, is readjusting itself to this new situation as it has done to previous reductions in orders from a specific sector of the market. Furthermore, according to the Office of Technology Assessment, which reports to Congress, local organisations scheduled to close can rely upon the legal requirements to provide federal funds and skilled advice to assist them to perform other functions locally after the closure. Furthermore, individuals scheduled for redundancy also have legally funded help with retraining and counselling to find new jobs.

Some Other Remarks Based on British Experience

If nationalised firms became competent to compete, why, it may be asked, was it necessary to privatise them? Leaving aside political dogma, a powerful argument is to be found in the separation of financial authority from the State and the ability to raise money in the open market without limitation of the Public Sector Borrowing Fund.

I was not alone amongst directors of nationalised firms to find in the British Treasury a certain lack of understanding of practicalities in matters of investment as well as lack of mental flexibility. Added to this was an inadequate grasp of all the issues, many of them highly technical and indeed scientifically difficult, by the civil servants, let alone Ministers in the departments of State to which one was responsible. It could not be otherwise; they were basically generalist administrators, perhaps advised by people who once had some experience of those matters.

A competent Board is composed of people who, together, command all the necessary skills and experience and know how to call upon their own as well as outside advisers for specialist detail and who are able to make professional assessments of that advice.

This is a rare ability amongst Government administrators. They are too removed from the realities of a fast-changing business to remain competent, if they ever were, to assess and set broad commercial policies, determine the right investment paths for capital investment and innovation and generally to perform as effective leaders even at a non-executive, supervisory level.

Another problem with a State-owned firm is that, generally speaking, the employees have more rights of tenure than is the case in private firms. It is therefore more difficult to persuade them to learn new attitudes and skills and indeed to move them either within the firm or to find new careers outside when it is found that they are no longer required.

Some French Experiences

This is also the case in France, where the State currently has problems with Air France. With its integrated and forward-looking planning system, basic consensus between the political parties and homogenously and well educated elite, France appears to have had fewer problems with national planning, with its energy, infrastructure of telecommunications, railways and roads than some other west European countries. All of these are currently still in public ownership.

The Government has had fewer problems with the necessary reductions in its nationally-owned defence industries. From the outside at least, firms like Dassault appear to have been well managed. They have been clever in anticipating the downturn of military orders. The French, under the slogan, "smaller body, bigger brain", are in the company of all major military powers who see the folly of creating and maintaining dinosaur armed forces. Dassault has over the past few years delegated more manufacture to contractors, retaining its R & D and design skills. The inevitable loss of jobs is planned to be accomplished through natural wastage and retirements.

The Case of Germany

Privatisation of the property of the former DDR presents an instructive lesson for both easterners and westerners. The West German Government expected to be able to attract western firms to invest in the factories of the DDR and were surprised when the facts did not fulfil their hopes. The degeneration of traditional German work values came as a shock; so did the conclusion of West German industry that it was more profitable to sell goods from their existing factories than to buy Soviet-style factories and make things there. An excellent report on the workings of the Treuhand appears in the Autumn number of the McKinsey Review for 1993. This report shows that privatisation has not been the success expected by its proponents. The economy of the former DDR is still very far behind that of the western Länder; it is supported at great cost to the West German economy and, let it be said, to other west European states.

Conclusions from the Western Experience

1- There are many models of a free market economy, with different patterns of ownership and control.

2- Many Western countries still retain some of their essential industries and services, including primary defence contractors, in State ownership.

3- British experience, in particular, shows that it is essential to prepare firms for private ownership and that the process of improving its business performance through transformation of its business culture and competence takes a very long time.

4- American experience suggests that restructuring primary defence contractors is unprofitable and that they are better closed. However, the American economy, as well as those of other NATO countries, can afford these closures, contractions and restructuring. This is because the defence industries occupy a very small part of the total manufacturing base of these countries. It is also true that their civilian technology at least matches and sometimes surpasses that dedicated to military purposes.

5- It is, regrettably, also true that military research and its resulting technology, whether in products or in production processes, is rarely adaptable to profitable civilian uses, in spite of the many attempts.

The Former Soviet Union and Their Former Partners in Eastern Europe

Backed by some western advisers, the reformers in these countries have pursued their objectives primarily by liberalising most prices, allowing relatively free exchange between their own currencies and hard currencies and by other macro-economic policies such as the promotion of privatisation.

These measures, however, have not been thoroughly thought out, consequently there is no firm legal, fiscal, financial basis which businessmen whether local or foreign can confidently rely on in order to be able to plan their business for even a year ahead. Some governments, including the Russian, Ukrainian and Belarussian, have imposed such crippling regimes of taxation, disposition of earned foreign currency that they have effectively forced businessmen into a grey or even black economy. The Governments have criminalised what could have been honest business.

Other Governments, such as those of Kazakhstan and Azerbaijan, set out to attract foreign investment in their oil and gas fields, but have failed to allow the foreign partners with whom they initialled agreements as long ago as two or three years back, to begin to implement these agreements, essential for the support of the local economies.

It was, of course, too much to expect from the Republics subsidiary to Russia to throw up leaders capable of creating coherent, sensible government since the locals had, till their independence, been subservient to Russian orders which went into immense detail as well as setting what passed for strategy and economic policy.[3] However, the Russian Government itself has proved to be no better at creating a reasonable structure and framework within which the economy, whether private or state owned, can develop.

Since the collapse of the USSR in 1991, the economy of the entire region has worsened and at an accelerating pace. In the interests of space I shall concentrate on the three Slav republics and Lithuania. The problems, situation and prospects for these countries are applicable to others, especially east and south of the Slav republics. Central and eastern European States, although they inherited, and still suffer from, the monolithic, integrated nature of the Soviet economic system as well as from the mentality of *Homo Sovieticus* show some significant differences. Albania is making sincere efforts to move toward a market economy and to apply intelligently western aid to create a good infrastructure. Estonia is strongly supported by the Scandinavians and Latvia is making progress, tying its currency to the Deutschmark. Romania was alone in not integrating its defence industry with that of Russia.

Whereas there are many varieties of a market economy there was only one model of a Communist Command economy in areas controlled by and in alliance with the CPSU(b).[4] On this basis it is possible to make general remarks, mainly based on the Slav Republics which are broadly applicable across the region.

The Communist Past

It was a centrally controlled economy aimed primarily at building the military capability of the State. The priorities of all industrial development were aimed at this goal. It is still not possible to establish with any degree of reliability the proportion of GDP devoted to defence and related activities such as space but it was probably around 30%. It also employed about 65% of all scientists and engineers.[5] One can truthfully say that the technical intelligentsia were never allowed to contribute to the improvement of the civilian infrastructure or the quality of life of the ordinary people. These remained backward by comparison with those of industrially developed countries.

The regime was also extremely inefficient. The Communist Party, its Nomenklatura and party appointees to the Soviets had no idea of running an efficient production and distribution system. Their aim was to fulfil the Plan, in output terms, regardless of the consequences. They interfered with the managerial and technical decisions of their competent people, even in the military sphere.[6] The drive to militarisation was pressed forward regardless of the costs. The system wasted all the material human and financial resources of the nation. Many of its factories were and still are value subtractors. That is to say that the materials and energy used could sell for more than the products in an open competitive market. The USSR traditionally exported raw materials, such as timber, minerals and gold and imported production equipment, turnkey factories and latterly consumer goods and food. Weaponry was bartered with the Socialist third world for cotton, sugar and once even for sweets! Soviet weaponry is indeed functionally effective but much of it, such as tanks, ships and aircraft, suffers, amongst other things, from a lack of safety for its crews.

By the time of Brezhnev's regime, the health of the people was deteriorating fast and the infrastructure crumbling. Agriculture yields were, in critical areas such as grain and potatoes, about a fifth of those of the USA and UK, in spite of massive investment in equipment, much of which was inappropriate to local conditions. On a per capita basis agriculture employs about 20 times more people than does the UK.

Communist propaganda boasted about its successes in science, high technology and superior weaponry. It is true that Soviet education did educate people well in science and engineering theory. The best of them are superb, especially in mathematics, computing software and physics. The fundamental weakness lies in the very abstraction of this education. Only in the military sphere were good scientists and engineers able to work closely with the users of their output as well as with the workshops making the prototypes and manufacturing the products delivered to the armed forces. The most highly integrated of the defence industries was the aircraft sector.[7]

In spite of this, soviet military aircraft engines were always well behind those of the west. As a result of the concentration on military engines with their need for after-burners required for rapid acceleration, the Soviets never developed fuel-efficient, high by-pass engines and therefore their civil aircraft are about 30% more fuel hungry than those of the west.

Soviet air defence industry also exhibits the weakness mentioned above of the Western defence industry in its difficulty in perceiving market needs and satisfying them. They are now making great efforts to penetrate the world's civil aircraft market but will not succeed without western participation in market intelligence, design, engines and avionics. Strangely enough, electronics, the essence of high technology as many people understand that term, provides the weakest section of Soviet weaponry and hence also of civilian radio-technical goods.

The efforts spent on genetics and biology still resulted in seed of poor quality delivered to farms.[8]

I started to work in Soviet research institutes in 1958 under the exchange agreement between the Royal Society and the USSR Academy of Sciences. It was exhilarating to work with the outstanding physicists and mathematicians of an older generation than I. But it was sad to see the cautionary approach of these people to their own work, which was frequently misunderstood by the Party dogmatists and might lead to loss of support, status and even liberty. It was plain then that a high proportion of "science" in non-classified areas open to me was routine, hack work and intended for no further use than publication leading perhaps to a trip abroad. Even work that in the West was directed at improving industrial processes and products was not organised in a fashion that made its application easy. As a result in my-then-fields of work, polymers and prosthetics the USSR is decades behind.

My recent experience in teaching and research establishments in Russia, Belarus and Ukraine does not, regrettably, allow me to alter my assessments. There are outstanding young mathematicians and physicists who collaborate with us and whose work in computing and nuclear physics is making very useful contributions to the west. Incidently some of their work also earns much needed hard currency for themselves and for their Institutes.

The old habit of exaggeration (vranyo in Russian), coupled with the ignorance and naivete that used to mark western academics also, persuades many of them to assert that their innovations are unique, world-beaters and must command high financial rewards in the west. Thus the job of western entrepreneurs seeking mutual benefits from sale of Soviet technology is made more onerous than it is in the west. Russian "inventions" need more thorough analysis and fewer of those offered will be commercialisable.

It is also essential to realise that factories may well be inadequately supported by scientists in academic institutes when it comes to profitable activity.

The basic orientation of Russian university education needs to move away from pure theory to a system allowing a close link between theory, practice and in a commercial environment.[9]

Manufacturing Industry in the Former Soviet Union

The purpose of production was always to satisfy the plan not the needs and wants of the market, except that of the military. The emphasis was on output; there were and still are no means of determining the amount of materials, energy or labour used, no means for determining costs of extraction of minerals, transporting them or processing them into goods. Transfer prices between enterprises are arbitrary, costs and prices bear no relation to fact and one cannot therefore make any sensible commercial decisions on profitability or on the worth of one investment opportunity versus another. There is no market in real estate.

On this basis therefore, it is not possible to determine the current value of an enterprise, although many people who work in the system will assert that the production equipment, together with the experience and skills of the work force and scientists, especially in the defence industries, represent the wealth of the country and must therefore be kept together.

Small wonder however that westerners find it hard to establish a basis for investment. They are accustomed to determining the worth of an investment by calculating the potential profit that it will generate. Most productive facilities and transport suffer from neglect and misuse. Most factories are poorly laid out and are inefficient users of resources. Contemporary civilian products are rarely competitive in western markets, they do not answer the requirements of international standards and would require considerable attention to detail in design and in provision of product support to satisfy western distributors.

Soviet factories are organised purely as manufacturing organisations, as well as providers of social services to the work force. They lack every other element of a western firm based on manufacture such as marketing in the full sense of business planning, finance, R & D, design, technical service, sales, quality assurance, safety and environmental control.

One must add to these deficiencies those at government level discussed above. These provide extra sources of anxiety concerning continuity of the conditions likely to allow a proper return on investment. The possibility of an authoritarian Government taking power again in the near future cannot be excluded and provides a political risk. It has to be noted that in every country of the region recent elections have returned to power former Communists, or their Agrarian allies, supported by the leaders of the military industrial complex and by nationalists.

Consequently prudence suggests that foreign investments will be restricted to those areas that are calculated to return the investment very quickly. Such areas include investment in extraction and transport of oil, gas, other minerals and metals, timber, precious stones such as diamonds and semi precious stones. These can be exported and sold on the world market to the mutual benefit of investors whether foreign or native. When there is a high local demand for a product such as cigarettes, western firms buy into or acquire totally existing plants and modernise them, frequently using their own brand names which are fashionable in fSU.

There is a considerable industry based on western magazines, financial houses and joint chambers of commerce which attempts to persuade potential western investors to move into fSU and other countries with excellent prospects. The facts show that the sum total of foreign investment is far below the claims and many investments are in quite modest amounts in small firms. The dinosaur factories are correctly seen by western firms as unattractive purchases for foreigners.

Some westerners conclude that the region is successfully moving toward a market economy because they see so many small, privately owned shops filled with western goods. In practice very few local people can afford them; purchasers are usually the rich, many of whom are criminals. A recent estimate in Russia estimated that 40% of all trade is in the hands of the Mafia. The flight of capital continues apace; some estimates put deposits abroad at over $80bn. In 1993 Russian tourists took abroad $1.5bn whilst incoming tourists brought only $800-1000 million.

Most internal privatisation of significant firms has been carried out through the voucher system where every citizen was issued with one that could be traded for a share in a commercial or industrial property on the occasion of its privatisation. But this is not privatisation which has a chance of improving the success of the factories. This is because the directors and managers have bought blocks of shares which sometimes give them control. Added to this the work force which also subscribed has been persuaded to give the directors first refusal on purchase of their shares. The old directors with all their deficiencies are thus ensconced in power. Provided they can continue to get government subsidies to support their hidden unemployment the firm will not be liquidated. Furthermore there are no sources of alternative, more competent directors, as there are in a market economy.

The defence factories are the best of manufacturing enterprises. The countries cannot afford to have them go bankrupt, they form the most important segment of the industrial base. It is essential that they be successfully restructured to serve the national economy as well as retaining a sufficiency for national defence needs. I have set out my own view as an experienced engineer and industrialist how this may be done in practice.[10] Privatisation appears later rather than earlier in the essential steps. I would wish that these views would be embraced by the present Governments.

Some of the defence factories have excellent, very up-to-date, mostly imported equipment. Most, however, have equipment which is about 10-30 years out of date and are poorly laid out. They are untidy in ramshackle and unsuitable multi-storey buildings which are costly to heat and in which it is almost impossible to set out efficient materials handling between operations. Their worst feature is the obsolete nature of the management style and system. These are discussed briefly above and at some length in my paper which is based on considerable personal experience in electronic and mechanical engineering factories across the region.

Their directors have often repeated a theme "our defence factories have very cheap labour, highly skilled workers, the best educated scientists and engineers and very high technology and therefore why does the West not invest in joint ventures in them?"

The answers briefly are these: the labour may be badly paid but their productivity is very low; rejects are many times greater than in the western or even Pacific Rim countries; the engineers and managers are not attuned to conditions of a market economy and are very slow to understand the proper work attitudes and methods, let alone to apply them; the manufacturing technology is rarely of high quality and is often poorly managed and maintained; and the product technology in civilian goods is primitive. Consequently, investment is unattractive.

In the last year or so one has heard this can plaint less often; some people are beginning to realise that they have to learn to do what is needed by themselves. However there is a dangerous undertone to this sense of reality. It is coupled with the following

"We are a proud people with a long history, foreign intervention in Russia has always led to disaster. We can manage alone yet again, as we did against the Intervention and in the Great Patriotic War. You do not understand us, you bring, with a sense of superiority, your prescriptions for success which may or may not have been successful abroad but take no account of our history traditions and current circumstances. Western advice has reduced the Russian people to beggary and is responsible for our current decline".

There is, sadly much truth in the last phrase. As a result the West is again being demonised and seen as hostile.

The West must revise the content, manner and level of advice if it is to be helpful.

Current Russian policies toward the defence industries are moving back to the aims and methods of the old Command Economy. Understandably the Government does not wish them to fall into the hands of the Mafia, foreigners or others who might be judged not to have the interests of the country at heart. To these sentiments are added the hope of selling arms abroad in sufficient quantities to provide a significant hard currency income, at least to the Government and perhaps also to the factories.

However, as Marshal of Aviation Shaposhnikov stated frankly in his article in Izvestia of May 11th 1994, the USSR never sold arms abroad and has no experience of competing with western arms manufacturers. As to the sums often quoted for the value of such sales, he admitted that it was rare for the customer to pay for them. Current sales of between $1-2 bn/annum are unlikely to return to the levels of 1988 when the claimed value was over $20bn. This policy is unlikely either to save the Russian economy nor to provide enough work for the estimated 6 million workers in the defence industry.[11]

Almost every pronouncement, publication and discussion, especially in the military press, in Russia about the defence industries insists that they must be retained in their present form and size and that further conversion would be a crime.

Conclusions for the fSU and for Eastern and Central Europe

1- Plainly the defence industries in Russia at least, which operated about 80% of the total defence industry of the fSU, are, understandably, a very sensitive issue and must be treated as a special case but at the same time must be assisted to a new and more supportive structure for the national economy. In this sense the defence industries should be considered as part of the essential restructuring of the entire resources of the fSU and of the region if they are to move toward a future of progress toward a better life for their people.

2- The other republics face similar problems but in a sense they are less able to analyse them properly. This is because their military leaders, just like their industrial directors, were accustomed to fitting in with the strategic requirements set from Moscow. Consequently few of them have the experience or indeed the ability to formulate correctly the threats facing their country, the required structure and size of the armed forces and what they need in terms of equipment. We see the same reluctance as in Russia to scale down their armed forces, coupled with a desire to retain their defence industries partly with the declared hope of aligning their standards with those of NATO and selling to the NATO national armed forces military products. At the same time some of these countries wish to build old fashioned armies designed to make threats non existent in the foreseeable future. If these intentions are carried the probable result will be yet another economic bankruptcy.

3- It is practical as well as essential for the defence industries of eastern Europe to be restructured. Some, as in the west, will face closure because there are inadequate markets for anything they could make. Help with retraining and finding other jobs will be essential. It is unfortunate that so little has been done since perestroika in these directions. Other factories must be rearranged, using their core skills to make things for their own civilian markets as well as for some export. This step will need detailed professional help from experienced practitioners working in the factories alongside their directors. Some of their present activities, especially the secondary ones, should be spun off and eventually formed into small competing sub-contractors serving the locality, as is done in Japan and in the West. Both such moves may logically result in private ownership.

4- The likelihood is that dual purpose workshops and those dedicated to arms development and production will remain in State hands for the near future. But their people will also have to learn, just as State employees have in the West, to be fully competitive on the world markets. If experience in the West and of the past seven years in the fSU is a guide, this will take a long time, probably some decades. However let it be remembered that in Britain we have not yet privatised the Post Office or the railways even after 15 years of a Conservative Government.

5- Privatisation at large is generally limited to trading, much of it in the hands of criminals. Their foreign earnings are sent abroad and cannot help the national economy. Their activities worry not only the decent ordinary citizens of the region but increasingly the Governments of western Europe and USA. It is a dangerous illusion to imagine that trade without viable manufacture can form the basis of a sound market economy.

FOOTNOTES

{1} As recently as the last Labour Government in Great Britain a Minister of State expressed his irritation to me, appointed to enquire into the failure of a firm into which his department had poured millions, when I told him that the businessman whom he had supported had merely assumed he could sell his product into an already over supplied market. He said the problem with consultants was that they always talked about the market and marketting.

{2} Rolls Royce was briefly nationalised, by a Conservative Government when it was feared that its innovative venture into the RB211 engine would force it into bankruptcy. In the view of some specialists in the aero engine business, this fear was wrong and the action was precipitate.

{3} It was Havel, then President of Czechoslovakia, who said "The only people whom I have to run this country are former journalists and dissidents. They do not even know what a tax law is"

{4} China had a different history and commercial tradition which allowed it to apply a different and apparently more successful set of reforms whilst still operating a largely State owned manufacturing industry.

{5} Comparable figures for NATO countries were about 4-5% of GDP. The USA and UK never employed in peace time more than 20% of scientists and engineers.

{6} The memoirs of the famous designer of fighter aircraft, Yakovlev, describe Stalin's interference, during the Second World War, in the detail of an endurance test of a prototype engine.

{7} Yakovlev, in the closing chapter of his excellent book, makes a passionate plea for this close cooperation, which has been routine for decades in the western chemical industry and increasingly, partly under Japanese influence, in the mechanical and electrical engineering industries.

{8} A British agricultural consultancy took its own seed, husbandry methods and some farm equipment to a Ukrainian Collective farm and on the 70 Ha it farmed, has in two years raised its yield by a factor of 2.7 times. Soviet farm equipment such as tractors are often too heavy for the soil conditions. Tractors have been designed to serve military as well as civilian needs.

{9} See my paper "Toward a rational philosophy for science and engineering in the fSU" It is available in both English and Russian from CSRC. RMA Sandhurst, Camberley, Surrey, England.

{10} "The Rehabilitation of a Russian Military factory"

{11} NB Shaposhnikov quotes 25 million but he must mean all dependents and workers in supply and subsidiary industries. The figure is an error.

PROBLEMS AND PROSPECTS FOR PRIVATIZATION IN POST-COMMUNIST COUNTRIES

Salvatore Zecchini

The fact that privatisation of state-owned entreprises - in both the East and West - has become a priority for governments is not a historical coincidence, says Salvatore Zecchini. Governments are now realising that privatization is a powerful instrument to help them revive economic growth. Privatization is not the main solution to problems affecting the defence industry. But it can be an important component of a multifaceted strategy. In the face of conflicting pressures, it is likely that privatization in the next five years will continue to be a gradual process and not the determinant factor behind the expansion of the private sector.

Salvatore Zecchini is Assistant Secretary-General of the OECD in Paris, and Director of the Centre for Co-operation with the Economies in Transition.

It is not a casual coincidence of history if, in this decade, privatisation stands high on the political and economic agenda of both several OECD countries and all the post-communist countries. It is rather the result of a fundamental conclusion drawn by governments in both areas, i.e. that privatisation is a major instrument to realise important welfare gains for the country as a whole because it revives economic initiative and promotes innovation and higher productivity, all factors that lead to sustained economic growth. A concurrent consideration common to both OECD countries and post-communist countries is that privatisation can help the government to generate resources or to save resources for the purpose of reducing budget deficits.

Not only in ultimate goals but also in the privatisation methods there are similarities as both country groups are privatising similar categories of public assets, i.e. land, manufacturing enterprises, financial institutions and individual production facilities. In spite of these similarities, privatisation in the CEECs and NIS is in many respects a process and a problem different from that which can currently be seen in the OECD area. It is not just a difference in the absolute and relative scale of this operation since the CEECs and NIS have to privatise the bulk of their productive assets. There are other more important differences.

CEECs stands for Central and Eastern European Countries, and NIS for New Independent States of the former Soviet Union.

The economic backdrop against which privatisation has been taking place is much more difficult than in the OECD area as all the reforming economies have experienced a deep reduction in the level of economic activity, living standards and savings. In addition, they have had to pursue a much more diversified set of privatisation objectives than merely disposing of public assets at the best price. They also lacked an institutional, legal and financial infrastructure that could ease the ownership transfer, protect private ownership and promote entrepreneurship. Last but not least, privatisation had to be carried out in a context of scarcity of domestic private capital and severe shortage of entrepreneurship and management skills.

All these differences make it doubtful whether these economies can duplicate or draw many useful lessons from the recent privatisation experience of OECD countries. To deal with the unusual aspects of their privatisation problems, the CEECs and NIS have had to do a fair amount of experimentation, to draw on each other's experience, and to carefully blend foreign technical expertise with their own assessment of the internal constraints to privatisation. But in one area that is essential to support privatisation and in which these countries have to take measures which are not needed in the OECD countries, their action has been below their possibilities. This area is the rapid reform of the legal and institutional system which presides over the carrying-out of economic activities.

Instead of continuing to dwell on a comparative analysis of the privatisation issues, I will concentrate my remarks on the state of privatisation in the CEECs and NIS, on the main problems which hamper privatisation, with a specific attention to the defence industry, and on the prospects for the next few years.

At the beginning of the transformation process, privatisation, together with economic liberalisation, was hailed by governments and people as the driving force to accelerate the change of the economic system and to inject dynamism into these lagging economies. In fact, after 3 or 4 years this expectation has not materialised in any of these countries in spite of the considerable planning effort.

In the last three years, it is the rapid output expansion in the private enterprise sector that has been the main factor to reverse or to slow down the general economic decline. In Poland, Hungary and the Czech Republic the private sector already contributes more than half to GDP formation. Such an expansion, however, has not critically depended on the pace and extent of enterprise privatisation. For instance, Poland has privatised only about 20% of its public firms and Hungary only 1/3 in terms of asset value. The disposal of individual or relatively small production assets outside enterprise privatisation has instead been important to allow many private entrepreneurs to build a minimum of capital base rapidly.

As the private sector could not afford large investment outlays, it has developed in low-capital-intensity activities in which it could use relatively small production facilities or assets, previously in public hands, in a new enterprise context in which it could achieve sharp productivity gains.

If in many segments of the services sector private enterprises are predominant in number and output and if the share of services in national output has risen sharply in all reforming economies at the expense mostly of industry's share, this is also due to the flow of relatively small public assets into private hands, while major assets and enterprises have remained in the public domain.

Of course, within this general picture of the role of privatisation, important differences exist. Progress in privatisation has been very uneven in terms of both countries and types of assets. Among the CEECs, the Czech Republic has progressed more than the other countries with more than 60% of public enterprises' assets already privatised or in the process of being privatised in the on-going second wave of voucher privatisation. Russia has been the most rapid country in privatisation: about 40% of large enterprises and more than half of small enterprises have changed hands in less than two years. Estonia and Lithuania have also advanced considerably in "large" and "small" privatisation. Ukraine and other NIS are instead lagging behind, still remaining at the beginning of this process.

The so-called "small privatisation", namely the one involving small firms operating in retail trade, catering services, transport and small construction businesses as well as small production units, is very advanced if not already completed in some countries. Furthermore, in Poland and Hungary, privatisation (de jure or de facto) of production assets as opposed to entire enterprises has been quite important, accounting for about half of privatised production assets. This has been performed, for instance, through "liquidation", whereby production assets are transferred to new entrepreneurs while the old public firm disappears and its liabilities are taken over by the public sector. Considerable delays instead characterise privatisation of large firms, with the exception of the Czech Republic and Russia which are the only countries that have made substantial progress in this respect.

The ownership change has not affected all economic sectors to the same extent. Heavy industries, utilities, energy, major transport firms and major chemical industries have so far largely escaped privatisation for reasons that cannot be related to the notion that potential market failures justify retaining these firms under direct public control.

To this effect, several countries have instead used the argument of the strategic nature of these industries or sectors; they have not considered the possibility of obtaining more efficient enterprises through privatisation coupled with a new model of industry regulation. Only lately there has been a change in attitude in Hungary, Poland and the Czech republic. They have privatised or are privatising public utilities, such as power generation, telecommunications and water supply. This can be explained with the increasing pressure on these governments to generate additional resources for the public budget and to improve the quality of these services and management. Banks and other financial institutions have been privatised to a very limited extent, particularly because they require extensive support by the government due to the insolvency of many of their debtors belonging to the public enterprise sector.

With the exception of Poland where agriculture was not nationalised under the previous regime, agricultural land is still to a large extent under public or old-co-operative ownership. Problems in partition of land and in some countries the unsettled question of restitution to original owners are adding to the delays. In those countries in which agricultural land ownership has been transferred to peasants or co-operatives, the impact on production has been generally negative so far, because the new private farmers have not been able to acquire needed farm equipment and inputs, and to develop models of farm enterprise which are a viable alternative to the old co-operatives. In spite of being relatively easier to implement, privatisation of housing is far from complete because of delays in reforming rent level determination and house purchase financing. The only exception is Hungary where a favourable financing scheme has accelerated this privatisation.

Overall, a large number of public assets are now in private hands in CEECs and Russia, but in spite of the considerable amount of preparatory work which has been done in most post-communist countries, the bulk of industrial, banking and large-scale enterprises has still to be privatised. Only the Czech Republic and Russia seem seriously determined to press ahead for the completion of this process in a short period. As to the other countries, it is not clear whether they will overcome the many obstacles encountered in this process and what will be the share of public ownership in the enterprise sector at the end of this decade and its importance for the development of these economies. At this juncture in the transformation of the post-communist economies what are the main problems hampering progress in privatisation?

Clearly, privatisation has not been hindered by the particular approach followed by these countries. After the initial professions of faith in one or the other approach, these governments have soon come to recognise that to deal with the complex reality of public firms dismissal it is necessary to use all available methods. All countries are currently resorting to a multiplicity of approaches, although there are differences among countries as to the choice of the predominant approach.

Mass privatisation, i.e. the unrequited transfer of ownership to the population at large, has either been adopted or is being considered by all countries. This is the only instrument that can accelerate the pace of privatisation because it does not discriminate among sections of the population in terms of who would benefit. Moreover, it avoids the difficulty raised by the capital requirement for the acquisition of ownership or the difficulties of having to restructure a firm before it is sold.

Therefore, it is not surprising that privatisation has progressed rapidly in those countries in which this method has been applied more extensively. The Czech Republic and Russia, which are the front-runners in privatisation, have transferred more than half of the book value of privatised firms through mass privatisation vouchers. Hungary, which has had difficulties in making privatisation advance, has recently introduced generous credit facilities for the purchase of firms by its population in order to obtain some of the benefits stemming from mass privatisation. Through this approach it can quicken the pace of ownership transfer.

It is evident that the public sector of these countries is not in a position to carry out a reorganisation or operational restructuring of its firms to make them competitive in the market place. These governments even lack the means to implement a financial restructuring aimed at helping the firm to achieve a balanced capital structure by reducing its excess leverage (i.e. eliminating its debt overhang). The public owner can instead be expected to "corporatise" its firms, and to break up large firms. Apart from these tasks, restructuring is to be obtained by private entrepreneurs once ownership has been transferred to their hands. Management contracts are just an approximation to this result. Poland is the country that more than any other has been engaged in pre-privatisation reorganisation, but this has been possible only for a relatively small number of firms. Extending this approach to the rest of large enterprises would imply a significant protraction of privatisation.

Management or employee buy-outs are the second most used instrument for privatisation. They have been linked to voucher schemes for mass privatisation or sales under preferential conditions. Both options have been widely applied in Russia, Poland and Lithuania on the request of the enterprises themselves.

Trade sales, i.e. the sale of firms to strategic investors through public tenders, closed tenders, direct sales, or various forms of auctions, are more difficult to implement than other methods because they require extensive preparation of the sale, a measure of restructuring of the enterprise to be privatised, and adequate financial support. Among the reforming countries, Hungary is the one which has chosen to rely mostly on this method as it accounts for about 3/4 of privatised firms by book value. As long as it followed only this approach Hungary made relatively slow progress in privatisation.

If the approach to privatisation is not at present the main problem in making progress, other factors constitute impediments. First, the initial enthusiasm and social and political pressures for privatisation are fading away in several countries, including Hungary and Poland. Political consensus is lacking because of the persistent fear of adverse social consequences of post-privatisation restructuring.

Two consequences have been a source of particular concern:

a) the radical change that privatisation induces in the distribution of wealth; this represents a major shock for societies used to decades of "egalitarianism";

b) the restructuring of the labour force and social services provided by the privatised firm which tends to eliminate the job and social guarantees of the old regime.

In the face of these concerns, governments tend to link privatisation to the fulfilment of a multitude of objectives other than achieving efficiency gains. These include distributing public assets to all the population since all have contributed to their build-up, creating new employment opportunities or limiting job destruction, obtaining guarantees of development of the firm's capital, favouring new entrepreneurs, and maximising proceeds.

These aims are not mutually compatible, and cannot be achieved by privatisation alone, even if the approach is diversified into alternative methods that are applied to different portions of public assets. To the extent that governments have not been able to establish an order of priority between conflicting aims, a compromise has been the necessary outcome and the easiest compromise of all was initially to delay the process. Of course, delays are not a viable solution as they lead to a deterioration of assets, abuse through mismanagement or misappropriation, and eventually to liquidation of firms.

Thus, after the initial stage, mass privatisation became the main solution to political and social impediments. But this is not the best solution for the economy because the development of these economies demands a certain degree of concentration of enterprise ownership in the hands of entrepreneurs who are fully committed to steer the course of their enterprises. Hence, a second stage of ownership adjustment is necessary after privatisation and this requires well functioning capital markets.

Nevertheless, as a second-best solution, mass privatisation is the easiest approach, and at the present juncture a number of lagging countries are moving in this direction. They are actually forced to privatise because there is less room in their budgets to sustain the cost of supporting public enterprises and past delays in privatisation have not led, as expected, to lower hardship for people and easier recovery for these economies. Even under these conditions, progress will depend on the capacity of governments to develop cost-effective social policies to smooth the enterprise restructuring process.

In this respect, two conditions must be fulfilled:

a) that the level of economic activity starts rising again;

b) that an active labour market policy is developed.

The second major problem is represented by the inadequacies of the institutional and financial framework of the economy and of privatisation itself. At the institutional level, the transfer of ownership is still taking place in a context in which property rights are not adequately protected and private enterprises operate in an uncertain legal and regulatory environment.

Enforcement of contractual obligations is doubtful and costly, while the hold of the old bureaucracy over economic activities is still pervasive. At the financial level, privatised enterprises face difficulties in meeting their financing requirements and in diversifying their capital sources in order to correct their currently-high financial leverage. Credit allocation by banks is still distorted in favour of firms holding public guarantees.

The possibility of reducing enterprises' debt ratio through debt/equity swaps with the creditor banks is limited because of the weak capital base of most banks. Financial markets are still at an early stage of development and are dominated by the financial instruments issued by the government. The general attitude of these countries has been to give priority to solving industrial crises on a case-by-case basis. Less emphasis has been placed on improving rapidly the economic environment, in easing rigidities on the employment of labour force, and in developing competitive markets for products and factors of production.

Under these framework conditions, it is difficult to expect that privatised enterprises can become competitive soon and that privatisation can bring about an early renewal of these economies.

Linked to this problem is a third one, i.e. the failure of privatisation in all the post-communist countries to attract large flows of foreign capital. Although there have been some restrictions or discriminations against foreign investors for the purpose of preventing a sell-off to foreigners, these measures do not seem to have constituted a major disincentive.

For instance, even in the case of Hungary, which is the largest recipient of FDI, only one third of foreign capital has been invested in the purchase of public firms, while the largest part has been oriented towards the establishment of "greenfield" enterprises. In fact, the same rigidities in capital and labour use that depress the profitability of domestic investment in public firms, discourage foreign participation in privatisation. Since these firms, like the others, need foreign capital and know-how to gain competitiveness and profitability, the government should consider what support to give to potential foreign investors in order to partly offset the disincentive stemming from these rigidities. In so doing, they would not discriminate against domestic investors because the latter already benefit from mass privatisation free of charge and other preferences.

A fourth problem is represented by the shortage of entrepreneurs. These countries have at their disposal a substantial number of good managers of production processes but have also a shortfall of entrepreneurs, i.e. people that are able to launch new production initiatives and manage business risk. The transfer of ownership into private hands does not lead, on its own, to a rapid conversion of good production managers into good entrepreneurs who are capable of maximising the value of their enterprise within the constraints of a competitive market economy. Therefore, to ensure that privatisation leads to development of viable enterprises, it has to be coupled with a government action aimed at promoting entrepreneurship on an economy-wide scale.

A fifth problem concerns the uneven quality of the enterprises which have still to be privatised. In the initial phase governments have disposed mostly of the firms which are in better conditions and can attract investors' attention. As privatisation advances, what are on offer are the less attractive firms and demand for them by private investors might be lacking. In this case governments are faced with the choice between liquidation and restructuring before privatisation.

Both options are costly and difficult to implement since they involve either dealing with the resulting unemployment and liability settlement, which also affects banks' solvency, or planning and implementing a business-oriented restructuring. Hence, with progress in privatisation, its interdependence with progress in other policies, such as industrial, social and financial policies, becomes critical for making further headway.

Privatisation of defence industries raises a number of problems that leave little in common with the general issue of privatisation. The difficulties in the defence sector derive basically from a shift in the composition of the demand in the economy: military procurement has been cut back sharply in a short period and government subventions to military industries have been curtailed. At the same time demand for civilian goods has risen but in a new context of markets open to competition and of a decline of per-capita income levels for large sections of the population.

Other peculiar difficulties are the exclusive dependence of the economy of certain regions on military industries, the relatively high incidence of laboratories and test facilities over total facilities, the secrecy surrounding many technologies and the coexistence within the military sector of a considerable production of consumer goods and machine tools. For instance, in the former Soviet Union, it is estimated that more than half of consumer goods were produced by the military-industrial complex. To assess the role and problems of privatisation in dealing with these difficulties the governments have, first, to clarify the objectives to be pursued.

Thus, the first problem to be tackled is to decide whether to pursue a reallocation of human and physical capital as well as technologies towards other sectors of the economy or other enterprises which are expanding in the new market-based economic system, or to continue investing in the military industries to produce the new range of goods and services requested by the market.

Related to this problem is a second one pertaining to the structure of ownership. The question is whether the government should retain ownership of facilities working for the market and aim at upgrading their management, or should transfer ownership to the private sector, being that more market- and business-oriented. Likewise, as to defence-oriented production facilities, the question is whether the national security concerns could be addressed through other means than direct government ownership of these facilities. In other words, should the government be only on the demand side of the economy, leaving the supply side for both military and civilian goods exclusively in private hands? Or should the government turn military industries into conglomerate companies which own both civilian and military-oriented companies and which can use resources generated in one group of companies to support the other.

Assuming that a certain portion of the current defence industry has to be privatised, another question emerges: whether to privatise individual assets, or entire plants, or to extend privatisation to military technology for the purpose of allowing their use in non-military sectors. All these questions have to receive an answer at the political level rather than at the military one since these involve many considerations which lie outside the military realm and also concern the future structure and development of the economy. From an economic point of view, it would seem appropriate that all facilities working for the market be transferred to the private sector because the latter is in the best position to compete in the market place.

It is not clear whether countries with a sizeable defence industry, such as Russia, have moved in the direction of drawing a clear demarcation line between the core defence activities to be retained in the public sector for security reasons and the other activities which can be privatised. By the end of 1993 Russia had privatised more than 270 defence-related enterprises and corporatised another 760. In the same period it is estimated that more than 1.8 million workers had left the defence sector.

In view of all these problems afflicting the defence industry, it does not seem that privatisation per se is the main solution. It is, however, an important component of a strategy which starts with "unbundling" the defence industry in to privatisable and non-privatisable assets, then proceeds with privatising all that is not related to "core" national security, and eventually leads to a restructuring of privatised enterprises by private entrepreneurs.

Enterprise restructuring is, nevertheless, a difficult task since it requires converting military firms to the logic and demands of the market. The experience of the US after the World War II and that of other OECD countries more recently shows that plant conversion seldom succeeds because the military enterprise culture does not encompass critical elements for being successful in the market place, such as cost-effectiveness, market analysis, financial management and marketing. It has often been the case that OECD countries, instead of converting or privatising defence plants, have found it more appropriate to liquidate these assets or to scrap them outright. Recent surveys of Western investors also confirm this conclusion as they indicate a clear preference for establishing new plants in the reforming economies rather than converting existing defence plants. Hence, it seems that the reforming countries should focus their response to the problems of their defence industry in directions other than enterprise privatisation. Specifically, they should aim at creating an environment conducive to the creation of new enterprises and new job opportunities. This has to be supported by consistent social, credit and labour-market policies directed to favour the reallocation of production factors. For regions which are particularly hit by defence expenditure cut-backs, it is also necessary to resort to regional development plans.

Leaving aside defence privatisation, what future can be envisaged for the general privatisation process in the next five years, starting from the present situation and the many problems already mentioned? In the countries that have made limited progress so far, an acceleration of the pace of privatisation seems unlikely unless a new high wave of mass privatisation for free is launched. As for the others, mainly the states of the former USSR who have lagged behind, an acceleration is possible. The pace of privatisation will likely depend on two conditions:

a) the stringency of the public budget constraint which might deprive public firms of critical support; and

b) the pace of output recovery since a revival of economic activities might ease the social costs of privatisation. Overall, only in one or two countries, such as the Czech Republic and Russia, enterprise privatisation is expected to be completed by 1997.

For the others, privatisation will continue to be a slow process, which might become hostage to social and political compromises, and might be restricted to a fraction of existing public enterprises. In contrast, a rise in the demand for the purchase of public firms could stem from the expected easing of the current constraints represented by the weakness of the legal and institutional framework of the economy, the shortage of domestic capital and the limitations in entrepreneurial skills. This is not, however, sufficient to spur the authorities to accelerate privatisation, unless significant benefits are expected, such as significant revenue for the currently strained public finances or considerable capital in-flows for the balance of payments.

In the face of these conflicting pressures, it is likely that in the next five years the development of the private sector would have to rely more on new entrepreneurial initiatives than on newly privatised public enterprises.

Surprisingly, it might be the case that the autonomous expansion of the private sector could offer a window of opportunity for facilitating speedier privatisation. By attracting labour currently employed in public firms, the private sector could alleviate the social impact of privatisation, and defuse its most contentious aspects. The outcome could be to bring to manageable proportions either the closing-down of public firms or their radical restructuring for the purpose of making them competitive. In other words, the problem of privatisation could disappear since public firms could either be liquidated and their production assets sold if not written off, or they could be turned into viable firms managed along business-oriented criteria and in no need of privatisation.

Regardless of whatever scenario would become reality, it is likely that in most of these countries the economic system would evolve in the coming years into a sort of "mixed capitalism", with private firms co-existing and competing with an important sector made out of firms owned by public authorities. In such a context, the major concerns for the purpose of attaining efficiency gains for the economy as a whole are both to create the framework conditions for private economic initiative to materialise and prosper, and to ensure evenhanded treatment for private firms and public ones so as not to distort competition. This would imply the discontinuation of the many preferences in financial and regulatory terms that public firms have so far enjoyed.

Among the various forms of privatisation, free ownership transfer and management or employee buy-out at national prices will continue to prevail over trade sales although the balance between them might shift towards sales if considerable proceeds or employment or investment guarantees will be provided by buyers outside the firm. In any case, the initial ownership transfer will be just the first phase of a process of ownership restructuring which will continue after privatisation. A new wave of ownership reshuffle is to be expected in the next five years with the result of a concentration of corporate governance in fewer hands than at the moment of privatisation.

The wide diffusion of shares among the population does not necessarily reflect people's desire to hold them and to exercise the inherent ownership rights over the way companies are managed. It is instead dictated by the two needs of dealing with concerns over the distribution of the accumulated social wealth and implanting a new economic culture among people. In spite of these needs, the reallocation of shares seems inevitable in order to allow a mechanism of control over and accountability of management to emerge in the face of the current fragmentation of ownership.

Three components are crucial to this end:
a) investment funds or mutual funds;
b) secondary markets;
c) the banking system.

Investment funds and similar institutions are bound to play a prominent role in controlling enterprises' management as intended by the authorities in launching mass privatisation. Building on these foundations, their role could easily develop into providing equity capital to new enterprises by attracting and mobilising private savings. Their ability to monitor the state of health of firms and their diversification of risks offer clear advantages to investors over a direct investment in enterprises' stocks.

Secondary markets for stocks and assets have begun to develop in these countries as the principal mechanism for adjusting the portfolio composition of investors and to provide liquidity to share holders. Their expansion has been hampered in some countries, such as Russia, by temporary preclusions of subsequent ownership transfers. With the progress in privatisation and a wider diffusion of shares, pressure for the abolition of these constraints will increase. A significant development of secondary markets could hence be envisaged. Such a development needs, however, to be sustained by improvements in the regulatory framework of markets and in the requirements for transparency of information on enterprises and financial institutions.

Apart from secondary markets, stock exchange markets could become an important instrument for privatisation by the end of this decade. So far only a small number of firms have been sold in the markets (15% of total book value privatised in Hungary and a lower percentage in Poland). As these markets mature, it can be expected that the number of public offerings of stocks will rise. This will concern both entire companies' stocks and minority stakes retained by governments after the initial privatisation. This trend is already evident: Hungary plans to sell large companies through the Budapest Stock Exchange and the Czech National Property Fund is selling shares retained after the first wave of voucher privatisation.

Despite its current weakness, the banking system is also essential in supporting both privatisation and post-privatisation. Its role will strengthen to the extent that banks are directly involved in the restructuring of the liabilities of the enterprises to be privatised. A certain number of debt/equity swaps will take place and the increasing presence of stocks among banks' assets will heavily influence the operational profile of the banking system: the model of "universal bank" might become the predominant one. Banks will also fulfil the essential function of supplying liquidity to investors and stock market participants. Without such support, secondary markets can hardly develop into efficient instruments for resources allocation and would remain rather unpredictable, with discontinuous patterns in price evolution.

As regards the role of foreign capital, there are now very few elements that might lead to an increasing interest of foreign companies in participating in privatisation, given several internal or operational constraints that accompany privatisation. The participation of foreign investors might instead rise in the post-privatisation reallocation of ownership, but this would demand major improvements in the performance of stock markets and financial intermediaries, such as investment funds.

Finally, two considerations on the expected benefits of privatisation. Welfare gains for the economy as a whole do not stem simply from privatisation but from its combination with competition. So far there has been limited support for demonopolisation prior to privatisation, particularly among those interested in acquiring public firms or that have already acquired them. Nor has liberalisation of foreign trade, profit regulations and competition laws been adequate to reduce the market power of monopolists. In the absence of demonopolisation authorities might refrain from relinquishing their ownership of de-facto monopolist firms. This does not seem the appropriate response because privatisation of predominant market suppliers might bring about higher efficiency gains than in the opposite case if it is accompanied by more stringent regulations aimed at reducing the market power of major domestic suppliers and by incentives for new competitors to enter the market. At any rate, the commitments taken by several CEECs and NIS to lower further their trade barriers in the next few years, particularly vis-a-vis European companies, is bound to make their markets much more competitive than at present by the end of this decade.

As to the impact on public finances, privatisation is not likely to generate large revenues for the budget, assuming the prevalence of methods other than trade sales. Some relief for public expenditure might however derive from the disposal or liquidation of firms, provided that the consequent social costs and social expenditures are not substantial. If some large enterprises are retained in the public sector for several years a hidden burden would remain in the budget. This will prompt the authorities to restructure these enterprises and to establish objective criteria for the accountability of management. Hungary, Poland and Romania are already considering entering into contracts with management groups to conduct operational restructuring and manage these enterprises. Such contracts, which include ownership incentives, might expand in the near future and prove successful in rehabilitating enterprises.

In conclusion, it has to be stressed that in a market economy, privately owned firms generally outperform public firms in cost-effectiveness, efficiency and competitiveness. Hence, in order to raise public welfare in the "mixed-capitalism" that will characterise these economies for at least this decade, privatisation has to remain a constant objective of governments and should continue to be pursued in spite of the difficulties.

In this respect, the main challenge for these governments is not just to achieve a successful restructuring of firms still kept under public ownership but to be able to recognise when the time has come for these firms to be privatised. If these governments fail in taking a timely decision in this sense, they will likely fall into the old trap of inefficiencies and subsidies. In other words, they will show that they have not learned enough from the experience of OECD countries that after decades of complacency are now forced by their economic ills to push privatisation through.

PANEL III

Defence Industry Privatization and National Security Requirements

Chair: Simon Lunn, Deputy Secretary General,
North Atlantic Assembly, Brussels

Panelists: Robert Farrand
Andrei N. Loginov
Katarzyna Zukrowska and Léon Turczynski
Nikolai Kulinich
Michael Bell

DEFENCE INDUSTRY PRIVATIZATION AND NATIONAL SECURITY REQUIREMENTS: THE UNITED STATES EXPERIENCE

Robert Farrand

The dilemma of how to beat swords into ploughshares in the wake of major armed conflicts has challenged humanity since the beginning of time. In describing the US defence industry privatization experience in the aftermath of war, Ambassador Robert W. Farrand and his colleagues explain that today's challenges for nations are to provide the level of national defence at a minimum cost. The question is not 'should we privatize?' because the United States technical/industrial base is and has virtually always been in the hands of private industry, but rather 'how can we continue to rely on our private sector defence industry in a time of war?'.

This paper was presented at the NATO Economics Colloquium by Ambassador Robert W. Farrand, International Affairs Advisor at the Industrial College of the Armed Forces (National Defense University), in Washington.

It was written jointly by Ambassador Farrand and the following specialists from the Industrial College of the Armed Forces:

Dr. Robert Scheina, Professor of History,
Department of Strategy (co-drafter);

Captain Fred L. Meyer, (USN, Ret.), Professor,
Department of Resources Management (co-drafter);

Mr. James R. Lecky, Research Fellow,
Department of Resources Management (co-drafter);

Commander Bernie Grover, Canadian Defence Force,

Bernard M. Baruch Professor of Economic and National Strategy,
Department of Resources Management (co-drafter);

Dr. Clair Blong, Federal Emergency Management Agency,
Professor of Industrial Relations, Department of Resources Management.

Foreword

This paper presents a view of privatization as it pertains to U.S. national security in a post-Cold War world.

In large measure, the future strength and prosperity of the American people will rest on the success of our Government and private industry working together to manage the process of converting industries heretofore dependent on weapons and defense-related production to the manufacture of civilian goods. We find ourselves at another decision point in history not unlike the end of the two world wars earlier in this century.

The ICAF faculty members from diverse academic and career backgrounds who collaborated on this paper have sought to summarize the history of defense production and procurement in the United States, cull lessons learned from that history, and pose the strategic questions currently confronting U.S. decision-makers in both government and industry.

The National Security Challenge

As a nation committed since its inception two centuries ago to the twin concepts of private property and free enterprise, the issue of privatization in the United States arises only in the context of governmental functions which the American people have decided must be performed by publicly owned, taxpayer-funded organizations and institutions. These functional areas have traditionally involved such sectors of the economy (and society) as government, education, municipal services, transportation infrastructure, and, most important, defense.

By and large, all other sectors in American life, including manufacturing and services, have been left to the initiative of private commercial enterprise. Thus, with some variation in emphasis on the part of our political parties as to the proper role of government in the economy, the question of privatization in the American context has been largely sorted out. By far the largest source of strength, innovation, and investment capital in the U.S. economy derives from the financial and intellectual resources of individual entrepreneurs and corporate managers.

The issue of privatization continues to be a vexing one, however, in the context of how a national economy based upon the free enterprise system where firms seek always to maximize profits can be relied upon to produce the materiel necessary for war.

Brief Historical Overview

The issue of how much national technical industrial base is adequate for security needs and how to guarantee that enough, but not too much, industrial base is preserved is a perennial challenge first confronted by the founding fathers of the United States in 1776.

The United States has fought ten wars since its Independence. In each of these wars to a lesser or greater extent the Government struggled to insure that the defense industrial base was adequate and ready enough to provide our forces in the field with the weapons, ordnance, food, clothing, and other physical assets necessary to prosecute the war.

In order to supply the Continental Army with enough cannons to fight the War for Independence, our early leaders found it necessary to establish a government arsenal in Massachusetts. To ensure the Army would be supplied with the necessary field pieces, therefore, the U.S. Government became an arms manufacturer at a very tender age. Alexander Hamilton, our first Secretary of the Treasury, however, did not consider the novel arsenal system adequate to meet the defense needs of the new nation.

In his 1791 "Report on Manufactures," Hamilton called for a national industrial policy which through tariffs would protect industries critical to the national defense (such as sail cloth production, the 18th century equivalent to nuclear propulsion) and create defense industries for which there was no parallel commercial market, i.e., no "dual-use" in today's parlance. The Congress, then controlled by the opposition party, saw Hamilton's suggestion as government interference in the free market system and therefore a policy concept to be avoided.

So throughout the first half of the 19th Century, the United States relied totally upon the yet-modest private sector to equip its small Army and Navy.

During the U.S. Civil War, President Abraham Lincoln found it expedient for a variety of political reasons to rely on state governors and not the National Congress to raise the Union army to fight the war. To increase the influence of the governors, the Union chose to leave production of war materiel in private hands and to divide the procurement spoils among the states loyal to the Union based roughly upon each state's contribution of men. One historian estimates that as a consequence the Union probably paid twice as much as it should have for equipment and supplies, but that was an acceptable cost of victory.

The military-industrial complex as we know it today first made its appearance in the United States in the late 19th century with the double birth of our new navy and a fledgling steel industry to support naval construction. The Government's boldest adventure was to the create an armor manufacturing plant with public funds. Long under debate and construction, however, the armor factory's completion, in an ironic twist of fate, coincided almost exactly with the signing of the Washington Naval Arms Limitation Treaty (1922) which placed a moratorium on the construction of battleships and, as a consequence, the taxpayer's investment in the armor factory was largely wasted.

But this loss was pennies compared to the total cost of the logistics fiasco of World War I. American industry was caught in 1917 wholly unprepared to support the U.S. forces. We fought World War I using French and British weapons because our industrial base simply could not respond in time. Indeed, when our factories finally started producing weapons, our shipyards had not completed the ships necessary to get them or our troops to Europe. The few weapons we were finally able to manufacture virtually never got to our troops. Our inadequate defense industrial mobilization of World War I actually led to the formation of the Army Industrial College, the forerunner of ICAF, to help ensure that the nation never finds itself in the same unprepared condition again.

The issue for the Government then became how to manage the build-down and how to be prepared the next time U.S. national security was threatened to build-up again in a timely manner. Thus, to address this double-edged challenge the following legislative and administrative initiatives were taken in the years following the Great War:

First, the Bureau of the Budget was created in 1921 within the legislative branch, thereby setting up an auditing function outside the executive branch;

Second, the Army Industrial College, now the Industrial College of the Armed Forces (ICAF), was established in 1924 so that the lessons learned during World War I would not be forgotten and the study of mobilization for war could be formalized;

Third, the Government subsidized in 1926 the designing of aircraft as well as plant and production equipment to assure the survival of the aircraft industry;

Fourth, the War Policies Commission was established in 1930 to give the government the capacity to regulate private property during war, thus eliminating the need for the Government to own a large number of production facilities.

Fifth, a limit was placed in 1934 on the amount of profit that could be made by a private firm when selling ships and aircraft to the government.

These measures and others adopted later in the 1930s were for the most part designed to reduce the need for the Government to own and operate costly, inefficient production facilities. The measures, taken as a whole, attempted to come to grips with the dilemma faced by a democratic government seeking to provide for defense without harming the system of free enterprise.

World War II again severely challenged the ability of the United States to fight a global war. But by the conflict's end, the United States had manufactured almost half of all that had been produced in the world during the war years. For example, by early 1945 the U.S. industrial machine, in private hands but under close Government supervision (and contracts), had manufactured from a virtual standing-start five years earlier the following amounts of war materiel, by category:

Aircraft	310,000
Tanks	88,000
Landing Craft	82,000
Rifles and Carbines	12,500,000
Trucks	2,400,000

To achieve this end, the Government had been required to enter into every conceivable ownership arrangement with the private sector in the United States. Although we conformed to our pattern of behavior following earlier wars by drastically reducing war production after 1945, the Korean War shocked us into facing the reality of an emerging Cold War. Recently abandoned manufacturing arrangements between the federal government and the private sector, based upon still existing legislation and agreements enacted during and before WWII, were renewed.

Down-Sizing in the Post-Cold War Era

The forty-year Cold War period which ensued saw as large a defense build-up and surge of technological research and weapons production as any comparable period in U.S. history. The Cold War's demise presents us all, the United States as well as other nations involved in the conflict, with a set of crucial decisions relating precisely to the topic of this colloquium. Since the vast bulk of U.S. defense industry remains in private hands, Government policy during the current "down-sizing" has been to leave the initiative on how to respond to reduced defense orders primarily in the hands of defense firms themselves. Government policy has had two primary aims, i.e., to attempt to:

- Identify critical defense technologies and capabilities deemed essential to our long-term security requirements. We are doing this through continued orders or by paying firms to maintain idle capacity and essential tooling. For example, Congress has approved funding for another submarine, even though there is no immediate operational requirement for it. By building the submarine, however, we are able to maintain our technology base, our unique manufacturing processes, and our highly specialized labor skills. Each of these capabilities would have been lost had we allowed normal market forces to work, and they would have been extremely costly and difficult to replace at some future point.
- Cushion the impact of reduced defense orders by creating a more favorable environment for defense plants and their workers. This initiative has taken several forms at the national and state levels, including:
  - Helping displaced workers find new employment through retraining, extended unemployment benefits, and employment information centers.
  - Assisting defense plants in finding civilian alternatives by providing consultation,

information, and small-scale funding of studies on how to restructure or redesign a given facility for alternative production.
- Providing tax advantages for new initiatives.
- Providing small amounts of funding to underwrite partially the cost of highly selective dual-use projects which have commercial utility and value, as well as defense applicability. (We will discuss more about dual-use technologies later in this paper).

As these changes are working through the economy, the U.S. Government continues to leave most of the initiative with individual firms and workers. In September 1993, then-Deputy Secretary of Defense William Perry said, "We've already lost hundreds of thousands of jobs (in the U.S. defense industry) and there are that many more ahead of us to lose. We clearly expect many defense companies to go out of business. And we will stand by and see that happen." In other words, the Government does not intend, under current post-Cold War conditions, to intervene in the market by centrally directing a detailed restructuring of defense production facilities from the national level. Instead, the Government is wrestling with the problems of identifying broad priorities and responding to strategic questions.

That said, the Government has not lost sight of the need to preserve essential production capabilities. The current industrial policy vision, in simple terms, is one that hopes to minimize the size of "defense-only" capacity and maximize the size of "dual-use" capabilities which can only be sustained by a healthier, more robust civilian economy.

International Competitiveness and Dual-Use Technology

The United States finds itself in the unique position of being a global power, while at the same time we are facing ever-increasing economic competition from the rest of the world, including significant competition from our traditional military allies. Our nation has strongly supported this increasingly open global trading system. The global trading system provided the basis for economic rebirth after World War II and increased opportunities for all, while increasing the standard of living for many.

The key to America's defense in this new global economic environment is international competitiveness. Relative economic power is often the ultimate constraint on a nation's foreign and military power. For the nation to remain strong, it must remain globally competitive in economic terms. The Government is addressing the need to be strong militarily, within the context of greatly reduced post-Cold War defense budgets, with the concomitant need to be strong economically. One option the Government is pursuing is to concentrate on "dual-use" technology, e.g., technology that has both defense application and the potential significantly to contribute to America's international economic competitiveness. Exploiting dual-use technology is leading to a new form of defense privatization.

In this new arrangement, the prime focus is on technologies — both product and process technologies — which will foster economic competitiveness, and thus will be of primary importance in the private sector. At the same time, the Government is concerned about maintaining a domestic technology capability, both to support current defense needs and to provide the weapons of the future. The Department of Defense (DoD), then, will work with private industry to foster, to nurture, chosen technologies in a way that supports both the military need and private sector competitiveness. In the process, both private sector firms and the military become winners.

Technology Reinvestment Program

Yet another "privatization" initiative involves the privatization of defense technology. This is an initiative wherein technology developed for military-unique application is being adapted for commercial use. For example, technology that heretofore was used in nuclear weapons production is being adapted to medical equipment applications. Federal government funding is being used to assist in this transition of technology which has the dual benefit of creating commercial value from what had been purely defense investments. U.S. firms will thus benefit from unique new, technologically advanced products for the global marketplace.

Strategic Issues of Industrial Organization

Once again the United States finds itself seeking answers to the following strategic questions:

How should the U.S. change its national security strategy in the new era?

What is the correct national defense strategy and related military force structure in the post-Cold War era?

How should the nation optimally reallocate its resources between political, economic, military and psycho-social elements of national power?

What are the desirable characteristics of the future national technology and industrial base (NTIB)?

In response to the latter question, the U.S. Office of Technology Assessment concludes that the NTIB characteristics should include:

* Advanced research and development capability
* Ready access to civilian technology
* Continuous design and prototyping capability
* Limited, efficient peacetime engineering and production

capabilities in key defense sectors
* Responsive production of ammunition, spares, and consumables for theater conflict
* Healthy, mobilizable civilian production capability
* Robust maintenance and overhaul capability
* Good, integrated management

What is the correct mix of national investment in current versus future military capabilities?

- To the extent that the U.S. faces an immediate military threat, the Department of Defense (DoD) will need to allocate resources for current capabilities. Current force structure must be maintained, obsolete systems replaced, and existing skills and facilities supported. Relevant policies would include: directly funding production over research and development (R&D);fostering weapons-specific manufacturing; and emphasizing weapon development over generic research and development.
- If the immediate threat recedes, as it likely will continue to do, then the DoD can shift investment toward the development of future military capabilities.

Related policies would include: shifting funding from production to R&D; emphasizing science and technology support; pursuing continuous prototyping; buying knowledge (as opposed to hardware); funding generic manufacturing advances; and emphasizing mobilization planning and the health of the broad national technical/industrial base.

Should the Nation continue to depend upon a NTIB which supports military-unique (i.e., status quo) or dual-use technologies for both products and processes?

• Military-unique technologies place performance first as the critical measure of effectiveness, require tight technology security, and generally have no civilian counterparts. To insure access to these technologies, the DoD would emphasize strict military design (rather than cost considerations), adopt commercial manufacturing practices which promote quality and efficiency, and fully fund R&D costs.

• Dual-use technologies, on the other hand, enhance the desirable goal of civil-military technological and industrial integration while lowering costs, increasing production capacity and the economic dimension of national security. Thus, implementing this "dual-use privatization" approach would: increase commercial competition; increase the use of items not solely developed for defense purposes; emphasize performance as well as cost considerations; adopt commercial manufacturing practices, including quality control standards; streamline government oversight to remove unnecessary rigidities; and lead to an improvement in the training and quality of government acquisition personnel.

In both the "military-unique" and "dual-use" technology approaches to maintaining current production and planning for future military capability, the Government must decide what level of public versus private national technology/industrial base (NTIB) is desirable;

- A decision to retain strong private-sector "contractor-owned/contractor operated" (COCO) facilities involvement in the NTIB would require rule changes to enable industry to earn profits commensurate with risks. Under this option, the nation could retain its overall strategy of relying primarily on the private sector, while maintaining some critical military - unique technology and manufacturing capabilities in "government-owned/government operated" (GOGO) and "government-owned/contractor-operated" (GOCO) organizations.
- If private-sector (COCO) industrial organizations are favored, some firms may have to be subsidized to main technology and manufacturing capabilities and profits must somehow be assured commensurate with risks to sustain the interest of public investors in the stock market.
- If the decision is made for "military-unique" technologies to promote R&D and manufacture in government facilities, then the Government will inevitably assume a greater share of the financial and technological risk.

During the Cold War era, the COCO/GOGO and GOCO industrial organizations were used in the U.S. with each one, singly or in combination, possessing unique advantages and disadvantages.

- The GOGO organization provided for full government ownership and control of capital plant and equipment and public financing of operations. This form of organization meant greater bureaucratic controls, while insuring stability of services and production, and maintaining critical skills;
- The GOCO organization permitted the Government to own the capital thus underwriting fixed costs of overhead while at the same time allowing "privatization" of the operations which increased reliance on market incentives to control variable costs of labor, materials, and the like;
- The COCO organization preserved the full incentives and advantages of the market place, controlled costs and encouraged industrial efficiency. This approach, used very successfully during the Cold War, injected more innovation, creativity and efficiency into the R&D processes than either the GOGO or GOCO models. The added burdens of laws, regulation and government oversight made the latter two NTIB organizations less efficient than their COCO commercial-product-counterpart organizations even when under the same private sector management.
- A key point to remember is that both the COCO and GOCO operations must provide the stimulus for adequate profit margins if these private sector enterprises are to stay healthy and viable.

(Figure 1 presents the three options discussed above for public/private sector industrial organization in matrix form).

The Office of Technology Assessment suggests that for reasons of cost, total capacity, and potential for innovation, the best options for post-Cold War industrial organization would be to increase the use of dual-use technologies, depend upon private ownership (COCO's) and competitive acquisitions. The next best option would be the GOCO-type operation providing for government ownership of overhead but private sector incentives to control direct, variable costs. Finally, for totally defense-unique manufacturing, and only as a last resort, the GOGO model option would be used.

Which strategic commodities should the United States purchase from private versus government manufacturing sources?

• The decision about the appropriate source from which to procure military products depends upon the item in question. Characteristics of products amenable to "privatized" sourcing would include: a unique military item nearly equivalent to a commercial item or which could be readily customized from a commercial item; a production process similar to the commercial process; an item from a lower manufacturing or technological tier (e.g., a commodity subcomponent). Examples of products which fit these characteristics are: commodities, foodstuffs, textiles, clothing, winches, laptop computers, satellites; global positioning systems, jet engines, cargo planes, food packaging.

Examples of dual-use items include: helicopter airframes, heavy trucks, jam-proof radar/radios, automatic test equipment, and general maintenance services.

Characteristics of defense goods or services which make them less amenable to integration with the commercial sector include those items where:

- There is no related commercial variant, (e.g., weapons).
- Production processes are highly specialized for performance or security reasons.
- They emerge from a higher manufacturing tier, especially prime vendor-level integration.
- They rely on cutting-edge technology having little or no commercial application.

Examples of such items are:

Large caliber ammunition; armored vehicles; specialty metals/composites; large gun barrels and their integration; nuclear weapons.

Finally, we are left with the question of how Government should respond to this industry perspective on defense down-sizing and industrial conversion:

"Defense private firms can transform themselves into competitive industries, given time, management persistence, and realistic expectations. Plant level conversion, however, is unlikely. Further, the implications for national security strategy of closing plants should not be minimized. Defense plants cannot be 'reconstituted' and once current defense production lines have been shut down, the time, political cost, and difficulties of restarting them will prove overwhelming."

Richard T. Minnich in "Defense Downsizing and Economic Conversion: An Industry Perspective." (1993)

The processes of "down-sizing," "right-sizing," defense conversion and privatization are complex and uncertain both in their implementation and in their outcomes. Even in the U.S., where the tradition of free market support of military security needs is centuries old, we continue to find the optimal solution to industrial organization for defense elusive. This paper has outlined U.S. industrial history and the flexible choices our system is pursuing to provide the industrial means to support the U.S. national security strategy.

Senior Government, industry and academic leaders continue to evaluate and debate the issues of "privatization" versus government ownership and operations. We will continue to experiment, learn from unsuccessful approaches and eventually settle upon strategy. Sharing our experience could benefit other nations facing the challenge of reallocating resources and human talents to solve a range of national problems to improve the well-being of their citizens while maintaining an acceptable level of military security.

Conclusion

The dilemma of how to beat swords into plowshares in the wake of major armed conflicts has bedeviled humanity for millennia.

The primal need of all peoples not to feel naked before their real or potential enemies is a powerful inhibitor to disarmament, even when levels of arms reach such proportions where they themselves pose a threat to the very security they were created to secure.

The questions raised and partially addressed in this paper have enormous import not only for the U.S. but for other nations, as well. With the world's population expanding with consequences for global security and standards of living, we must find a way of providing for our national defense at minimum cost. As experience has shown, wealth expended upon arms cannot simultaneously be applied to the amelioration of society's ills which, in the United States, are large and clamoring for attention.

The challenge for U.S. policymakers and their counterparts throughout the democratic world is how to strike a just and workable balance between defense and social needs. The ICAF faculty members who contributed to this paper trust that in some small way they have been able to shed light on this question, one of the most pressing of our time.

FIGURE 1

Three Options

Option	Benefits	Cost
Govt Owned & Operated (GO/GO)	Maximize Control & Stability	Lose Market Efficiency
Contractor Owned & Operated (CO/CO)	Maximize Efficiency	Less Control, Subsidies Necessary
Govt Owned/ Contractor Operated (GO/CO)	Reduce Risk For Private Sector More Efficient Than GO/GO	Less Control Than GO/GO, Less Efficient Than CO/CO

The analysis and opinions expressed or implied herein are those of the faculty members of the Industrial College of the Armed Forces who collaborated in this study and do not necessarily represent the views of the National Defense University or its constituent colleges, the Department of Defense, or any other U.S. Government agency. This material does not imply Department of Defense endorsement of factual accuracy or opinion.

PRIVATIZATION IN RUSSIA: RESULTS AND PROSPECTS

Andrei N. Loginov

Slowly but surely, privatisation is changing the economic culture in Russia. People are getting over their initial suspicion. Demand for legal and business advice has soared, and so has enrolment in business classes. The clock can't be turned back now, especially if the economy picks up in 1994/5. But the approach to the defence industry is more cautious. A big segment will be sold off this year, but the government is protecting key enterprises, and kept a majority share in others. An estimated US $150-300 billion is needed for Russian's defence conversion.

Andrei N. Loginov is a Senior Research Fellow at the Economic Department of Russia's Institute for Strategic Studies in Moscow.

Dynamics of Privatization

The process of privatization in Russia is unprecedented in scale and volume. It would not be an exaggeration to say that during the last 18 months property relations have endured a real revolution. The background to reforming property relations in Russia is the very deep and still continuing economic recession. Probably only Russia could sustain such difficulties and carry on with social, economic and political transformations.

94,300 enterprises had been privatized by April 1, 1994: out of 19,000 largest enterprises 15,000 have been transformed into joint-stock companies and 12,000 have been privatized. The total value of privatized properties accounted for 1200 billion rubles. Up to 40 million people (more than a half the Russian adult population) became shareholders of privatized enterprises. Over 50% of chemical and petrochemical, ferrous metal industry enterprises, 98,6% of light industry enterprises and 33% of non-ferrous metal industry, building material industry enterprises were privatized. About 900 enterprises were being privatized each month during 1993 and up to 2000 over the first quarter of 1994. More than 29 million workers (that is 41% of the labour force in the Russian economy) were employed at privatized enterprises, and the production of non-government enterprises increased to 47,8% of total industry output in 1993.

The last months of voucher privatization saw the involvement of middle and large enterprises in the process. The average value of a privatized enterprise rose from 21,5 million rubles in 1993 to 52 million rubles in the first quarter 1994, and the average number of employees in one enterprise increased from 260 workers to 310 during the same period. This trend was intensified during the first quarter of 1994 when the largest enterprises such as Gasprom and GAZ (Autoplant at Nizhny Novgorod).

Such high rates of privatization overwhelmed the Russian economy and the mentality of Russian people and became one of the reasons for some negative attitudes. So fast an attack on state property without adequate and deep transformations in the economy could very soon exhaust its potential. This threat had been realized by the Russian Government and now it is changing the priorities of its privatization policy, paying more attention to quality rather than to quantity.

Estimates of the Results

The results of privatization became the subject of political disputes rather more often than the theme of economic analysis. The general results of voucher privatization could be stated as follows:
- Private ownership in the Russian economy has been rehabilitated and passed the point of no return.
- Conditions for the next redistribution of property and forming of an effective and functional business capital were created;
- Support has been provided for the creation and development of market backgrounds (institutional reorganization, change in society's mentality).

Other goals set forth in the Government Privatization Programme (1993) could not be said to have been achieved. Even the 40 million who shareholders emerged in Russia could not be considered as a wide group which unconditionally supports private ownership. Privatization today means a simple juridical re-registration of the owner's rights on the enterprise assets and is not linked to the involvement of large private financial resources. There may be wide social disappointment with the results of privatization in the case of massive bankruptcies of joint-stock enterprises and investment funds, which accumulated now up to 50% of issued vouchers.

The hope of the Government to get substantial revenues from privatization to cover budget deficit and finance the most acute social problems also has failed so far. On the contrary, methods of the evaluation of the state property are widely criticized. Very often the opposition is promoting the idea that "Russia is being sold off to the foreigners", despite the fact that foreign investors are more prudent in the approach to the Russian market.

At the same time according to official estimates, foreign companies have purchased 10% of privatized state property, giving Russia US$1 billion. Proceeding from this figure one could estimate the whole value of the state property of Russia as only US$20 billion - which is obviously untrue. It is clear that the methods of evaluation of the state property need improvement.

The other thesis very popular among opponents is that "the privatization means 'pumping over' the state ownership to the former nomenklatura, criminal elements and newly appeared dubious entrepreneurs". It is impossible to believe seriously that the majority of 40 million Russian shareholders who got the largest part of privatized state property could be considered in this way.

However, this thesis may not be fully groundless. From January 1993 to February 1994 Goscomimutshestvo (The State Committee of Property Management) examined 278 cases of improper privatization. As a result six cases were delivered to the Procurator office, five to the Ministry of Security, four to the Ministry of Internal Affairs and four to the Department of Tax Inspection. Against a background of 90,000 privatized enterprises it is a drop in the ocean. Such a small share of abuse can be explained by the insufficient attention to its prevention or by the lack of proper penalty legislation. Even the governmental bodies that carry out the privatization themselves recognize the abuses in privatization.

Meanwhile, voucher privatization has not caused the restructuring of the Russian economy. One of the reasons is a lack of investments. According to the Privatization Program, vouchers could be used only in the cases of changing the titles of ownership. And enterprises could not use them at the market to purchase equipment , technology, services, etc.

The lack of information and a weak explanatory campaign have given a push to negative social reaction. The privatization authorities have begun the check-holder awareness campaign among the public too late. After the well-known scandal with the check investment fund "Techinvest" the people realized that the risk of voucher fraud is very high. The government has found an opportunity to help the shareholders of "Techinvest". Their stocks were changed to the stocks of other investments funds. But the results of the next fraud case with "NeftAlmazinvest" (which is not yet closed) would not be so safely resolved for thousands of stockholders. Only during the last months have the mass media opened a wide range explanatory and awareness campaign among the public.

It seems too early today to make final positive or negative estimation of the economic, social and political results of voucher privatization in Russia.

Privatization and Creation of a Market Economy

One could not overestimate the role of privatization in creating the backgrounds of a market economy. Some new market institutions appeared due to it and others got strong boosts for their development. Check investment funds (CIF) have appeared to support the voucher' circulation. Nowadays there are more than 200 CIFs in Russia. They have accumulated up to 50 million vouchers (33% of the emission) and invested them into privatized enterprises. They would be transformed into ordinary investment funds and companies after the end of voucher privatization.

High rates of privatization present a wide opportunity for the development of a new and important sector - an independent juridical and economic consultation sector. Enterprises often had no ability (a lack of experts or time) for preparing the whole documents for their privatization. And they needed the support of such specialized and experienced companies. The success of privatization would create brilliant conditions for prosperity of this sector of the Russian economy.

Vouchers greatly contributed to the formation of a stock exchange in Russia. Their liquidity was one of the highest among the securities. The largest part of the security exchange turnover falls on the deals with vouchers. The second stage of privatization (with sales of state-owned stocks and new share issuing of privatized enterprises) would lead to a security exchange boom. This would stimulate the creation and development of a security exchange infrastructure.

Privatization considerably influenced the mentality and economic behaviour of people. The lack of knowledge was compensated by special literature, seminars and courses. Management and accounting are the most popular themes. Economic self-education is widespread. The economic behaviour of people is changing. They have to find the answers to a lot of new questions. They realize that property means also responsibility.

New aspects of the problem of the effective functioning of enterprises were raised by privatization. Up to 80% of Russian stock-companies have been privatized according to the "second option", when workers received 51% of all stock capital. The prominent Russian economist Grigoriy Yavlinsky named these companies "industrial kolkhoz". The main threat for such companies is the spending of working capital on non-productive purposes. New shareholders have to prevent such a development and to find a mechanism of strict control over the managers and stimulating the productivity of labour of the employees. This problem could not be solved within a short period. But it could be handled by the support of foreign investors participating in privatization.

Post-voucher Privatization

The second stage of privatization in Russia will begin on July 1, 1994. The main goals and methods of it have been adopted by the Government and stated in the Concept of Post-Check Privatization. Most attention will be paid to the following problems:
- Stimulating of the effectiveness of new privatized enterprises on the base's of their reconstruction.
- The formation of a group of the strategic owners who will invest their capital in production.
- Involving new enterprises and state property in the privatization process.

- Accumulating financial resources to solve urgent social problems and to cut budget deficit especially by decreasing the outlays for supporting the former state enterprises.

The beginning of land privatization, the introducing of the bankruptcy mechanism, the organizational and consulting support of privatized enterprises, and the widening of the rights of regional funds of state property are important elements of post-voucher privatization. The most arguable point of the new program is the essential cutting back of the preferential treatment of employees and managers of privatized enterprises.

Sales of the shares which now belong to Goskomimutshestvo (20-30% of each enterprise or even more) would be an important source of investment for joint-stock enterprises. The distribution of income of further privatization would be as is shown in the table below:

The distribution of income from privatization of federal, oblast and municipal property (%)

Recipient of the income	Enterprises which					
	have sold more then 75% of its shares			have sold less then 75% of its shares		
	federal	oblast	municipal	federal	oblast	municipal
Local budget	-	-	90			80
Republic'Kray Oblast'budget	-	-	-	50~	50~	-
Federal budget	-	-	-	30	30	-
The Goskom-imutshestvo	10	10	10	10	10	10
Privatized enterprise	70	70	-	10	10	10

~ The income will be directed to the budget wich will finance the social infrastructure of the privatized enterprise.

The further issue of shares of privatized enterprises could become the other strong source of investments. The problem is to find those who will support this stock issue.

Accumulated capital of new Russian entrepreneurs abroad are officially estimated in US$20 billion. (The unofficial estimate equals US$30-35 billion and rises by one billion each year). New commercial structures in Russia (banks, trading houses, financial companies, etc.) also accumulated enough capital for investing in production. The leaders of Russian business have repeatedly announced that they are ready to finance industry if the investment climate (especially taxes) is changed.

Besides this, the reviving of the Russian economy would also attract new foreign investments. Even today, foreign investors possess 10% of stocks of privatized enterprises. According to some analysts, this share could be increased to 15-20% in 1994-1995.

The problem of investments is very closely linked to the problem of creation of strategic owners. By this term the Government means a proprietor who could achieve a more effective functioning of the enterprise. All methods of privatization (money auction, investment contest, special plans for super-large enterprises, etc.) are aimed at the realization of this goal. Preference would be given to the investors who would buy 50% or more of stocks of the privatized enterprise. This strategic aim would be achieved also by selling about 30% of shares of large enterprises to small shareholders. The dispersal of joint stock would give an opportunity of controlling the enterprise with holding less then 50% of shares.

There is one more peculiarity of the new privatization program - there are no limits to its period. One may suppose that privatization would be completed with greater expediency. The interests of the state as a property owner could be observed more carefully. First of all it touches on the methods of evaluation of the property which must be changed.

The future of the privatization process in Russia depends on various economic, social and political factors. This process could be greatly transformed but not reversed. The experience of the previous stage of privatization, the significant shift in society mentality, and the expectations of macroeconomic stabilization in 1994-1995 present an opportunity for the optimistic scenario.

Privatization of Defence Industry

Today the Russian defence industry consists of 2000 enterprises with 4.5 million employees including 800 thousand in research and development. The defence complex includes more than 70 single-company towns. The majority of the defence industry's enterprises which possess the most modern and valuable equipment were privatized during the first half of 1994. Only 0.3% of 2000 defence industry enterprises were privatized in 1992. Last year the share of private enterprises in the defence industry increased to 10%. During the first 4 months of 1994 about 500 defence industry enterprises were privatized and 640 were transformed into joint-stock companies. The whole privatization of the defence industry should be completed by the end of 1994.

According to the Government Privatization Program, all the enterprises of Russian defence industry are divided into three groups. The first one includes 437 state enterprises which will be wholly financed from the budget and strictly controlled by the Government. They are playing and will continue to play the key role in arms and military equipment production.

The second group consists of joint (private-state) enterprises. Private owners could buy shares and finance their development, but 51% of capital stock will belong to the State. These enterprises should be obliged to follow their previous production profile. And this will be the only limit on their activity introduced by the Government.

All other enterprises of Russian defence industry would be privatized in a year. The Government could influence their activity only by state contracts and arms purchasing.

Privatization of Russia's defence industry should go along with its conversion. This makes the problem of investments rather urgent. According to various estimations modernization and conversion of all the defence industry will cost US$150-300 billion.

Some experts consider that only Russian business (banks, investment companies, financial-industrial groups) could solve this problem. Thirty to forty financial-industrial groups are to be created. They will include financial, industrial, trade, insurance companies. The production and export of the most competitive military equipment will be the main aim of their activity. Such firms as "Antey", "Almaz", chemical plant at Biysk are named among the most perspective centers for such financial-industrial groups. There was an idea of creating a Military Industry Export-Import Bank and a Military Insurance Company to provide the independence of the privatized enterprises in defence industry from the State.

Other experts consider that the problem of financing conversion and maintaining the level of high technology production in the defence industry could be solved mainly by more close cooperation with foreign partners. A rise in arms exports to US$3-5 billion a year could also be regarded as a source of investment.

It seems that the best solution could be obtained if all these sources are used simultaneously.

The privatization of the defence industry in Russia is closely connected with the issues of national security and especially with aspects like military and economic security.

Privatization leads usually to changes in the production profile of the enterprise meeting the demand of the armed forces. But this demand should be provided by the state-owned and state-controlled enterprises of defence industry.

The high rate of specialists leaving the defence industry could lead to the closing of a number of high technology productions. But this outcome appears more as a result of macroeconomic situation but not of privatization itself.

Possible threats to national security are connected with the social aspects of privatization of defence industry. The rise in "latent" unemployment in military towns-plants could cause serious social disturbances. A sharp reduction of employees without alternate training and any social guarantees could create a group of militants dissatisfied with reforms.

In general the problem of the interrelation and correlation of privatization and national security needs greater attention and a more complex approach. The new privatization program could be added to by a special block of measures concerning defence industry, where all urgent issues would be taken into account.

Andrei N. Loginov

References

1. Privatization in 1993. Reforma. The Bulletin of Russia's Fund of Federal Property. N 23, May, Moscow, 1994.
2. Assecritov S., Yuriev Day of Privatization. Business World, 28 May, Moscow, 1994.
3. Alternative Views on Privatization Policy. The Discussion. Voprosy Economiky. NN 10,11,12, Moscow, 1993.
4. Khromov Yu., Foreign Investment and Privatization in Russia. Report. Russian Institute for Strategic Studies. Moscow. 1994.
5. Kotov A., The Freedom without Limits? Economica i zhizn. N 51, December, Moscow, 1993.
6. Larionov I., The Results and Prospects of Privatization. Birgevye Vedomosty. N 14, April, Moscow, 1994.
7. New Priorities of Auctioneering: the Concept of Post-check Privatization. The Goskomimutshestvo of Russian Federation. Rossiyskay Gazeta, 21 April, Moscow, 1994.
8. The Privatization of Defence Industry. Chelovek i karyera. N 5, Moscow, 1994.
9. The Results of Privatization. Kommersant. NN 13, 14, April, Moscow, 1994.
10. Russian Federation: economic and social situation. Vestnik economiky. April, Moscow, 1994.

OWNERSHIP CHANGES IN THE POLISH ARMS INDUSTRY: SECURITY ISSUES

Katarzyna Zukrowska and Léon Turczynski

Because many of Poland's arms producers were also producing civilian goods, they had a relatively easy switch to consumer market production. But the bigger companies had bigger problems. Economically, they face the same difficulties as their civilian counterparts, with demand shrinking at home and abroad. Politically, they need to cope with the changes in the international scene, and their implications for national security. Katarzyna Zukrowska and Leon Turczynski are clear as to what their country's long-term aims are: full membership of NATO, and closer co-operation in arms manufacture so that the east and west European defence systems can be fully compatible. The key to it all, they say, is patience and planning.

Katarzyna Zukrowska is a Senior Researcher at the Institute for Development and Strategic Studies, Central Office of Planning, in Warsaw.

Col. Leon Turczynski is a Senior Researcher at the Central Office of Planning in Warsaw.

Ownership changes in the arms industry cannot be studied apart from the ownership changes in the whole economy. They are also closely interlinked with structural changes of the industry, which are introduced in the framework of macrostabilization, liberalization of prices and international turnover, institutional changes and macroeconomic restructuring.

National security is one of the aspects that has to be taken into consideration in defining the strategy of structural changes (both in macro and micro scale) in the arms industry.

The period of transformation in Eastern European countries brings about new threats for internal and external stabilization of a country, that derive directly from the scale of changes introduced in the region. They cover such issues as controversies in the socio-economic sphere, political sphere and the national sphere. Despite the fact that such problems do not occur equally in all the countries of the region, their repercussions can be felt also outside the borders.

International economic cooperation is one of the main tools fostering a dynamic development in economic relations between countries. The effectiveness of this instrument depends on the number of disciplines it embraces. Military production cannot be left out of this cooperation. Arguments supporting this concept cover such issues as the idea of creating a European Security System, demands of standardization of military equipment in national armies and the creation of compatible defence systems. Catching up with the army structures and equipment of NATO partnership countries also matters and can gain momentum in international cooperation of the arms industries.

The internationalization of defence industry should be accompanied by the construction of a pan-European international security infrastructure. This concept will have a doublefold influence on the improvement of international security in Europe. Generally such a development would have a direct and indirect impact on security issues.

On the one hand it will create new opportunities of employment for the manpower released from the military production and increase effectiveness of utilization of financial resources. While on the other hand direct linkages between the industries will bring closer together cooperating producers, which in turn would help to eliminate all the existing prejudices among them.

Structural Changes in Poland's Arms Industry

Structural changes in the arms industry began in the second half of the 1980s as a result of improvements in international relations and the diminishing intensity of the East-West confrontation, that was followed by a qualitatively new stage in disarmament negotiations.

Since that time, things have happened at an accelerated speed and what took place five or more years ago seems to be ancient history. It is impossible to show in detail how all the events occurred and in what sequence.

We concentrate therefore on the latest series of events with small comments that throw some light on what has happened in the past.

Arms production in the late 1980s could be characterized by reduced military spending (Table 1), limited scope of arms production and shrinking export markets.[1] The role of government intervention in this sector has totally vanished. All that was followed by an increase in unutilized capacities of the producers, significant lay-offs, and a reduction of the number of enterprises engaged in arms production. Industrial potential were utilized by 10-30%. The number of enterprises engaged involved was reduced from 120 final producers to 90. It is planned that at the end of the restructuring process the Polish arms industry will consist of 28 enterprises, organized in a set of four branch holdings.

Poland's arms industry experienced a market-driven strategy of structural changes with all its consequences. Government policy towards arms producers in the period of 1989-1994 could be labelled as contradictory. On the one hand, producers were told that their production is needed and they have to survive; on the other hand they had difficulties in adjusting to new unfriendly conditions (shrinking orders, limited credits and independence in decision-making) as well as to unknown market conditions.

Although there is no one universal pattern of transition from one system to another, some results and findings deriving from the Polish experience could be interesting for other countries from East Central Europe (ECE), which are following the same path.[2] The importance of the Polish experience is growing when one has to take into account the fact that ECE countries very often are facing the complexity of decisions of choice that have to be taken on both levels: by the government and the enterprise. More often those choices are influenced or even forced by newly born interest groups.

In the transition period contradictions and paradoxes could be found everywhere in each single field of the economy.

As far as the arms producers are concerned - most of the contradictions concern difficulties in reconciliation of short and long term goals. The second group embraces choices between social goals and security goals. Although choices are never made between sharply divided alternatives, most of the time it is necessary to meet partially two ends at the same time.

A paternalistic approach of the government towards the arms industry in the short term could ease the burden of transition - but at the same time it could prolong the transition period.

Protection could facilitate the financial standing of companies and their workers in the short run, but in a longer perspective this would mean bigger problems for the future. In practice this would only be a postponement of reaching aims with growing competition and burdens. Moreover, protection is not conducive towards restructuring what undoubtedly becomes a necessity in all ECE economies. Lack of protection does not mean lack of control but it needs to be done with new instruments and specific institutions which are being developed.[3]

Arms production is the most politicized field of the economy. This meant that political decisions about the future of Polish arms producers were postponed several times. The government made decisions to give help to the arms producers but the budget constraints did not allow the plans to be carried out. Enterprises left in a state of suspension had to find their own way in the new conditions.

Finally in May 1993, after several sittings, the Economic Committee of Council of Minister's (KSERM) decided that all the arms producers have to change their ownership status, according to a following schedule:

- One-holder stock companies owned by the State Treasury. This group will consist of ten enterprises being the most important in Polish arms industry. The following companies will fall into this category: Zaklady Metalowe MESKO in Skarzysko Kamienna, and Przemyslowe Centrum Optyki in Warsaw.
- Joint-stock companies with majority of shares controlled by the State Treasury. This group will consist of 18 enterprises including 6 main Polish aircraft producers. Such enterprises will fall into this category: WSK PZL Mielec, Bumarkabedy, PZL Warszawa Okecie and WSK Swidnik.

- Private enterprises and limited liability companies. The rest of the companies, representing five different branches can proceed with their own restructuring without any interference from the government. The outcome of their production will be created by market demands. This category will encompass such enterprises as those specializing in: transport, communication, anti-chemical defence, logistics and engineering works.

Table 1
Polish Military Expenditure, 1986-1994
Figures in billion zlotys, and constant prices

Year	Military expenditure	Dynamics, in percentages	
		Change compared to the previous year	Change compared to 1986
1986	110,1	NA	NA
1987	106,9	2,9	2,9
1988	99,6	6,8	9,5
1989	89,7	10,0	18,6
1990	80,7	10,0	26,7
1991	52,5	35,0	52,4
1992	50,4	4,0	54,5
1993	48,8	3,2	55,7
1994	47,9	1,8	56,5

Source: M. Perczyski, P. Wieczorek, K. Zukrowska, The Current Situation in Polish Arms Industry, manuscript Warsaw 1994.

Table 2
Value of Polish arms exports, 1984-1993
(in million rubles and million dollars)

Exports	1985	1988	1989	1990	1991	1992	1993
rubles	100,5	113,6	992,5	768,2	-	-	50-
US$	118,4	258,2	188,3	64,9	386,2	60,0	60

Source: as in Table (1), based on estimates from CENZIN.

In parallel with the reduction of the number of enterprises engaged in arms production, changes will also include a new organization of the sector. The change in the structure of the arms industry will be conducted in two stages. In the first stage all the enterprises will be transferred into one-holder stock companies owned by the Treasury. In the second one, newly-born companies will be organized into four following holdings:

- Conventional weapons producers, which would embrace producers of ammunition, missiles and explosives. They will include 14 enterprises, employing about 32,000 people in all.
- Aircraft producers, embracing 5 enterprises "PZL", employing about 24,000 people.
- Producers of radar equipment, opto-electronics and electronics, which will consist of 5 enterprises, employing about 10,000 people.
- Armoured vehicles producers, consisting of 5 enterprises, employing 22,000 people.

Primary changes in the Polish arms industry were possible mainly thanks to the low involvement of the producers in arms deliveries. In other words the reduction of number of arms producers was conducted mainly by switching into civilian deliveries. This was possible only in the companies with high share of diversified production, where military production was only a small fraction.

Conversion or further changes in the arms industry are limited mainly by lack of available financial resources that could be utilized for such purposes. Those limits are the result of poor financial standing and often a lack of financial liquidity; limited options for self-financing (shrinking domestic and foreign markets); difficulties in obtaining credits for restructuring;central budget limitations; and limited demand on the civilian market in the first period of transition.

In an open market economy survival of the producers is no longer solely defined by domestic orders. This rule does not concern only civilian production, where it was proven in full.

The Ministry of Defence (MoD) and other central institutions are marking out only the required shape of the production but the survival of each of the enterprises heavily depends on external relations, both in production and exports. Such are the tough rules of the open market economy. This finding is clear in civilian production and it happens also in the military sphere, whether we like it or not.

In the new conditions the role of the government in Poland was limited to such fields as initiating changes, preparing legal infrastructure, working out political climate for launching the worked out strategy and intervention only where it amounted to fire-fighting.

The government was no longer able to support the enterprises financially. This role was taken over by the developing banking system. Money was given to enterprises only in drastic situations and such a solution became a rule while the political and economic system was transformed.

Security Questions in the Transition Period

Historic changes that have taken place in the late 1980s in European and international politics have decisively influenced (improved) the state of security in Poland. The security concerns have shifted from external to internal dangers, although one cannot say that external threats were fully eliminated.[5]

Despite the fact that the transformation period has eliminated some old threats, at the same time it created some new ones. Those threats are rather complex and are differently rooted. It is rather difficult to predict all of them and estimate their consequences. Moreover, ways of reducing the newly-born tensions are not only limited but also time-consuming.

A successful attempt to present this issue can be found in one of the latest SIPRI publications on ECE countries, entitled Central and Eastern Europe The Challenge of Transition, edited by Regina Cowen Karp.[6] It is said there that:

"The picture that emerges does not suggest an easy or short path to building security in Europe. The continent is in the midst of historical changes. Relationships between countries are unsettled as are domestic relations between rivalling political groups. There is continuing danger of states breaking apart and ethnic tensions escalating into open conflict.

Collective security offers the only means of encompassing the whole of Europe and integrating its still disparate parts. Collective incrementalism as currently practised is unlikely to lead to collective security proper. It raises expectations for a security order that states are not yet willing to adopt. Without a clear recognition that peace in Europe is in the national interest of each and every state, sceptics concerning the notion of a collective security order will be proven right and the concept will remain a desirable but unachievable objective."

Into trying to throw some light on new security threats in ECE countries, it would be wise to distinguish external and internal dangers and political, economic, national and social tensions.

There is no need to characterize more closely the external threats of ECE countries as they are obvious and well known to all economists and political scientists. The most complex example comes from the separate republics of former Yugoslavia. Still more examples on this specific issue are produced by the events taking place in the republics of the former USSR. No-one knows how internal tensions in Ukraine, Azerbaijan, Georgia, or Kazakhstan will finally develop. It is clear that if they do lead towards some kind of explosion of civil war, the results of it could overpass all the startling events that happened in former Yugoslavia.

The external security of a country is not only defined by political factors; the economy also matters. Several economic determinants have influenced the transformation process of each ECE country.

• The rise in prices of raw materials, including especially oil prices.

- The disintegration of the old economic ties.
- The collapse of trade with former COMECON countries.
- The increased competition on internal and world market.
- The economic slow-down in all partnership countries (old and new customers).

As was mentioned at the beginning of this chapter the accent on the security issues has been moved from external factors towards internal ones. In such circumstances there is no need to comment closer on the external security determinants as their meaning is minor and temporary. Their impact is strongest at the beginning of the transformation process and with time passing and advancement of the reforms the weight of enumerated factors fades. The growing significance of internal factors merits closer examination.

Factors that can undermine internal security embrace such issues:

- Unemployment.
- National tensions in multinational countries and in countries with national minorities.
- Economic and social costs of the transition.
- Political tensions.
- Costs of emigration and immigration.
- Hyperinflation.

The list of external and internal factors that determine security of each ECE country shows that both market economies and economies in transition are facing similar problems but the scale of the problems is different.

Although we can speak with the same language about our economic problems the difference lies in the fact that some of the phenomena did not appear in those economies in the post-war period, and ECE countries in many cases do not have the tools to master them effectively - or when they do have them they are too weak to act in a desired direction.

The transformation period generated a conflict between macro-and microeconomic policies, with the microeconomic policy reducing the macroeconomic effectiveness.

All this increases frustration and produces political duels. Often the lack of proper information in the mass media increases the possibilities of manipulating the society.

These problems are being overcome with the advancement of the reform, when problems are removed and attempts made to fulfil the existing gaps. Nevertheless, it is necessary to notice that such problems do exist in early stages of transformation and it is necessary to overcome them. Very often overcoming them requires direct support from the outside (international institution or foreign experts), but as the Polish experience shows this can not be done without the agreement of the government.

Security and the economy are closely intertwined. Linkage between them gains importance in the transition period and depends heavily on the strategy applied by a country.

The Role of the North Atlantic Cooperation Council (NACC) and the Partnership for Peace (PFP)

Most of the ECE countries try to get under the security umbrella created by NATO membership, fulfilling thus the security vacuum that emerged after the end of the Cold War and the decision to dismantle the Warsaw Pact. It is clear that before obtaining full membership they have to adjust their defence systems towards the requirements of NATO. This will embrace all the quantitative changes within the CFE Treaty, alongside qualitative changes that will lead towards closer compatibility of defence systems.

The argument of ECE countries supporting the idea of NATO membership is well known and there is no need to repeat it here. On the other hand Western countries say that NATO is in the process of restructuring, that both sides are still not ready for the enlargement, that security architecture in Europe is in a flux, etc... In other words it is clear that the would-be members have to proceed through a transition period almost like a quarantine during which they will restructure their defence systems, bringing them closer to the NATO requirements.

Such adjustments need time. They are not only limited to technical replacement of one system by others but, more importantly, require deep mental changes on both sides.

Both NATO and Cooperating Partners are in the process of accepting that they are not enemies any more. They have to weed out the old habits of being too suspicious. This does not eliminate national interests, although in some specific cases international interests can override national ones. Moreover, it is necessary to understand that European security in the future relies deeply on political and economic cooperation from which defence industry cannot be excluded.

NATO has prepared an expanding program which could be compared to a corridor leading towards full membership for ECE countries. This program embraces the NACC and the PFP. These initiatives are the result of evolution in perception of the processes of systemic changes in ECE commenced after 1989. NATO has followed carefully all the events taking place in the ECE countries, as is reflected by declarations in official documents beginning with the Brussels Declaration dated 30 May 1989. All official documents and declarations from NATO that appeared since that date show the responsibility of NATO for the course of events in Eastern Europe.

The best proof for that can be found in the following quotation from the "Rome Declaration on Peace and Cooperation":

"We have consistently encouraged the development of democracy in the Soviet Union and other countries of Central and Eastern Europe". and further in the same point "...We will support all steps in the countries of Central and Eastern Europe towards reform and will give practical assistance to help them succeed in this difficult transition. This is based on our conviction that our own security is inseparably linked to that of all other states in Europe."

The same declaration has introduced a closer institutional relationship in consultations and cooperation on political and security issues, proposing the following activities:

- Annual meetings with the North Atlantic Council at Ministerial level, called the North Atlantic Cooperation Council.
- Periodic meetings with North Atlantic Council at Ambassadorial level.
- Additional meetings with the North Atlantic Council at Ministerial and Ambassadorial level as circumstances warrant.
- Regular meetings, at intervals to be mutually agreed, with NATO subordinate committees, including the Political and Economic Committees, the Military Committee and under its direction, other NATO Military Authorities".[8]

In a short time, these proposals were put into life in the North Atlantic Cooperation Council Statement on Dialogue, Partnership and Cooperation, signed in Brussels on 20 December 1991.

With time passing, simple institutions were supported with new initiatives of more sophisticated character, giving new momentum to the cooperation and mutual alliances.

On 10 January 1994, Heads of State and Government participating in the Meeting of the North Atlantic Council held at NATO Headquarters, issued an "Invitation to Partnership for Peace", in which we read that "...the Alliance, as provided for in Article 10 of the Washington Treaty, remains open to the membership of other European states in a position to further the principles of the Treaty and to contribute to the security of the North Atlantic area." and further "...we therefore invite the other states participating in the NACC and other CSCE countries able and willing to contribute to this program, to join with us in this partnership."[9]

The new initiative did not meet fully the desires of the ECE countries, but finally they accepted it as it brought them closer towards NATO than all the former offered steps.

Within the framework of the PFP, subscribing countries will cooperate with NATO in pursuing the following objectives: facilitation of transparency, ensuring democratic control of defence forces; readiness to participate in operations under the UN or CSCE authority; and the development of cooperative military relations. Participation in this program is financed by the partner country, but in specific areas support can be available from NATO.

What good is the PFP? The most interesting thing in the program is that it gives each country the opportunity to work out its own path leading towards NATO membership, which can be done at a speed set by the country itself.

The bad side of the PFP concerns its costs. The shorter the route, the higher the expenses of covering the distance towards full membership. Within the framework of the PFP each country has to prepare its presentation document in which it will state how it wants to fulfil the objectives defined in the document and in what time this has to be done. Such a document is a preliminary step in getting acceptance for the program from NATO.

Table 2
Chronology of signing the PFP program by cooperating countries

Date	Country	Who has signed
26 January	Romania	Minister of Foreign Affairs: Teodor Viarel Melescanu
27 January	Lithuania	President: Algidras Brazauskas
2 February	Poland	Prime Minister: Waldemar Pawlak
3 February	Estonia	Minister of Foreign Affairs: Juri Luik
8 February	Hungary	Minister of Foreign Affairs: Geza Jeszenszky
8 February	Ukraine	Minister of Foreign Affairs: Anatoly Zlenko
9 February	Slovakia	Prime Minister: Vladimir Meciar
14 February	Bulgaria	President: Jelu Jelev
14 February	Latvia	Prime Minister: Vladis Birkavs
23 February	Albania	President: Sali Berisha
10 March	Czech Republic	Prime Minister: Vaclav Klaus
16 March	Moldovia	President: Mircea Snegur
23 March	Georgia	Prime Minister: Alexander Chikvaidze
30 March	Slovenia	Prime Minister: Janoz Drnovsek
4 May	Azerbaijan	President: Geidar Aliyev
10 May	Turkmenistan	Deputy Prime Minister:
		Boris Shikmuradov
27 May	Kazakhstan	Foreign Minister: Kanat Saudabaev
1 June	Kyrgyzstan	President: Askar Akayev
22 June	Russia	Foreign Minister: Andrei Kozyrev

Source: NATO Review, June 1994, and NATO Press Service. (The table does not contain Sweden and Finland which also have joined the PFP).

History is happening just now and we are creating it. It is very difficult to comment on latest events without having a distance towards them but for sure NACC and PFP means more confidence not only among former enemies but also among former allies. One of the goals is being reached.

What Can be Done - a Model of Recommended Solutions

The beginning of the 1980s has marked a new turning point among the European nations. What are the new factors that describe contemporary relations between Western and Eastern countries?
• New relations could be described as cooperative instead of antagonistic deterrence from the past.
• The new period is characterized by breaking divisions and building bridges.
• The newly-built ties are increasing international interdependence among two groups of countries which in turn has its impact on redefining of national interests.
All those processes are complicated and time-consuming. Moreover they cannot be carried out without a wide variety of costs embracing not only finances but also social and psychological burdens which are beyond simple estimation.

As was said, national security in ECE countries heavily depends on the development of events inside each of the countries, while increasing interdependence changes the role of the international environment in the security question.

What can be done and which path should we follow in order to increase security in Europe? There is no doubt that the direction pointed out in NACC and PFP is a correct one and leads us in a desired direction. All the partnership countries can choose between different speeds and paths, which they define on their own. This idea gets to the point, but it is necessary to accept the fact that newly born democracies are impatient. This impatience is caused by the eagerness to cover the development and civilization gap. It is also deeply rooted in the past when all plans had to be fulfilled on time, no matter what were the costs of such an undertaking.

We have to follow the idea of defining long-term goals.
- NATO membership.
- Closer cooperation in arms production that will lead towards an international military complex.
- Building an international net for security infrastructure.
- Fulfilling the ideas presented in NACC and PFP.
- Bringing defence systems closer to each other by increasing their compatibility.
How can this be done? This question has to be answered by the specialists: politicians, military and scientists from different disciplines. Our aim is to

formulate ideas and create a climate in which those ideas can mature and be brought to life. Such ideas as the NACC and the PFP are creating conditions in which the desired goals can be fulfilled, but we cannot stop at this stage. We have to go further, widening our horizons.

Notes

1. A. Falkowski, National Economic Development and Defence Budget of the Republic of Poland, paper prepared for Economic Committee Meeting with Cooperation Partners, Budapest, April 1994.
2. D. Hübner, Transformation and Growth 1990-1993, IRiSS Working Papers 1994.
3. A. Falkowski, Control of the execution of the Defence Budget, paper prepared for the Economic Committee Meeting with Cooperation Partners, Budapest, April 1994.
4. For details look: W. Karpinska-Mizielinska, T. Smuga, Zmiany stosunków wlasnosciowych w procesie tworzenia strategii gospodarczej, IRiSS, Raporty, Studia nad strategia 1994.
5. J. Walker, Security and Arms Control in Post-Confrontation Europe, SIPRI, Oxford University Press 1994, p. 14.
6. Central and Eastern Europe The Challenge of Transition, ed. R. Cowen Karp, SIPRI, Oxford University Press 1993.
7. For more details look: NATO -1990-1992. Otwarcie Sojuszu na Wschód. Dokumenty przygotowane w ramach Zespolu analiz strategicznych,PISM, lipiec 1992.
8. Rome Declaration on Peace and Cooperation, Issued by the Heads of State and Government participating in the meeting of the North Atlantic Council in Rome on 7-8 November 1991. Signed at Rome on 8 November 1991. Quoted after: J. Walker, Security and Arms Control in post-confrontation Europe. SIPRI, Oxford University Press 1994.
9. NATO Partnership for Peace. Brussels, 10 January 1994. Press Service.

DEFENCE INDUSTRY PRIVATIZATION AND NATIONAL SECURITY REQUIREMENTS: THE UKRAINIAN CASE

Nikolai Kulinich

Defence conversion in the Ukraine started when the country was part of the USSR, and one third of the Soviet military complex was on Ukrainian soil.
Nikolai Kulinich says this has left the country with too many weapons it doesn't need, and a defence industry still dependent on the former Soviet Union. Despite these problems, conversion has made good progress and more consumer goods are being made. But old habits die hard. No defence companies were included in the first wave of privatisation, and none will be sold off in the second wave. The Ukraine wants the international community to contribute to the financing of its conversion programme.

Nikolai Kulinich is the head of the Department of International Organizations and Diplomatic Service at the Institute of International Relations, Kiev University.

The conversion of defence industry is one of the most complicated problems directly connected with the Ukrainian National Security Issue. The dimensions of defence conversion must be dictated by the military security requirements of Ukraine, the peculiarities of the defence industry, weapons production technologies, and equipment for the National army.

Sovereignty and independence, and the territorial integrity and invulnerability of its borders have to be maintained. Ukraine considers that the threat of war has not yet disappeared. Possible reasons of conflict can be of political, territorial, national-ethnic, religious origin based on real existing disputes which not always are settled by states in friendly way. We're all witnesses to that.

That's why Ukraine considers it necessary to have both its armed forces to ensure its national security and national defence industry which will meet its requirements in weapons and equipment at a sufficient level.

The problem is to evaluate the "sufficient level" of national defence industry. This is the crucial issue facing Ukrainian national security and economy. The conversion of military industry of Ukraine was started in 1988 within the framework of the former USSR. The last five-year state program of conversion was meant to reduce military output, increase the production of civilian goods, and improve the quality of manufactured goods able to compete on the world market. Thus the program of conversion was planned to ensure a more or less gradual transition to output of civilian goods using a wide network of co-operative deliveries from all 15 republics of the former USSR.

By the time of the collapse of the USSR 30% of all the USSR military-industrial complex (MIC) enterprises were located on Ukrainian soil. That means 15-20 enterprises from each of nine All-Union ministries dealing with the USSR defence industry. These enterprises together with enterprises of seven former All-Union machine building ministries form the basis of the Ministry of Machine Building, Military-Industrial Complex and Conversion of independent Ukraine (MINMASHPROM). This Ministry was created in 1992 [1].

By January 1, 1993 MINMASHPROM Ukraine managed approximately 3590 enterprises which comprised 2056 industrial enterprises, 479 scientific centres, and 246 project design centres [2].

Purely military industry was represented by 700 enterprises with a total number of approximately 1450000 employees. By the time of the Soviet Union's collapse, the proportion of Ukrainian involvement in armament construction and supply was :

- In complete (finished) armament supply - 15% (compared with Russia - 79%).
- In complete (finished) armament construction and development - 7% (Russia 91%).
- In armament sales (abroad) - 14% (Russia - 71%).

At that time, 50% of the Soviet military fleet warships, ICBMs, tanks, radio-electronic equipment were built on Ukrainian territory [3].

Some negative features of the Ukrainian Military-Industrial Complex (MIC) still exist.

- Excessive resources devoted to armament construction areas such as rocket launchers, warships, and battle-tanks.
- The lack of full-circle military industry in manufacturing the majority types of armament.
- The great dependence on external armament procurements and order (basically from Russia).
- The high level of dependence for spare parts supply and co-operation with MIC on the CIS. Eighty per cent of components for military manufacturing are supplied from the CIS. For example, in order to complete the construction of the cruiser, "Ulianovsk", at Ukrainian naval shipyards, spare parts and components from 2500 CIS military enterprises were needed.

Obviously, the type of military-industrial complex we have does not fit the concept of Ukrainian national security, or the concept of an efficient market economy.

In 1992 on the initiative of the MINMASHPROM and other departments, enterprises and organizations, the State Conversion Program was developed; it consists of more than 540 conversion sub-programs.

Taking into consideration the experience of other countries and national interests, these sub-programs have been radically revised. They were regrouped into 22 complex programs. More clear priorities were provided and the basis for economic encouragement (preferable credits taxation etc.) was formed.

The acute (3 times) reduction in the output of military equipment and weapons by 1993, has been matched by a significant growth in the output of civilian goods. The rate of the growth was 115% [4].

Conversion is aimed at producing civilian goods which are of high demand in the national economy. State regulation of the conversion process allows us to avoid chaos in restructuring military industry and ensure more efficient distribution of scarce financial and raw material resources.

Sometimes, partial conversion of plants and factories using former organizations and structures requires additional investments for mastering civilian goods production. Here it is very difficult to estimate actual expenditure and enterprises do not have the incentives for modification and improvement in the quality of their products, etc. Converted plants have to orient themselves towards many buyers instead of one - the state. In this case they bear the overall expenses in the process of products replacement. They lack flexibility in use of equipment,and they cannot properly define output volumes in good time. This significantly slows down development of the conversion process.

There are two ways of increasing the effectiveness of MIC. One is through the privatization of military industrial enterprises; the second is by increasing investment into state-managed military industrial enterprises.

Let's review the first possibility in the context of the current realities of Ukrainian economy. Three months ago the "first wave" of privatization of state-managed enterprises began in Ukraine. One hundred and fifty enterprises of the medium and small scale were designed to be privatized. There is not one enterprise from the MIC in this list. It is evident that there are no essential plans of privatization of MIC enterprises for the forthcoming future in the MINMASHPROM.

The second way is the most acceptable for the Ukrainian government. Volumes of investments in conversion and foreign investment in particular are not sufficient. To carry out conversion together with the simultaneous formation of a free-market economy without foreign assistance may take an unacceptably long time.

The Ukrainian government has some ideas as to how to accelerate the conversion with foreign support and assistance.

- The implementation of UN Institute on Problems of Disarmament (Institute Report No. 47 to the UN General Assembly) on the organization of international assistance through technical consultations, equipment etc. for the purpose of transition of post-communist countries to a market economy;
- The formation of International Conversion Assistance Center;

- The formation of the UN "Register of significant military enterprises subjected to conversion" for assisting them financially from international sources.

The Ukrainian government is sure that the International Community, the West, in particular, will benefit from allocating now necessary funds. Such an allocation will also promote regional and international security.

[1] V. Antonov. "Oboronka" Ukrainy vibraet svoy put. "Krasnaya zveda" 26.02.1993
[2] V. Antonov. konversia vojennogo proizvodstva. "Uriadovy kurier" No. 25-26 18.02.1993
[3] V. Antonov. ukrainiski put konversil. "Uriadovy kurie" No. 9, 10 21.01.1993
[4] V. Durdinets. Vice-Speaker, Verkhovna Rada of Ukraine. Modern Ukraine and security in Europe. Speech at International Seminar. June 1993.

DEFENCE INDUSTRY PRIVATIZATION: THE BRITISH CASE

Michael Bell

Defence companies in the UK were treated differently from other nationalised industries in the UK's privatization programme. They were sold or floated on the stock market, some as a whole, and some broken up. The government retains a 'Golden Share' in three key companies to protect the national interest but the bottom line is that the market rules, and this has been reinforced by the Ministry of Defence's adoption of procurement policies based on competition. This process has not been painless in an era of falling defence budgets; jobs have gone and sites have closed. But the companies have become leaner and more customer-focused. Export orders were a record last year - at no cost to the taxpayer.

Michael Bell is Britain's Deputy Under-Secretary of State for Defence Procurement, Ministry of Defence

The present privatisation initiatives are commonly regarded as being the result of policies introduced by the Conservative Party which came to power in 1979. Their intentions for privatisation went much wider than defence, though naturally this presentation deals only with defence. If we look at their manifesto we see that it "strongly opposes" the Labour Party's nationalisation plans and that it will "offer to sell back into private ownership the recently nationalised aerospace and shipbuilding concerns, giving their employees the opportunity to purchase shares".

It said that in order to become more prosperous, Britain must become more productive and the British people must be given more incentive. State spending was to be reduced and instead of relying on state intervention, industries were to become more responsive to market forces. The three key factors in the strategy, which was designed to revolutionise UK industry, were relaxation of state controls and increased privatisation and competition.

However, there was no distinct policy for privatisation with clear set objectives. At that time, privatisation perhaps more accurately described an approach to industrial policy rather than a policy in its own right. The implications of this approach meant that British industry faced a period of tremendous cultural change. It had to change a lot of things at the same time, and quickly, in order to become more competitive and survive. Today's management gurus describe this as "discontinuous change". Defence equipment producers and suppliers were to be treated in the same way as those in other industrial sectors - they were not singled out as a special case. In the eyes of the government, there was no overpowering reason why defence equipment and services had to be provided by nationalised organisations.

However, the story goes back even further than that. In 1968, the Mallabar Committee was asked to investigate efficiency in government industrial establishments, with a view to determining whether the existing organisation and systems of control and accountability presented impediments to achieving full efficiency and how these impediments should be removed. In its report in 1971, the committee recommended that the Royal Ordnance Factories and The Royal Dockyards should be given a financial structure more like that of a commercial undertaking and should be placed on a Trading Fund basis of accounting. Consequently, the ROF's were placed on a Trading Fund basis on 1 July 1974, but a decision on the future of the Dockyards was delayed.

Fifteen years on, it is possible to say that the major objectives of privatisation have evolved as:
- Reducing government involvement in the decision-making of industry.
- Permitting industry to raise funds from the capital market on commercial terms and without government guarantee.
- Raising revenue and reducing the public sector borrowing requirement (the PSBR).
- Promoting wide share ownership.
- Creating an "enterprise culture".
- Encouraging workers' share ownership in their companies.
- Increasing competition and efficiency.
- Replacing ownership and financial controls with a more effective system of economic regulation designed to ensure that benefits of greater efficiency are passed on to consumers.

So how was this privatisation achieved? The main ways are by being sold to the highest bidder, floated on the stock market or by being split up into smaller units which are then floated or sold off. Other avenues which have been used include management buy-outs and employment of management contractors. These methods, used in defence privatisation, have also been applied to the privatisation of UK national utilities. In each case advice was sought from financial experts on the best method to use.

In 1981, British Aerospace (BAe) became incorporated as a public limited company and at that time half of the shares were sold to the general public. In 1985 the Government sold its remaining ordinary shares in BAe.

We have a similar story for Rolls Royce, which became a public limited company in '85, and was floated on the stock market in May 1987.

The favoured route to privatising Royal Ordnance was initially that it also should be floated on the Stock Market. However, this was impractical within the timescale involved and instead it was decided that it should be sold as a package by way of private sale to the highest bidder. ROF Leeds, which made tanks, was sold separately to Vickers in July 1986, so that the business could be reshaped to meet future requirements. A number of companies submitted bids for the rest of the company. The number of bids was reduced in stages and eventually the company was sold to British Aerospace in July 1986.

In October 1989, Shorts of Belfast was sold to the highest bidder, Bombardier of Canada. Prior to privatisation, in a memorandum to the House of Commons Trade and Industry Committee, Shorts stated that "the company is in favour of privatisation because it believes that decisions on investment, and on re-equipment and future development of the business, are best taken in a business environment, based on sound commercial reasoning and without constant involvement of Government/political considerations."

In the shipbuilding world, the yards which made up British Shipbuilders were sold off separately by various means, including management buy-outs, during the mid-1980s.

As mentioned previously, the Mallabar Committee had recommended that the Royal Dockyards of Rosyth and Devonport, should operate on a Trading Fund basis. The option which was chosen in this case was to appoint a company or companies, to be responsible for the commercial management of the yards. Following open competition, seven-year contracts were awarded in April 1987 to Devonport Management Ltd for the management of Devonport Dockyard, and to Babcock Thorn Ltd for the management of Rosyth. These contracts are almost completed and in May this year we advertised the dockyards for sale. In the interim, the seven-year management contracts have been extended for up to a year.

Although the Government has relinquished control of the privatised defence companies, in a few cases special arrangements have been put in place to protect essential national interests. This has been done through the mechanism of a 'special share' which the Government continues to hold in some of the privatised defence companies, BAe, Rolls Royce and VSEL. These special shares give the Government the power to veto certain changes to the fundamental rules of each company which are contained in their Articles of Association. The special shares thus ensure some measure of control against the company coming under foreign control, by allowing the Government to restrict the proportion of shares owned by non-UK interests, and to stipulate that the companies' boards have a majority of UK directors.

So now we have a situation whereby almost all of our defence industry is in the private sector and although the British Government does hold a 'special share' in Rolls Royce, British Aerospace and VSEL, these give no say in the management, development and profitability of the business, which are entirely for the Board and the ordinary shareholders. These companies have had to undertake a very thorough self-examination to make sure that they are in the right market, producing the right goods and that their shareholders, many of whom we must remember are employees, receive the best possible return for their investment.

This is counterbalanced with the aims of the Ministry of Defence in buying equipment, which is to achieve best value for money for the taxpayer. At the same time as industry was adjusting to the changes brought about by privatisation, the Department began to increase its use of competitive tendering for contracts. This does not mean that the intention was always to select the cheapest option. When we reach the stage of assessing competitive tenders, we take a whole range of factors, one of which is price, into consideration. We have to determine the best option from those put forward and to assess the risks involved. We need to decide whether we can rely on the tenderer to deliver and whether they have the technical and managerial capability to do a good job to the required standards.

When we do look at price we do so within the context of these other factors.

The Department's move to competitive, usually fixed price, contracts means that companies have to assess very carefully the costs they are likely to incur. They should be able to make a reasonable profit, but if all other factors are equal, then obviously the company which can do the job the most economically stands a better chance of being awarded the contract. In order to become more competitive as a result of increased exposure to market forces, defence enterprises have had to restructure. Some have had to change direction, many now have radically different cultures and it is significant that they have reorganised their businesses to become more customer-oriented.

From the Government's perspective, privatisation has enabled us to pursue our policy of opening up defence procurement as fully as possible to competitive pressures, by removing the inevitable distortion of competition which arises when the Government is both the customer and one of the potential suppliers. The much greater use of competition in defence procurement has produced substantial economies to the defence budget in recent years.

It has also ensured that the process of adjustment within the defence industry as a result of the changed international situation is being shaped by commercial and industrial logic to a much greater extent than it would have been had large sections of the UK defence industry remained in public ownership.

Divesting ourselves of ownership of suppliers in this way has meant that we have been able to draw a clear line between ourselves as customers and the defence industry as suppliers, and to leave industry free to take the decisions which are properly theirs to make about their future direction and strategy.

The culture change which has occurred in the privatised defence industries was well summed up recently by the Chairman of British Aerospace, when he said that the company had changed from a "cost-plus" business to a "cost-conscious" one.

This brings us to another benefit which has arisen from privatisation: increased accountability, which applies both to employees and to products. Workers are being given the responsibility to ensure that their own work is of the required standard and are being encouraged to put forward new ideas and to feel that they have a valuable contribution to make to the success of the enterprise.

The sharpening up of the UK industry which has come about through competitive procurement policies has not just meant much better value for money for the taxpayer when buying the equipment our Armed Forces require; it has also meant that the UK defence industry has also become much more competitive internationally. 1993 was a record year for UK defence export orders which amounted to more than £6 billion.

Turning to strategic capability, we must not confuse loss of capacity with loss of capability. The UK is not in the business of using scarce resources to fund overproduction or inefficiency in the defence sector - private or public. By keeping suppliers informed, we aim to ensure that our needs will be accommodated. We have not lost any strategic capability as a result of the reduction in capacity which has been a commercial decision taken by the managers of these enterprises.

To summarise, the UK has found that industry performs more efficiently, effectively and economically if companies are left to run their businesses without the interference of government. There has been a cultural change from 'cost-plus to cost-conscious'.

Government will continue to give high priority to maintaining an effective range of well equipped forces.

In a time of change it is important to provide industry with as much visibility as possible of our requirements. We have taken a number of steps to ensure that industry are provided with all the information necessary to enable them to make sound commercial judgements so that they can remain competitive and successful in both domestic and overseas markets.

By setting up a customer-supplier relationship with the Department, industry is able to make commercial decisions which will enable us to obtain best value for money for the taxpayer when buying the equipment our Armed Forces require.

By giving companies the freedom to exercise their commercial judgement on how to adapt to changing market circumstances, they are in a position to ensure that they have a strong basis for future growth.

PANEL IV

Impact of Privatization of Defence Industry on the Labour Market, Taking into Account Privatization Experiences in other Fields

Chair: Allen Keiswetter, Deputy Assistant Secretary General for Political Affairs, NATO

Panelists: Lajos Héthy
Yuri V. Andreev
Igor Kosir
Edward Gorczynski
Jean-Hugues Monier
Franz-Lothar Altmann

EMPLOYMENT, PRIVATIZATION AND RESTRUCTURING IN CENTRAL AND EASTERN EUROPE

Lajos Héthy

Finding creative solutions to combat the increased job losses across Central and Eastern Europe will be one of the primary challenges for governments over the coming years, says Lajos Héthy. Even in countries such as Poland, where economic decline has ceased, unemployment can still increase due to the privatization and restructuring processes which are currently underway. Perhaps the most innovative approach to date comes from the Czech Republic, which encourages the unemployed to become self-employed, by offering them considerable financial subsidies.

Dr. Lajos Héthy is the Director of the Institute of Labour Research in Budapest.

In Central-Eastern Europe the arrival of mass unemployment is a major shock: while in most of the region (registered) unemployment was unknown until the middle of 1990, its rate - after a sharp rise in 1991 - had gone up to around 15 % by the end of 1993 in some countries; it was 17,04 % in Bulgaria, 14.9 % in Poland, 14.4 % Slovakia, 14.4 in Slovenia, 12.1 % in Hungary. Having in mind that these countries (with the exception of Bulgaria) are the "early starters" of economic transformation, there is good reason to think that the "late starters" - Romania, Albania, the countries of the former Soviet Union - will follow up as economic reforms gain impetus (In Ukraine in 1993 the rate was still below the incredible 1%).[1] There is also good reason to believe that mass unemployment - on a much higher rate than in Western Europe - will last for a long period of time. (The Czech Republic is, at least for the moment, a notable exception: in 1991 it had only 4.1 % and in 1992 - after a decline - only 2.8 % unemployment!)

Mass unemployment, as it appears, is primarily linked with economic decline: radical drops have occurred both in GDP and in industrial output. In Western Europe stagnation, or 1-2 % decline in GDP, is interpreted as "recession": in Central-Eastern Europe there was a radical drop in the GDP; even in Hungary, in a relatively good situation, this index was about minus 20-25 %. The region has been faced with a situation which could be best compared with Europe's 1930 Great Depression. The enormous fall in GDP could be attributed to a considerable extent to the collapse of the internal (past COMECON) trade within the region, to the shrinking national markets coupled with the impacts of energy price rises as a result of the Gulf War and the recession in the Western industrialised market economies.

In this context, it is noteworthy that drops in employment (i.e. the growth of unemployment) have not followed up the decline in GDP: i.e. productivity has deteriorated plunging to even lower levels than it had been before the change. (The first signs of GDP growth appeared in 1993 in Poland.)

Economic decline has been closely related with macroeconomic stabilisation and economic restructuring; they have had their influence felt both over the general level and structural changes in employment:

1) privatization, which is given a great emphasis all over the region, has resulted in shifts between the state and private sectors: while the number of those employed in the private sector (and that of the self-employed) has kept growing, a large proportion of the labour force has been still in the state (or quasi-private) sector.

2) The predominance of the economies by large (state-owned) enterprises, concentrating large numbers of labour force has been weakening as a result of their collapse (or serious financial problems) and the mushroom growth of SMEs.

(The partial survival of these big state enterprises has alleviated tensions in employment even if at the expense of productivity until now).[2]

3) Shifts have taken place, in most countries, from the artificially maintained "material production" to services, from heavy industry (as well as the military industry), manufacturing and agriculture to commerce and other services. While certain industries (such as metallurgy, arms industry) have been obviously collapsing, this trend has not been compensated, however, by dynamic growth in other ones.

While we have reliable data on employment in the shrinking state sector, information about it in the private sector is unreliable and often based on estimates.

According to a multinational study employment growth in private business in the period between the end of 1991 and 1992 was as follows: in Slovakia from 15,7 % to 17,2 %, in the Czech Republic from 17,6 % to 27,8 %, in Poland from 47,2 % to 58,4 %, in Hungary from 8-10 % (in 1989) to 38 %.[3] The above figures, however are much debated: in Hungary e.g. some experts claim a 49 % share for the private sector in employment, while others refer to about 30 % share only.[4] (The debates are rooted in the definition of "private sector": whether earlier state-owned enterprises transformed into share or limited companies with the maintenance of the majority - although indirect - ownership by the state belong to the private or to the state sector?)

The impact of privatization on employment seems to be fairly complex, depending on what is meant by it:

a) the new private sector is primarily constituted by small undertakings, involving self-employment; they suffer a shortage of capital and their capacity to create jobs is very much limited; they seem to function as a source of labour shedding as much as of employment.[5]

b) the establishment of new private firms of bigger size and relying on sufficient resources (such as "greenfield investments" by multinationals) tend to create new jobs but these are rather few; c) the privatisation of past state owned companies, at the same time, may involve considerable losses in jobs, as cutting production and costs includes reduction in the (redundant) labour force and the badly needed technological development (the substitution of the mostly obsolete old technology with "high tech") tends to be "labour saving" as well.

Such consequences, however, are unlikely to occur right away after the (legal) ownership change but as a longer term outcome of the emerging new business strategies in a narrow market. They are also subject to the power-play of local and national industrial relations and political actors (unions, employers, government, political parties, legislation etc.). On the part of the labour unions it has been a general demand to build in guarantees for the maintenance of jobs into the process of privatization: such guarantees, however, tend to create difficulties for this troublesome process.

In Central-Eastern Europe the labour market situation, while it differs from country to country, has the following major common features:

1) there is growing labour - market - related poverty: neither guaranteed minimum wages nor unemployment benefits are linked with minimum costs of living: minimum wages in general,[6] unemployment benefits for most, are inferior to them.

2) unemployment seems to be regionally concentrated; there are regions (e.g. most capitals and their surroundings) which suffer from it much less and there are "crisis regions" (earlier dominated by such shrinking or collapsing branches as agriculture, metallurgy, mining or arms industry).

3) there exists a growing labour market segmentation: unemployment of (ethnic) minorities has arisen alarmingly (in Slovakia e.g. the official rate among Gipsies was over 30 %, in Bulgaria 50 % of the Turkish minority and 80 % of the Gipsies were jobless). Women, in several countries, have lost jobs in greater number than men (Germany, Russia, Bulgaria).

4) A vulnerable group facing difficulties in employment are young people (past Czechoslovakia, Poland).[7]

5) Long-term unemployment, especially for the most vulnerable groups, seems to be part of the gloomy perspectives of our days and the future.

We de not have reliable empirical evidence for changes in employment in the arms industry of the region: this sector has been more strongly hit, probably, by losses in jobs than other fields, as the administered exchange (trade) of arms within the Warsaw Pact arrived at an end, production suffered a more radical drop than industrial output, military expenditure was cut all over the region etc. The geographical (regional) concentration of arms production and its collapse, there is good reason to think, is a major factor in the appearance of "crisis regions" in some countries (e.g. Slovakia).

The context of enormous drops of the (depressed) GDP have created a "vicious circle" for employment: it is a major contributor to it (and its consequences are far from being fully felt as yet) and - at the same time - it has set close limits for the financial resources which could be mobilized for both restructuring and the alleviation of labour market tensions.[8]

A major challenge for governments is to pursue overall governmental programmes to deal with mass unemployment. Most experts seem to agree that results can be expected from coordinated measures in such seemingly distant and isolated policies and fields as price and wage liberalisation, promotion of exports and exchange rates, education, social security or even defence, having their impact felt on demand and supply in the labour market. The best employment policy, in this approach, is economic policy promoting growth and thus generating demand for labour.

Such coordinated governmental policies are faced, however, with immense difficulties:

1) before economic restructuring has taken place, a switch back to growth risks with further imbalances in the economy (in the budget, in the balances of trade and payments etc) thus undermining the ongoing efforts of macroeconomic stabilisation.

2) the priority of reducing unemployment often collides with those of other policies (e.g. to reduce social costs e.g. by the extension of the age of pension, to reduce military costs by reducing the armed forces, to achieve rapid privatization etc.).

3) overexpenditure by the budget also sets close financial limits for such possible long-run strategic programmes that could serve both employment and economic growth (the development of infrastructure, education etc.).[9]

4) The international financial organisations (the World Bank, IMF) keep exercising permanent pressure on most governments to cut budgetary deficits.

5) There is a painful lack of coordination of governmental policies, their programmes are (as a necessity) dominated by fiscal approaches and priorities of employment (tacitly) are thrust into the background.

Governmental efforts to fight unemployment, in this context, are limited to employment policies pursued by the isolated labour administration mostly left on its own. In addition liberal economic approaches, aimed at stabilisation tend to downgrade the problem of unemployment and look upon it as an issue of "social charity". While there can be little if any doubt that employment is heavily dependent on the economy, it can be much debated whether only social policies are sufficient to deal with the problem. Anyway: at present no effective overall governmental programmes to fight mass unemployment seem to exist in the region.

Employment policies in the region rely on:

a) legal protection against the termination of employment (with special respect for mass-layoffs): in case of layoffs severance payments are often more generous than in Western Europe although bankrupt companies often cannot afford to pay them. (In Hungary e.g. they may amount to six month earnings and collective or individual work contracts often include even more favourable terms from the point of view of workers).

b) passive and active employment policy measures (such as unemployment benefits, job creation and public utility works, subsidies for enterpreuneurship, early retirement and shortened working hours, special programmes targeted at regional unemployment, young people, disabled people, long term unemployed etc.).

c) a network of manpower services.

The establishment of labour market institutions is under way. (The process started in Hungary as early as the end of the 1980s, in the rest the of the countries in the early 1990s.) The governments have introduced both active and passive labour market policy measures - following Western European examples - to deal with unemployment. Political commitments are related (and political lipservice paid) to active measures. There are however, disquieting open questions: to what extent can active measures can prove to be effective to promote success in the specific economic (and employment) situation of sharp GDP drop in the region?

How can these (rather expensive) measures be financed in the tight budgetary and economic context? What one could witness in the region for the past few years is a double process:

a) governmental efforts to divide the financial costs of employment policy measures (by imposing growing obligatory contributions to them on both employers and workers).

b) to reduce social benefits offered for those unemployed.

In spending there has been a shift from active to passive measures: in 1990 both Hungary and Poland spent considerable sums (30 % and 60 % of the employment budget) on active policy; as unemployment started to grow rapidly and more and more jobless people asked for benefits, in 1991 the share of active measures in spending declined (to 30% in Hungary, to 20 % in Poland) and this process continued in 1992. A notable exception was the Czech Republic - with the lowest unemployment rate - where an increased emphasis has been laid on reemployment. Financial resources spent on active measures were primarily concentrated on the support of training and retraining in Hungary, on job creation in Czechoslovakia and on retraining in Poland in 1991/92. Thus the major thrust of employment policies in 1991/92 in Czechoslovakia was the creation of new jobs and the promotion of self employment by considerable financial subsidies. These efforts were supported also by the tripartite General Agreements in 1991 and 1992.[10]

To limit overexpenditure by the budget (and overtaxation) unemployment benefits have been gradually cut all over the region in the past years. They are still relatively generous in Hungary (benefits are paid for a 12 month period at 75 and 60 % level of the earlier earnings) but much less so in other countries. The most radical cuts have taken place in the Czech Republic. Long term unemployed, after the expiration of benefits, may apply for social subsidies - which are, however, much more uncertain and fixed at much depressed levels. It should also be noted, that growing clandestine employment and invisible income, in several countries, have had a part in the subsistence of many jobless people. Clandestine employment is often related with the processes of (illegal) migration of labour from the economically most depressed countries (e.g. Romania, Ukraine) to those which are relatively well-off. (Hungary, Poland etc.)

Without trying to diminish the importance of governmental policies one should be aware of the growing importance of the autonomous decisions of employers in this field, including such private employers in increasing numbers over which the state has no direct control any more. In this context labour relations - negotiations and agreements among employers, workers (unions) and the government - may become as strong an instrument in the maintenance or promotion of employment as governmental policies.

In this respect two major issues have appeared:

a) the trade unions' participation in the control of privatization.

b) the trade unions' say in the formulation of employment policies. The labour organisations in a set of countries (e.g. Czechoslovakia, Hungary) have been excluded from the privatization process while national (tripartite) negotiations have mostly covered employment: the agreements achieved, however, have not resulted as yet in any solid guarantees against mass unemployment. (Labour unions, in general, exercise considerable pressure to achieve wage increases regardless of their possible consequences for jobs.)[11]

Employment prospects for the coming years are gloomy: even if the GDP drop arrives at a halt (as it did in 1993 in Poland) unemployment tends to grow further as other processes (privatization, restructuring) continue to generate it. One should not forget that labour hoarding around 1989/90 amounted to an estimated 15-30 % in the number of those employed at a higher level of both production and productivity. It is still an open question: whether and when will this redundant labour appear in its full dimension as jobless people in the labour market? It is a question which all of the countries in the region have to face in the future including those where unemployment presently is on a very low level in Western European standards.

Footnotes:

1. The present paper draws upon the national contributions prepared for the Conference "Employment Policy and Programmes in CEE". (Budapest, June 2-3, 1994, ILO): Czech Republic (V. Uldrichova), Slovakia (P. Ochotnicky); Poland (M. Góra); Slovenia (S. Drobnic), Romania (C. Zamfir); Ukraine (V. Yatsenko) and Hungary (M. Frey.)

2. Héthy, L.: Enterprise Level Industrial Relations under Economic and Political Pressure. The Case of Past Big State Enterprises. WORC, Tilburg, March 1994.

3. Koltay, J.: Munkanélküliség és foglalkoztatáspolitika Közép és Kelet Európában. (Unemployment and employment policy in Central and Eastern Europe.) Közgazdasági Szemle, Budapest, No 2. 1993. p. 154.

4. Kolosi, T.: The poor and the rich in Hungary. Institute of Economics, Budapest, Transit Club Series. No 7. 1993. Laky, T.: A munkaerôpiac keresletét és kínálatát alakító folyamatok (Processes shaping supply and demand in the labour market.) Institute of Labour Research, Budapest, 1993. p. 14.

5. Koltay, ibid. p. 154.

6. Vaughan-Whitehead, D.: Minimum Wage in Central and Eastern Europe: Slippage of the Anchor. ILO/CEET Reports No 4. Budapest, Oct. 1993.

7. Standing, G.: Labour Market Developments in Eastern and Central Europe. ILO/CEET Policy Papers, No 1. Budapest, Jan. 1993. Koltay, ibid. p. 157.

8. Before the drop Central-Eastern Europe already had depressed GDP levels. GDP/capita in 1990 (USA = 100%) was as follows: Hungary 29.1 %, Czechoslovakia 36.9 %, Poland 18.6 %, Romania 16 %. Calculations by E. Ehrlich. Ehrlich, E., Révész, G.: A jelen és egy lehetséges jövô Magyarországon. 1985-2005. Budapest, 1993. p. 222-223.

9. Compare: A Programme for Full Employment in the 1990s. Report of the Kreisky Commission on Employment Issues in Europe. Pergamon Press, Oxford, 1989.

10. Koltay, ibid, p. 163.

11. Héthy, L.: Tripartism in Eastern Europe. In: (Ferner, A. - Hyman, R.: New Frontiers in European Industrial Relations. Blackwell, Oxford - Cambridge (Mass.) (forthcoming)

A VIEW FROM RUSSIA

Yuri V. Andreev

Knowledge was power in the Soviet Union - and the Party kept a tight hold on both. Yuri Andreev says that the biggest obstacle to restructuring Russia's defence industry is that nobody really knows how big it is. Secrecy and inefficiency have combined to make the statistics unreliable. National security means that the state should still have a big say in the industry's future, but the private sector must also come in - and it won't unless it knows exactly what it is getting into.

Professor Yuri V. Andreev is the Academic Secretary for the Russian Peace Research Institute at the Russian Academy of Sciences, and the Secretary of the Russian Commission for Promotion of Conversion.

Before we start analyzing the impact of privatization of the defence industry on the labour market some general basic comments have to be made.

The statistics available in present-day Russia leave much to be desired.

Any analysis requires sufficient and reliable information about the entire economy, but especially about the military-industrial part of this economy. When we talk about the share of military expenditure in the GNP, we know that in the USA it takes about 5%. But if we try to assess the same in the Former Soviet Union (FSU) or even in the Russia of today, we get tremendously different figures and practically no official statistics. According to the former Gosplan (State planning ministry) of the USSR, military expenditure made up around 10% of GNP, but Mr.. Gorbachev used to refer to 18% of national income in late 1980s.

The American economist Birman, who emigrated from the USSR some time ago, gave 25% of GNP as a result of his evaluations. Two Russian economists, Perwyshin and Lagutenko, went as high as 52% and 50%, respectively.

What is important is that nobody showed any statistical basis for their appraisals; that is why it is hard to prove anything. My judgment tends to be, that most probably around 20% of GNP of FSU should be considered as close to reality. But the major problem still remains - we need reliable statistics that could give a clear and transparent answer to this basic question, especially in present-day Russia.

Take a smaller question - how many factories are there in the Russian military-industrial complex [MIC] or were there in the MIC of the FSU? Some experts claimed about five thousand such units in FSU; others even put it at ten thousand. At the same time many officials name 1500 factories and 200 or more research bureaux in MIC of present Russia, which, according to available information,

215

makes about 70% of the FSU figures. These last figures correspond to our own assessment of the place of the MIC in the economy of the FSU and present-day Russia. But again, we need official data; without them correct evaluation and proper programming are not possible.

We are not debating here the ways and means of privatization in Russia, its general strategy. This could and should be a subject of another, special discussion.

I am against privatising the Russian defence industry in general at present. My approach is based on determining the part of current Russian MIC necessary for maintenance of national security, converting the rest of MIC into civilian production, and privatizing this part of MIC.

The first and most important question consists in considering the correlation between conversion and the national security doctrine, strategy and policy of the country. Only after agreement about this doctrine could the country put aside the capacities needed for military production and R&D. The rest could be clearly considered as available for conversion and privatization. In Russia, such a military doctrine is already adopted. However, it makes up only part of national security doctrine, which is still under debate at present. The result of this debate will decisively influence the limits of, and the entire terrain for, the conversion of military production and R&D in Russia and their further privatization.

The defence industry as such should remain in state hands: according to available information around 400 such factories, which will be engaged only in military production, are already picked out. A private defence industry in Russia could create, in my judgment, a lot of troubles domestically and internationally. As for diversified firms, which produce both military and civilian goods, they should be in mixed [public and private] enterprises.

According to the available information privatization is going rather slowly. Of all factories and research bureaux only about one hundred changed hands. At the same time, the state plans to speed up the process and to sell about 69% of all MIC enterprises before the end of the voucher privatization, including some big and well-known firms.

As for the labour market, we know that employment in the defense industries of Russia has decreased by 19% in 1993 as compared with 1991. However, there is considerable hidden unemployment in the industry. The factories and research institutions still keep a lot of workers and researchers on their payroll [salaries are very low anyway] in the hope that they might get contracts one day. In fact, the real decrease in the number of working people is most probably much higher than officially stated. It has to be pointed out that the MIC has already lost a great part of its most dynamic, industrious and young people, who went into businesses often totally disconnected with military production.

According to the statistics, for the first three months of 1994 5000 factories had shut-downs of a sizable duration, 428 out of them are closed altogether. At the end of the first quarter of 1994, the number of unemployed reached 4.4 million people; by the end of 1994 it could become 8.8 million or 11% of the labour force. A considerable part of these factories and unemployed people belongs to the Russian MIC.

According to our analysis of this problem, the impact of slow-going privatization in this area on the labour problems of Russia's MIC is quite negligible. The problems are caused not by privatization, but by other processes. They are a result of something popularly known as "conversion", but in fact of the lack of conversion. Russian military production stopped or decreased totally by 48% in 1993 as compared to 1991. However, for many reasons, civilian production did not start instead - it even decreased in the same period by 13%.conversion and privatization.

Conversion and privatization are closely connected. Privatization should follow the conversion of that part of the Russian MIC, which is in excess of national security needs.

In the years of the Cold War, the military-industrial complex of the USSR consumed up to 4/5 of all national financial, human and technical resources. As a result, 60% (according to some other estimates- 80%) of the industry was connected with the military. In Russia alone, with approximately 70% of the military-industrial complex of the FSU, about 7 million people are employed in defence-oriented industries (indirectly, counting the subcontractors, up to 16 million). In the basic sciences, half of all expenditure was connected with the military; in space research, about 70%. Half of all firms in Moscow and about 3/4 in St. Petersburg belong to the MIC. Russia has ten so-called "secret" towns totally devoted to nuclear defense production. In Arzamas-16, Chelyabinsk-70, Penza-19, Tomsk-7, Sverdlovsk-44, Krasnoyarsk-26 and other such towns live about 700.000-900.000 people. There are also dozens of smaller secret towns producing other types of armaments.

We badly need programs for conversion, and for privatization in a country where the economy still bears signs of over-militarization. Sometimes one could hear, that some programs, maybe even many, already exist. If, as in the case of the State Program on Conversion of the USSR, signed in 1990, they remain secret and unpublished, they might expect the same, not very bright fate.

Conversion and privatization need also corresponding legislative backing. The law on conversion of defense industries in Russia was adopted in March 1992. The social side of the law is especially important - it regulates the problems of the employed personnel in a country where one fifth is in one way or another connected with the military-industrial complex. But it is only the first step in creating a comprehensive legal basis in this area.

How could privatization exercise a positive influence on, and promote a solution to, the labour problems of the Russian MIC? New private firms born out of MIC could present some ample possibilities for new employment, but they seldom do so. The retraining of unemployed or potentially unemployed labour force from MIC has not really started in full swing yet. In this area the role of the private sector could be extremely important.

It is extremely important to develop mutually beneficial international cooperation in the field of conversion and privatization. The first steps have already been made. Considerable work was undertaken by Russian on one side and American, German, Italian, French partners on the other. In June 1992, a joint Russian-American declaration on defense conversion was signed which envisages the establishment of a US-Russian Defense Conversion Committee to facilitate conversion through expanded trade and investment.

Of course, there are many obstacles in the way. Some difficulties spring from systemic differences and a lot of effort is needed to harmonize the economic bases of our countries. Other difficulties are connected with bureaucracy, the inefficiency of our management, and the tremendous corruption. As a result only a few hundred million dollars of foreign money are invested in the Russian MIC at the moment.

We need concepts and models of international cooperation in the field of conversion, worked out together by experts of respective countries. Some coordinating bodies for that already exist and should be activated. The UN system which showed great interest in this problem could be more actively involved in the process. The concept of cooperation in this field ought to be based on the following grounds:

- No help is needed, except in extreme situations.
- Cooperation should be mutually beneficial.
- It is better to develop such cooperation with fully converted factories.
- It is preferable [but not a "must"] to develop such a cooperation with privatized, fully converted firms.

However, instead of developing mutually beneficial cooperation including investment, we get a lot of advice whose value leaves much to be desired. Take, for example, the article "Defense conversion: bulldozing the management", published by K. Adelman and N. Augustine in "Foreign Affairs" in 1992. They give the Russians a lot of recommendations and design a number of models, although they state at the beginning of the article, that conversion in the US has "a discouraging history of failure". They cite an expert's report that says that "successful examples of such conversion [of the military production of the USA] are difficult to find. Detailed research has not identified a successful product in our economy today which was developed through a military-to-civilian approach. As of 1990 there are very few concrete examples of actual conversion". Therefore it seems to me quite questionable to recommend models based on such results.

It is clear that conversion in Russia must go on even without any cooperation and of course without any help. The military-industrial complex of the FSU was created independently. Russia can survive without help and cooperation, but we will hardly survive without conversion and most probably without privatization of a considerable part of MIC.

SLOVAK DEFENCE INDUSTRY CONVERSION: A KEY TO ECONOMIC AND SOCIAL TRANSFORMATION

Igor Kosir

After the Velvet Revolution came the peaceful creation of the Czech and Slovak Republics as separate states. Having inherited 60 percent of the military production of the former Czechoslovakia, the Slovak Republic's biggest challenge is to manage the transition of this sector as effectively as possible, says Igor Kosir. Today, progress is slow and much outside investment is needed, but this republic's privatization efforts are encouraged by a Number One priority: full integration into the European Union as a final strategic goal.

Igor Kosir is the Director for the Centre for Strategic Studies at the Slovak Republic in Bratislava.

In spite of the serious and complex transformation problems of Central and Eastern European Countries the transition period is a real challenge for their nations, for the whole of Europe and its future integration, for our civilization and its peaceful and continuous development.

The new economic growth in several developed countries and anticipated further period of longer economic growth in a big group of economies will play a very positive role in accelerating transformation of the economy and society in this part of our continent.

1994 is only the second year of the relatively short era of Slovak independence, but Slovakia is already ranked among the democratic European nations. Despite a lot of very negative forecasts about our future after independence day and thanks to our more critical attitude toward all events and positive development problems, Slovakia has achieved a quite good position among the European economies in transition.

As an independent state, the Slovak Republic has a legitimate right to formulate its own transformation and development strategy and to realize it in cooperation with its neighbours - the more developed European nations and other democratic states. The Slovakian parliament and all main non-parliament political parties and movements support its European orientation as the Number One strategic priority. The symbol of this strategic orientation of the Slovak policy and economy is the Slovakian membership in the Council of Europe, participation in the NACC and WEU activities, associate membership and cooperation with the European Union - with full membership as a final strategic goal.

This goal is connected with a very important reorientation of our country's foreign trade and active international cooperation.

The peaceful, very cultural and democratic division of the former Czecho-Slovakian federation approved by both chambers of the former federal parliament is without precedent in European history. This political and social event with a very strong economic context was not a real danger for stability of our continent. Slovakia and the Czech Republic are leaders of the transformation process in Central and Eastern Europe. For Slovakia, the real economic growth of 4,1% in the first quarter of the 1994 is a very positive sign. Slovakia wants to use all positive aspects of this heritage, built on more than 74 years of coexistence with the Czech nation. Now, under its own responsibility and national identity, Slovakia is an equal partner in the family of democratic nations.

Transformation of the Economy and Society of Slovakia and the Conversion Process

The conversion process is connected with global changes and restructuring in the world economy after the end of the cold war period. It is a big challenge for our civilization.

In the Central and Eastern European countries, this process is more complex. It represents a very important and complicated part of the topical transformation toward the democratization of society and a market-driven economic system. In spite of a very optimistic picture of transformation in 1990-1991, the reality is that natural transformation was slow because the huge systematic social change in the former socialist countries was a real-life case, not a laboratory scenario.

The pillars of this process are: liberalization of prices and foreign trade activities, implementation of internal convertibility of national currency, and economic restructuring connected with privatization. This represents a historical ownership change in this area of Europe and requires maintenance of social peace as an important condition for the success of the entire transformation process and economic reform.

Achieving economic and social reform is more complicated because of serious conversion and environmental problems of several countries, including Slovakia. The Slovak economy faces this problem more than the average of the Central and Eastern European Countries (CEECs) because of its specific economic evolution after World War II. Slovaks wanted a new federal structure (former Czecho-Slovakia) but it was impossible after 1948 because a very centralized state system was the main feature of the Communist Party regime.

But a huge country-wide industrialization process was realized in the 1950s and 1960s which aimed to strike a balance between the two parts of the country.

The first Czecho-Slovakian Republic (1918-1938/39) was economically very unbalanced. The Czech country brought to the new European state an important heritage from monarchy, the feature of the most industrialized country of this side of the world.

Slovakia was a classical agrarian country without any important industry. The well-known economic crisis of 1929-1933 represented a real national catastrophe, sparking a huge emigration to the western part of this continent and, especially, to the USA and Canada. In comparison with that period the postwar industrialization process was a positive step. But the centrally-planned economy made a lot of mistakes. It reached a very unbalanced production structure for many internal and external reasons. Former Czecho-Slovakia was one of the most industrialized socialist countries and naturally it became a strong center of defense industry, not only for national security reasons but also as a supplier to the entire Warsaw Pact. Slovakia played a very specific role in this economy.

In general, Slovakia was not specialized in final industrial production. This advantage was enjoyed by the of the Czech part of country. But Slovakia became an important center of armaments production for the Warsaw pact countries for its geographic strategic location. In addition, this system centralized all activities of decision making, production planning and a huge concentration of foreign trade activities in the country capital. The Slovak part of the Czecho-Slovakian economy was the functional appendix to the traditionally more developed Czech one.

The Prague spring movement of 1968 brought a better situation. Czechs and Slovaks agreed the federalization of the country, the creation of two national republics, but a "normalization" process after April 1969 recreated a very centralized state regime. The Velvet Revolution of November 1989 created a new space, and the new democracy enabled us to realize these old aims. Confederation of two equal partners was not accepted by Prague' political structures after elections of June 1992 because of the advantage of the transformation progress enjoyed by the independent Czech Republic.

The result of the political discussions between the main election winners was an agreement about the coordinated division of Czecho-Slovakian federation. And this agreement was realized by both sides very seriously. For the new Czech Republic it brought the progress of transformation and for Slovakia, realization of national identity for Slovaks and a new space for state and national development in a European context. A short disintegration process was immediately replaced by the integration of both our independent republics.

The first year of independence, 1993, was relatively complicated for continued international relations in terms of the future Slovak orientation and the destiny of economic reform which began in 1991. But all Slovak governments were stressing its strategic orientation on the European integration process. Slovakia is not interested in a new split of our continent.

There was some mistrust concerning the conversion process in Slovakia, but a real decline of the Slovak defense industry production from 100% in 1988 (historical maximum of production volume of CSK 19,3 billion - Czecho-Slovak crowns) - 24% of the total production of the Slovak machinery and electrical engineering) to only 9-10% of that volume in 1992 was a convincing symbol of a very dynamic continuation of country conversion process.[1]

There was a vast discussion about the speed of abolition of the Slovak defence industry production. This was mainly due to a different industrial structure between the two republics, which caused a more negative impact on the labour market - as an absolutely new social and economic phenomenon in Slovakia after more than 40 years. Unemployment became a very sensitive aspect of the whole transformation process. Connected with important loss of the former stable CMEA markets, with decisive concentration of foreign investors in Prague and other Czech firms, with a crucial state of under-capitalization of the economy and relatively high debt among the Slovak state-owned enterprises and increasing inflation - the conversion problem caused a feeling that Slovakia required its own economic policy which focused on its national interest.

In spite of a very complex internal and external situation concerning the division of Czecho-Slovakia (unexpected a few years ago in the international community) the peaceful divorce, which was achieved in a very cultural way, influenced the attitude of the international community to the new European states.

The basic approach of the Slovak government to conversion was and is positive. Decreasing of expenditures to the defence sector releases a huge amount of resources, creating the possibility to solve other important social and economic problems. But at the same time it evokes a need to restructure - to convert the military-industrial complex.

The conversion process is not just an ownership change. It must be considered as a complex restructuring of production on the basis of the civil economy (non-military), its modernization, increasing of its competitiveness and export orientation. It is valid not only for economically small and medium countries. And a huge ownership change in terms of private sector orientation is an important tool concerning the final aim to reach a new quality, a new efficiency of production.

There are a lot of serious problems with the conversion process in the Central and Eastern European countries in transition. In addition to the above-mentioned factors which complicate this process in every country, there is another very important influencing factor: conversion requires a lot of money.

The undercapitalization stage of all transforming economies connects this process with foreign financial resources. But in the global recession stage there was not a big motivation to invest into converting defence industries of the CEECs. Some CSK 152,9 million of foreign capital participated in the Slovakian conversion projects in the 1991-1992 period. But this represented only 3,1%

of conversion cost.[2] From the viewpoint of market forces, it is not advantageous for the CEECs that this process is now occurring in all countries at the same time. The total cost is too high.

Basic Data about Conversion in Slovakia

1. The defence industry in Slovakia represented approximately 60% of the Czecho-Slovakian defence industry production.
2. The former Czecho-Slovakian army ranked among the best armies of the world because of training and equipment (armament). The Czecho-Slovakian defence industry delivered 60% of the latter.
3. The defence industry played an important role in foreign trade activities of the federation (volume of exports to the Warsaw Pact countries was two times higher than domestic deliveries). Armament export was an important resource of foreign currency. One fourth of the export oriented to the Warsaw pact area was realized in the developing countries.
4. The Slovak export volume of CSK 84 billion in the period of 1976-1988 represented 58% of the total defence industry volume of production.
5. Defence industry in Slovakia represented 24 percent of production share of machinery and electrical engineering.
6. Slovakia reached its top of armament production in 1988 - CSK 19,3 billion.[3]

There were some indicators of the future conversion process in the eighties. But it was not prepared seriously by the centrally planned system from many objective and subjective reasons before 1989. One result of several decisions of the federal government of Czecho-Slovakia (No. 84/1989, No. 103/1989 and No. 42/1990) was the Slovak defence industry decline to a 1992 volume of production of 1,8 billion CSK.[4] It was connected with an important dismissal of labour force (30 000).

(x) Slovakia is very interested in foreign participation in its conversion projects. In the 1991-1993 period, foreign capital participated in 11 projects from 100 total.[5] Without an abolition of debt of defence oriented enterprises (4,087 billion Slovak crown - Sk) in 1993 a majority of these firms was going to collapse because the speed of abolition of this kind of industry was too dynamic, and because of a loss of 70-80 percent of former markets. The government decision was a step to assist the Slovak armament firms to may to restructure their production into civilian one. But it is a longer process than was expected. And Slovakia believes that one of the most efficient ways will be a substantial and very useful cooperation with NATO countries participating in the NACC activities and on the joint activities with WEU. That is why a privatization process in this kind of industry may have some specific features. The role of the state is important, especially in the small and medium countries (for example in Switzerland).

The share of the private sector in Slovakia is different: in the first quarter of 1994 its participation on the GDP creation was 40 percent (39% in 1993) including the cooperative private sector. The participation in industrial production in the first quarter of the 1994 was 25,5% (1993: 22,1%), in construction it reached 59,3% share (1993: 49,6%), in transport 51,7% (1993: 49,8%), in retail trade 85,7% (1993: 85,1%), in services 66,8% (1993: 66,7%) and in agriculture (without cooperatives) 25,8%.[6]

National and International Context of Existing Defence Industry in Slovakia

The necessity of existence of the Slovak defence industry and its cooperation with NACC partners results from the following circumstances:

1. A strategic priority of Slovakia is full membership in the economic and political structures of integrated Europe.
2. The new Army of the Slovak Republic should be supplied with essential equipment needed to defend and secure the country.
3. The top level of this kind of industry stimulates a real development of the civilian industrial sector, too.
4. The conversion process needs time and a lot of money and this kind of industry may secure some additional resources itself in cooperation with some NATO countries on a bilateral basis.
5. Privatisation of the defence industry is a very important issue. It will be achieved with the entire transformation process, the concrete social climate (the unemployment rate in April 1994 reached 14,17 percent but in some districts more than 25%), and with state and foreign participation.[7]

The conversion process continues but in a more realistic way, in a climate of confidence and useful cooperation among the NACC and WEU partners.

Resources:

1. KOVACIK, J.: Ku konverzii zbrojárskeho priemyslu v Slovenskej republike. Materiál Ministerstva obrany SR. 1994. (x) - p. 52, (XX) - p. 54, (xxx) - p. 47 and 51.
2. Statistická správa o základných vyvojových tendenciách v národnom hospodárstve SR v 1. stvrtroku 1994 a ich predikcii na rok 1994. Bratislava, jún 1994. (xxxx) - p. 20.
3. Statistické vysledky o nezamesnanosti v Slovenskej republike za apríl 1994. Správa sluzieb zamestnanosti Bratislava. Bratislava, máj 1994. (xxxxx) - p. 1.
4. GREENBERG, M.E. - HEINTZ, S.B.: Odstranovanie bariér. Stratégia pomoci dlhodobo nezamestnanym. IEWS, European Studies Center, Prague 1994.
5. Návrh obrannej doktríny Slovenskej republiky. Materiál Ministerstva obrany SR. Bratislava 1994.
6. Projekt priblízenia SR k NATO. Materiál Ministerstva zahranicnych vecí SR. Bratislava 1993.
7. Partnerstvo za mier. Prezentacny dokument Slovenskej republiky. Bratislava, máj 1994.

RESTRUCTURING POLAND'S DEFENCE INDUSTRY

Edward Gorczynski

Prior to the fall of communism, Poland's defence industry was designed to protect the Soviet Union and the Warsaw Pact, rather than Poland. Edward Gorczynski discusses how the government has set about slimming down the industry to make it more efficient, and to allocate more resources to civilian production. They also have in mind to return the industry to its more traditional function - supplying the arms and equipment to defend Poland itself.

Lt.Col. Edward Gorczynski is a chief expert at the Department of Defence Affairs in the Polish Ministry of Industry and Trade

The Polish Army should be supplied with essential equipment needed to defend and secure our country, and some production capabilities should be provided to ensure a degree of defence self-sufficiency, the defence industry should be able to import advanced defence technology by using its exportable surplus,and it should stimulate technological development in the civilian industrial sector.

Poland's defence industry structure should be adopted to our present defence doctrine in the following ways:
- Its production capabilities should meet the present needs of the Polish Army and the State's financial capabilities.
- Its new technical and organizational structure should comply with new tasks.
- Its non-production and social infrastructure expanded in the past years should be managed.
- It should give jobs for highy-skill specialists.

The restructuring process should also aim at creating the production potential suited to our present defence doctrine and able to adopt new technologies and standards resulting from present aspirations and priorities of the Polish Army and State; converting the redundant capabilities and social structures into civil production; and making the effectiveness of our defence sector higher by introducing both the privatization process and training in management.

Step 1: 1989-1991

At the end of the 1980s demand for Polish defence equipment was considerably reduced, not only in Poland but also in other markets. The Polish defence industry consisted of more than 80 state enterprises employing about 200,000 people. Defence production in those enterprises, depending on which branch, was between 10 and 80%. The production capabilities, developed mainly to meet the demands of the former Soviet Union and Warsaw Pact, turned out to be too large, both in proportion to our present needs and to the State's financial abilities.

Total defence production in Poland decreased twice in the 1988-1989 period. In July 1989 and then at the end of 1991, the Polish Ministry of Industry and Trade recommended developing individual restructuring programs and introducing them into some defence branches. These programs consisted in changing and limiting defence production profiles. Surplus capacity was planned to be diverted to civil production. The activity was concentrated on only those enterprises where existing production lines could be adapted easily to new needs. It had no significant effects on market production because of the recession taking place in our country. Beside the personnel were extremely dissatisfied because they were facing dismissals (even group dismissals in some enterprises).

Today, the failure can be explained by the lack of funds to convert the production profiles from military to civilian activity, the recession taking place in Poland, and the country's lack of experience in realizing such a transformation.

Step 2: 1992-1994

At the end of 1991, after a detailed analysis of the first step in the restructuring process, the Department of Defence Affairs prepared the complex program for all defence enterprises and submitted it to the Government on January 28, 1992.
- The Main points of this program were:
- Concentration of production - this means the separation of specified productive capabilities in each of 31 enterprises, which are of particular significance for national security.
- Change of organizational structure - this means both the privatization process in which the above capabilities will be transformed into four Treasury-run production divisions according to the production profile. By the end of 1993, five of 31 enterprises were fully switched, the others are to be converted by the end of 1994 or a bit later.
- Cancelling the debts of defence enterprises to the budget - this means negotiating with banks in order to find the best way of debt repayment.
- Continuation of the individual restructuring programs - this means the successfully completion of the programs with continuous cooperation with consulting firms.

- Defence-to-civil conversion - this means that a considerable part of redundant, non-production and social capabilities and assets belonging to the enterprises will be sold, put on lease or converted into civil production.

The program was prepared in two variants: an optimum variant of restructuring prepared according to the national defence needs, with the necessary funds guaranteed by the budget; and a budget variant of restructuring prepared with the funds provided for by the budget. The Government chose the budget variant.

Present Condition of Polish Defence Industry

The Polish Defence Industry consists of 31 enterprises. Five of them have already been converted into the Treasury-run companies. The others will be transformed by the end of this year according to the plan and algorithm prepared by the Ministry of Industry and Trade. The individual programs for particular enterprises are in progress. Official negotiations with banks to find the best way of debt repayment have been completed. A considerable part of redundant and non-productive assets belonging to the enterprises has been sold or put on lease. Based on the existing labour power, new market production with a wider assortment has been started. A program of defence production concentration is just in progress, and employment in the defence sector has been reduced (in relation to the 1990 level) by more than 50% (see table and charts). Average efficiency (sales to employment ratio) of both civil and defence sectors for 31 enterprises is increasing. The legislative process has been completed and the real process of ownership and structural transformations is under way.

Restructuring, Step 3: 1995 - 1996

The new organizational structure of Polish defence industry, as one of the essential elements of the restructuring process, will be the most important part of future activities (1995 -1996).

The program mentioned above includes establishing four production divisions based on the Industrial Groups made up of the manufacturers having the approximate production profiles :

- Aircraft division.
- Conventional arms, ammunition, missiles and explosives
 division.
- Radar, electronic and opto-electronic division.
- Armoured equipment division.

However, there are several conditions that should be met to carry this program into effect successfully. The target needs of main customers should be defined. This condition is closely connected with the structural reorganization of the Polish Army because it will be the prime customer of the defence industry.

The privatization and the debt cancelling process of the defence industry should be completed successfully; and all barriers for export (except the limitations resulting from UN resolutions) of Polish defence products should be cancelled. Funds required to carry out the process should be provided by the Government.

The restructuring process of Poland's defence industry was based on individual programs and business plans prepared by the enterprises with close cooperation with consulting firms

The Ministry of Industry and Trade (Department of Defence Affairs) is acting as a coordinator of the process and an institution responsible for creating the legal base for the restructuring.

All activities undertaken are limited to 31 enterprises only, which make up the base needed to create the national defence industry with the production potential suitable to our present defence doctrine and able to adopt new technologies and standards resulting from present aspirations and priorities of the Polish Army and State.

Individual programs also include the cooperation links with both local and foreign partners. Now, the enterprises can cooperate with foreign companies directly. They can buy licences, carry out technology transfer, establish joint ventures and organize seminars and managerial training.

The present economic condition of the enterprises is still below expectations but there are some things that speak well for the processes just being carried out. Fourteen of the thirty-one enterprises made gross and net profits at the end of 1993, and 26 of them increased their incomes in relation to 1992.The average sales-to-employment ratio of both civil and defence sectors increased, and employment in the defence sector was reduced by more than 50%.

The term "restructuring" used here is the general one and it includes all activities (also privatization and conversion) undertaken to increase effectiveness of the defence industry and to adjust its capacity to the needs resulting from the defence doctrine.

Polish Defence Industry (%)

ITEM	PARAMETER	1990	1991	1992	1993
1	TOTAL SALES*	100	81,97	83,76	109,64
2	DEFENCE SALES*	100	90,75	41,05	56,09
3	TOTAL EMPLOYMENT	100	79,51	66,51	59,24
4	DEFENCE SECTOR EMPLOYMENT*	100	69,49	51,64	46,75
5	TOTAL SALES TO EMPLOYMENT*	100	103,02	125,84	184,95
6	DEFENCE SALES TO EMPLOYMENT*	100	130,59	79,52	119,31
7	DEFENCE TO TOTAL SALES	27,57	30,52	13,51	14,11
8	DEFENCE TO TOTAL EMPLOYMENT	35,52	31,04	27,58	28,03

* *1990 = 100%, 31 enterprises*

TOTAL SALES(1) and DEFENCE SALES (2)

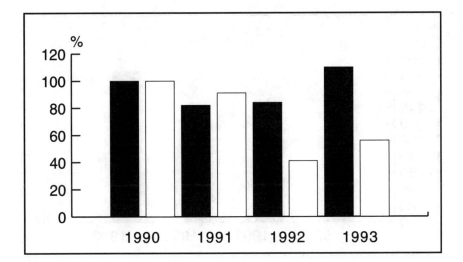

TOTAL EMPLOYMENT (3) and DEFENCE SECTOR EMPLOYMENT (4)

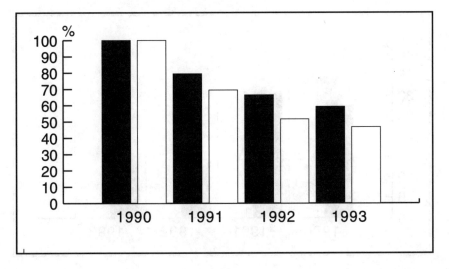

TOTAL (5) and DEFENCE (6) SALES TO EMPLOYMENT

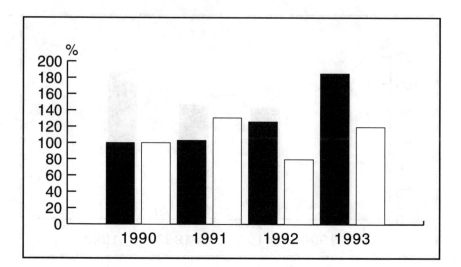

DEFENCE TO TOTAL SALES (7) and EMPLOYMENT (8)

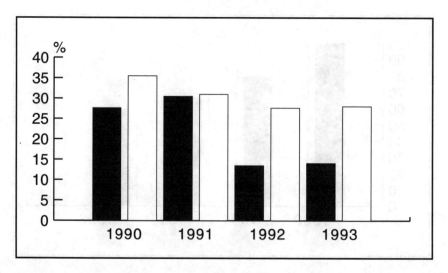

LA TRANSFORMATION DU STATUT DU GIAT: POURQUOI? COMMENT? QUELS RESULTATS?

Jean-Hugues Monier

Ces dernières années, les structures industrielles de défense ont beaucoup évolué en France. L'événement le plus significatif à cet égard est sans doute la désétatisation au plan juridique du GIAT (Groupement Industriel des Armements Terrestres) qui a été concrétisée le 1er juillet 1990 par la création de GIAT Industries. Pourquoi et comment cette transformation s'est-elle opérée et quel est le bilan qu'on peut dresser quatre ans et demi plus tard? C'est ce que Jean-Hugues Monier a expliqué dans son intervention au Colloque Economique de l'OTAN. Une expérience qui devrait principalement intéresser les pays d'Europe de l'Est où plusieurs entreprises de défense sont encore des arsenaux d'Etat.

Jean-Hugues Monier réprésente la Délégation générale pour l'armement du Ministère de la Défense de la France.

En France, il existe plusieurs types d'acteurs industriels qui exercent une activité dans le domaine de la défense. Le contrôle de l'Etat sur ces entreprises s'exerce bien évidemment de manière différente lorsque l'on s'adresse à des entreprises privées ou publiques. Mon propos a pour objet d'exposer une expérience française dans le domaine de l'évolution des structures industrielles de défense.

En effet, en s'inspirant de la situation que connaissent aujourd'hui les pays d'Europe de l'Est où beaucoup d'entreprises de défense sont encore des arsenaux d'état, il me semble intéressant d'expliquer l'opération que les services officiels français ont effectuée en 1990 en créant la société Giat Industries dans le domaine des armements terrestres. Comme l'indique le titre de cette table ronde, mon propos s'intéressera en particulier à l'impact de cette opération sur les personnels.

Le Contexte Général.

En 1971 a été créé le Groupement Industriel des Armements Terrestres (GIAT), ensemble industriel puissant polyvalent et intégré de quelques 17 000 personnes, chargé de la maîtrise d'oeuvre de systèmes d'armes complexes (véhicules blindés et artillerie), de l'étude et de la fabrication des munitions et armements associés.

L'objectif de cette création était de séparer au sein de la Direction des Armements Terrestres (DAT) de la Délégation Générale pour l'Armement du Ministère de la Défense, les activités industrielles (études, développement, fabrication) des missions de l'Etat-client et puissance publique assurées par la partie restante dite étatique de la DAT. Ainsi étaient clarifiées les responsabilités.

Puis le 1er juillet 1990 voyait la naissance de l'entreprise nationale GIAT Industries, résultat non pas d'une privatisation du GIAT, mais d'une désétatisation du GIAT au plan juridique, le capital de la société étant détenu en quasi-totalité par l'Etat.

Pourquoi en est-on arrivé là ? Comment a été réalisée cette transformation et quels sont les résultats après 4 ans et demi de fonctionnement de GIAT Industries ? Telles sont les questions auxquelles cette intervention va s'efforcer de répondre.

Pourquoi la Transformation du Statut du GIAT ?

La réponse simple et globale est la suivante : lorsque le marché est porteur, il est possible de s'accommoder des rigidités des règles de l'administration qui n'ont pas été conçues pour des activités de production et de commercialisation mais pour garantir la régularité d'activités d'approvisionnement. Lorsque la situation devient difficile, les handicaps et les faisceaux de contraintes obérant l'efficacité deviennent insurmontables, par rapport à des concurrents agressifs et qui n'ont pas à faire face à ces mêmes handicaps.

Quels sont donc les handicaps du GIAT, partie intégrante de l'administration? On peut schématiquement les classer en six catégories :

- l'isolement industriel, le GIAT en tant que partie intégrante de l'Etat sans personnalité juridique propre n'était pas capable de se comporter comme un industriel à part entière dans ses relations avec l'industrie française et a fortiori étrangère. Ce statut devenait en particulier un obstacle insurmontable à la prise de participations dans des sociétés françaises ;
- les handicaps en matière de personnel, les règles budgétaires nécessitent de prévoir les besoins en matière de personnel, lesquels pour des contingences financières ne peuvent souvent pas être satisfaits. Dans la plupart des cas, ces règles ne permettent les recrutements que par concours : elles ne sont donc pas adaptées aux besoins éminemment fluctuants aux plans qualitatifs et quantitatifs d'une activité industrielle internationale. La gestion de ces personnels est extrêmement lourde compte tenu de la multiplicité des catégories. Même lorsque les droits d'embauche peuvent être obtenus, il faut pouvoir rémunérer les candidats aux prix du marché, ce que ne permettent souvent pas les règles de la fonction publique. C'est pour de tels motifs que le GIAT s'est ainsi retrouvé depuis toujours avec un pourcentage d'ingénieurs par rapport à l'effectif total bien inférieur à celui d'industriels similaires.

Inversement, lorsque les perspectives d'activité l'ont rendu nécessaire, il a fallu une très longue concertation interministérielle avant de pouvoir aboutir à des dégagements des cadres ;
- la dépendance et la lourdeur commerciales: GIAT commercialisait ses produits à l'exportation au travers de sociétés spécialisées qui avaient le monopole de la commercialisation des produits du GIAT sur leur zone géographique, mais qui travaillaient aussi au bénéfice d'autres industriels. GIAT n'avait donc pas d'autonomie commerciale et il pouvait apparaître des divergences d'intérêts ;
- l'absence d'autonomie financière: le GIAT ne pouvait pas emprunter ce qui limitait ses ambitions en matière d'anticipation, d'investissement ;
- les contraintes en matière de diversification civile: la loi d'Allarde de 1791 interdit aux arsenaux de concurrencer l'industrie privée pour des besoins autres que ceux de l'Etat. De ce fait, le GIAT se trouvait être l'un des rares industriels dont l'activité était à 100 % orientée vers l'armement avec les handicaps que cette situation représente lorsque le marché est en contraction ;
- les lourdeurs administratives, outre celles déjà citées en matière de personnels ou de commercialisation par exemple, l'application du code des marchés publics, les contrôles a priori des marchés entraînent des délais en matière d'acquisition, y compris pour les besoins export, incompatibles avec la rapidité de réaction exigée d'un industriel. En particulier, GIAT ne pouvait pas facilement faire preuve de solidarité durable vis-à-vis d'un partenaire industriel qui lui aurait permis d'accéder à un contrat à l'exportation. Les règles de gestion administrative se cumulaient avec les règles de gestion industrielle.

Comment s'est fait la Transformation du Statut ?

Mi 1988, un plan stratégique a été élaboré pour le GIAT. Celui-ci faisait l'état des lieux et analysait notamment les causes de la situation actuelle, les objectifs que doit avoir le GIAT rénové et les axes stratégiques pour atteindre ceux-ci.

Parallèlement une intense concertation avec les organisations syndicales était organisée au niveau du Ministre. Durant cette concertation, le plan stratégique a été discuté et amendé, les possibilités d'évolution du GIAT examinées, les orientations en matière de régime d'emploi des différentes catégories de personnels et les mesures d'adaptation des effectifs précisées, les principes de l'accord d'entreprise et les dispositions en matière de formation arrêtés.

En particulier, il a été prévu que les personnels bénéficient d'un délai important avant d'opter pour la société (ou de demander une autre affectation) pendant lequel ils étaient mis à disposition de la société. Un protocole d'accord relatif aux conséquences pour les personnels civils de GIAT de la création d'une société nationale a été signé en janvier 1990 par le Délégué Général pour l'Armement et trois organisations syndicales.

Le Ministère de la défense a procédé à deux opérations de déflation des effectifs ouvriers (indépendantes du changement de statut car liées à la charge actuelle et prévisible). L'une décidée en juin 1987 portant sur 2.850 postes, l'autre en mars 1989 portant sur 1.200 postes, se traduisant par des retraites anticipées au-delà de 55 ans avec bonification d'ancienneté, des mutations et des départs volontaires. Un dispositif incitatif a été mis en place (indemnités de conversion et de départ volontaire). Ces déflations se sont effectuées jusqu'en 1992 inclus.

Dès l'annonce de la décision du Ministre, les réflexions préliminaires au sein du ministère ont été amplifiées et un certain nombre de travaux d'évaluation ont été entrepris ainsi que des simulations économiques diverses. Ces évaluations ont nécessité l'intervention de divers organismes extérieurs : sociétés d'audit, cabinets conseil, les commissaires aux apports ... Elles ont permis l'établissement du bilan d'entrée et des comptes d'exploitation prévisionnels de la nouvelle société.

Par ailleurs, des travaux sur l'impact budgétaire de cette transformation étaient conduits. En effet, l'attribution à la société d'une marge bénéficiaire et d'une marge pour études libres, le coût du renforcement en matière grise et des évolutions de charges sociales de même que l'assujettissement de la nouvelle société à la TVA suivant le régime de droit commun induisent une augmentation de coût pour le client budgétaire. Certains de ces surcoûts tels le supplément de TVA sont neutres pour le Budget de l'Etat puisqu'ils se traduisent par des recettes supplémentaires.

Ces différents travaux ont nécessité de nombreux contacts avec d'autres départements ministériels, notamment la Fonction Publique pour les aspects personnels et le Ministère des Finances pour les aspects budgétaires et financiers. Ces divers contacts ont abouti notamment :
- à l'élaboration d'un projet de loi qui a été présenté le 16/08/89 en Conseil des Ministres, discuté et voté en novembre et décembre 89 par le Parlement, la loi étant promulguée le 27/12/89 ;
- à la constitution effective de la société : décrets autorisant la participation financière de l'Etat, nomination au Conseil d'Administration, première réunion du Conseil le 26/06/90, nomination du président, arrêté fixant la liste des droits, biens et obligations attachés aux activités des établissements industriels de la DAT constituant le GIAT et apportés à la société GIAT industries, assemblées générales ordinaire et extraordinaire ;
- à la fixation de la dotation en capital de la société à 1000 MF pris sur le budget de la Défense.

La création de GIAT industrie au 1er juillet 1990 a en outre nécessité de procéder à un arrêté des comptes du GIAT et donc d'établir les documents comptables réglementaires habituellement produits en fin d'exercice.

De nombreux autres textes contractuels ont par ailleurs dû être rédigés sur des sujets très divers : formation dans les écoles, redevances d'étude et de contrôle, mise à disposition de matériels appartenant aux armées, utilisation de pistes, remboursement par GIAT Industries des dépenses relatives aux personnels mis à sa disposition et le fonctionnement des antennes étatiques... Cette dernière convention traite en particulier les relations avec GIAT industries des antennes étatiques instaurées dans les établissements de l'ex-GIAT et chargées de divers travaux transitoirement restés à la charge de l'Etat : gestion et rémunération des personnels étatiques restés à disposition de GIAT industries, indemnisations des personnels mutés ou dégagés des cadres de la fonction publique, apurement d'opérations comptables et financières des établissements du GIAT non reprises par la société.

Quelques premiers résultats.

Il serait présomptueux de vouloir dresser dès aujourd'hui un bilan définitif du changement de statut du GIAT pour au moins deux raisons :
- les résultats d'une telle opération ne peuvent s'apprécier que sur la durée tant les bouleversements dans l'organisation et ceux liés aux diverses restructurations sont importantes. Encore convient-il de noter que le paysage budgétaire s'est assombri par rapport à celui qui prévalait lors de la préparation du changement de statut, avec les réductions importantes des budgets de la Défense qui ont eu des répercussions non négligeables sur GIAT industries : annulation de commandes, réduction de cadence, étalement de programmes
- la difficulté est par ailleurs de comparer la situation de GIAT industries aujourd'hui, non pas avec celle du GIAT au 30 juillet 1990 mais avec la situation que connaîtrait le GIAT aujourd'hui si le changement de statut n'était pas intervenu, alors que le besoin de souplesse et de réactivité n'a fait que s'amplifier.

Le changement de statut devait créer les conditions permettant à GIAT Industries de se développer et de s'adapter à la conjoncture nationale et internationale. On ne peut nier que ce résultat ait été obtenu et un certain nombre de résultats positifs ont été atteints en particulier parce que GIAT industries a pu procéder autour de lui à une restructuration du paysage de l'armement terrestre français. Un certain nombre d'acquisitions ou de participations ont également concerné des sociétés étrangères. Ces acquisitions ont permis la rationalisation, la diversification et l'accroissement des forces commerciales. Naturellement beaucoup reste à faire au sein de l'Europe qui, par exemple, dispose de surcapacités importantes dans les domaines des munitions et des véhicules blindés.

Dans le domaine du personnel, GIAT s'est considérablement renforcé en matière grise, son effectif de cadres passant en deux ans de 1200 à 1600.

L'effort de diversification s'est traduit par la création d'une branche spéciale GITECH qui a poursuivi les efforts déjà engagés (shelters par exemple) et s'est développée dans les métiers nouveaux et complémentaires (robotique par exemple) pour le bénéfice de secteurs variés.

On notera également 3 autres domaines où GIAT industries a fait un effort important :

- en matière de recherche et de développement, les dépenses ont représenté l'an dernier environ 15 % du chiffre d'affaires dont près de la moitié en autofinancement ;
- en matière d'action commerciale, l'effort s'est traduit par d'importantes prises de commande à l'exportation ;
- en matière de politique d'achats, une action vigoureuse a été conduite avec l'objectif de peser sur les coûts de série, l'effort s'étant porté en priorité sur le programme de char de combat Leclerc.

A côté de ces éléments incontestablement positifs, plusieurs point noirs demeurent. On peut en particulier regretter que cette opération n'ait pas pu être réalisée quelques années plus tôt lorsque la conjoncture était meilleure.

THE IMPACT OF DEFENCE INDUSTRY PRIVATIZATION ON THE LABOUR MARKET: A WESTERN VIEW

Franz-Lothar Altmann

While it is virtually impossible to compare the defence infrastructures of each of the former East Bloc and Soviet economies on common ground, there are some similarities which help us understand the defence privatization challenge more clearly. Franz-Lothar Altmann says that the regional and "monocultural" implantation of defence industries in these regions, and the potential negative political/security impact of rapid defence privatization if it is done too hastily today, are the reality which the East and West must face.

Dr. Franz-Lothar Altmann is the Deputy Director of the Südost-Institut in Munich.

Privatization and Employment

Does there necessarily exist a close correlation between privatization of state owned enterprises (SOEs) and the increase of unemployment? In theory this question will be answered "yes": It is common knowledge that in socialist state enterprises excess employment is normal, and every private owner will first try to diminish those costs which can be reduced without any capital infusion. However, the term "privatization" is often used just for the formal change of the legal framework of the enterprises, i.e. the transformation of a state enterprise directly administered by a ministry into a joint stock company where at least for some time the state still holds the majority - if not all - of the shares. In such a (pre-)privatization case, which e.g. in Poland is called "commercialization" - the management will think about reduced employment only if from the state, the capital owner, distinct pressure is exerted. This, however, cannot really be expected since the politicians want to be reelected, and therefore they will not be very eager to announce unpopular decisions like workers' layoffs.

But the situation becomes different if private capital takes over, as the interest of the investor will be oriented towards profit-making, and any reduction of costs - here labour costs - will and must be examined. A different situation also occurs if the shares of the company - after commercialization - are distributed among the employees. In this case, of course, even so-called privatization should not lead to large layoffs. Who will act against his/her own employment interest?

Unemployment in Eastern Europe

In fact, overall employment decreased already before privatization of the large SOEs became a serious issue. It started in most of the former socialist countries due to the drastic decline in output which followed the collapse of the Eastern trade cooperation system, CMEA. Massive unemployment is primarily linked with economic decline, a conclusion which we can derive also from developments in Western market economies where private ownership of production predominates.

If we look at the following table, it seems that the highest increases in unemployment in the former socialist countries appear where the loss of markets and lack of competitiveness were/are greatest (Albania, Bulgaria, Croatia, Slovenia, the Slovak Republic, Romania), or where restructuring had really started earlier but only half-heartedly (Poland, Hungary?), or where no specific protective accompanying measures had been applied, like the introduction of a very favorite rate of exchange in the then Czech and Slovak Federal Republic.

Country	Change of Employment 1990-92	Rate of Unemployment end 1993	Number (1000s) of Unemployed, end 1993
Albania	- 21,7	25 (?)	301,3
Bulgaria	- 28,7	16,4	626,1
Croatia	- 22,1	16,9	243,1
Czech Republic	- 8,8	3,5	185,2
Slovak Republic	- 13,5	14,4	368,1
Hungary	- 12,1	12,1	632,1
Poland	- 12,6	15,7	2889,6
Romania	- 4,5	10,1	1170,0
Slovenia	- 13,5	14,9	137,1
Russia	- 4,2**	1,1**	835,5**
Ukraine	- 5,6*	0,4*	83,9*
Belarus	- 6,0*	1,3*	66,2*
Baltic States	- 4,3	3,2	123,4

* These are official data. Estimates on real unemployment are of course much higher due to hidden unemployment.

** These figures cannot be taken seriously. They were reported officially to the ECE-secretariat. However, the Ministry of Labour released information in mid-July 1994 that the total number of unemployed was approaching the 10 million level, which equals an unemployment rate of 13 percent! Russian TV, 20 July 1994.

Source: ECE, Economic Survey of Europe in 1993-1994 and national statistics.

So far no direct correlation between progress in large scale privatization and the increase in unemployment can be definitely assessed. In particular, if we compare the Czech Republic and Bulgaria we can see that privatization of state-owned enterprises in the former has been pushed ahead in an amazing way, whereas too many political and other barriers have blocked progress in privatization in the latter so far. However, the unemployment figures present the Czech Republic as the transformation society with by the far lowest percentage (if we do not take the unemployment percentages of the CIS-countries as real), and Bulgaria is ranking among the three top countries with regard to unemployment!

But this observation does not mean that there is no correlation between privatization and increase in unemployment. In general, of course, the unquestioned excess employment in former big socialist industry will have to be reduced to improve productivity and competitiveness, but the core question seems to be how well prepared the respective countries are to face mass privatization, and what kind of structural deficiencies have to be overcome. Of course, there are substantial differences, as the relative weight of problematic heavy industry enterprises varies from country to country. It is obvious that privatization of these companies threatens employment much more than does privatization of industries that are closer to consumers' needs. Consumer industries have a better chance of restructuring their production patterns according to international competition and acquiring foreign capital than heavy industries, as the latter has overproduction in all these countries. This means that in countries with already high (open or hidden) unemployment the threat of a possible increase of unemployment as a result of further privatization is a highly sensitive political issue. This is in particularly true if we see that these are the countries where privatization is limping forward.

Defence Industry in the Former CMEA - a Special Case?

In all countries, both West and East, the defence industry has been and still is a special case - with regard to the relationship between producer and buyer, the employment situation, and the share of private entrepreneurship in decision-making. However, where the West has competition, this was not the case in the East. Here, a distinct division of labour was established, apart from the all-dominating hegemonical Soviet military production complex which had to secure the absolute independence and self-sufficiency of the procurement of the Soviet army. On the other hand it was obvious that self-sufficiency was not possible for any of the socialist satellite countries. What emerged was that very different patterns of weapons industries developed according to traditional experiences (e.g. Czechoslovakia) and to the specific requirements derived from the socialist division of labour.

The Employment Dimension

First of all it is striking how much the employment dimensions in the respective former Warsaw Pact countries vary. Although a general caveat must be placed, because statistical data on weapons industry employment were and to some extent still are subject to political motives and intentions, most of the countries concerned now tend to give rather correct figures. Variations, however, must occur when general figures are quoted representing the employment which either directly or indirectly is related to the military industries. The following figures should be taken as direct employment in weapons industries.

Thus, in 1990 in the then CSFR, 250,000 persons were said to be employed in the defence industry representing approximately 3.5 percent of overall employment. There was a clear concentration on the Slovak Republic where about 150,000 people worked in these industries making up 6.2 percent of overall employment and about 20 percent of the output of the machinery industry of that part of the Czechoslovak Federation![1] This regional concentration had several reasons. One was that Slovakia was more distant from the Western enemy border and closer to the neighbouring Warsaw Pact countries Poland Soviet Union and Hungary. But it was also a means of developmental strategy to build up new industries - and new factories were erected for the construction of T-Tanks and other heavy Warsaw Pact arms - in the underdeveloped regions of Slovakia to improve the employment situation there. In good old socialist years the Slovaks did not at all complain about these industries, in particular because they provided also excellent export opportunities. But already in the late 1980s scepticism came up when some of the foreign buyers had problems with payment (Libya, Syria, Iraq), and prospects for further export development became rather doubtful. Due to the political decision in Prague to stop exports of weapons and because of these payment difficulties, arms production in Slovakia was severely hit and employment decreased considerably. This was mainly because conversion to civilian production turned out to be much more complicated in Slovakia than in the Czech lands, and also the Slovak product-mix is much worse suited for general export than that of the Czech Republic. The latter even seems to have good chances to sell its L-139 airplane to the US Forces[2], whereas, for example, work force in ZTS Dubnica, one of the biggest arms factories, declined from 14,000 in 1988 to 7,000 in 1993[3]. But this occurred - not after privatization - but just because of diminished demand.

For Poland in 1990, employment in the weapons industry reached about 260,000 persons[4] which corresponded to 1.6 percent of overall employment. As in Czechoslovakia enterprises producing military equipment were not supervised by the Ministry of Defence but by the Ministry of Trade and Industry which means that no real protection against reduction of production existed. The output of the Polish defence industry fell by 77 percent between 1988 and end of 1992[5] as a result of budgetary constraints, heavy cuts in military expenditures and an extreme slump in exports. But it must be stressed that most of these firms also produced civilian goods.

Bulgaria had 110,000 people employed in its arms industry in 1989[6] which totalled about 2.5 percent of overall employment. As in Poland, the Bulgarian Ministry of Industry was responsible for the regular production of the military enterprises whereas the Ministry of Defence supervised only repair activities. The serious economic problems that struck the Bulgarian economy in the early 1990s included controversial discussions on increases or rather decreases of arms exports. This cost Ludzehev - the first civilian minister of defence, who defended the exports - his post. This situation also caused reductions in production and thus unemployment threats which led to several demonstrations of concerned workers as early as 1992.

The Hungarian defence industry reached the peak of its development in the mid-1980s when it employed between 20,000 and 30,000 people[7], representing about 0.6 percent of overall employment. The value of military production at that time (20 billion forint) corresponded to less than 2 percent of industrial output. Eighty percent of the output of Hungary's defence industry was exported, 12 percent of sales went to countries outside the Warsaw Pact contributing successfully to the country's hard currency incomes. This explains why the end of the CMEA and Warsaw Pact hit Hungary's defence industry more than those of the partner countries. However, it had the advantage that most of these enterprises had a product-mix where the greater part of the production was civilian oriented. This could be supportive for the necessary conversion attempts of today. Anyhow the value of defence production had decreased dramatically: in 1993 it was only 6 billion Ft of which 95 percent were exported[8].

At this NATO conference Daniel Daianu stated that approximately 100,000 people are employed in the defence-related factories in Romania. Considering that former president Ceausescu had declared, at the end of the 1970s, that the country had reached self-sufficiency in the production of military hardware[9], and since then that military experts have argued that 75 percent of Romania's armament requirements for its 200,000 man army were achieved, by domestic production[10], this figure seems relatively small. But observers also pointed out that the Romanian army was rather poorly equipped[11]. Of course, the economic downfall of Romania has already impacted its defence industry and thus defence employment. For example, it was reported that one of the three defence industry "regies autonomes" (state-owned concerns into which these factories had been organized, which are not foreseen for privatization. Law 15/1990), GIARA, reduced employment from 21,000 in 1991 to 18,000 at the end of 1993[12]!

As Keith Bush has stated in an article published in spring 1994[13] figures on the size of the Soviet military-industrial complex were treated as state secrets, giving good reasons for extremely diverging estimates. Already the number of factories belonging to the military industry, which officials would like to see at around 1,500 (plus some 200 research institutions), sometimes even reaches

10,000. Even more diverse exist documenting the number of people employed in this sector. In his article Bush quotes some officials who spoke about only 4.5 million people, but he also mentioned ITAR-TASS which reported some 15-20 million[14]. Finally he quoted newspapers[15] with "authoritative sources" who spoke of "some 40 million people currently employed in the overall sphere of ensuring the country's defence capability and security".

Yuri Andreev is probably close to reality when he speaks in his conference paper of some seven million people directly employed (and 16 million indirectly) in the defence-oriented industry of Russia which itself inherited about 70 per cent of the capacities of the former Soviet Union. Half of all firms in Moscow and three-quarters of those in St. Petersburg belong to the military-industrial complex! The complicated financial situation already caused substantial reductions in the production volume of these enterprises. News reports from Chelyabinsk, where more than 30 defence-oriented enterprises are located, say that employment has already been reduced by 50 percent through unpaid holidays. The firms did not have the money to pay the wages because the government did not pay for the production ordered from Moscow[16].

These rather cursory attempts to quantify the employment factor of the defence industries in some of the former socialist countries have disclosed two aspects. Firstly, all quantitative statements on employment in the defence industries must be handled with extreme caution. During the time of the Cold War confrontation this sector belonged to that part of the economy which was kept secret in terms of production as well as of employment. Furthermore, many of the respective factories performed dual production (civilian and military). But when the agenda turns to defence industry employment, it is never clearly explained whether the respective employment figures relate to each enterprise, or only to its defence-related part. Substantial understating is therefore very easy, depending on the purpose and target of the statement.

The second finding is that - regardless of the above-mentioned uncertainties concerning the data - the quantitative dimension of defence-related employment in industry varies significantly from country to country. This means that the importance for overall employment differs dramatically, as does the political dimension - i.e. the possible barrier to further restructuring or even privatization of these industries.

Privatization versus National Sovereignty/Security

The end of the Cold War confrontation and the dissolution of the Warsaw Pact did not do away with all security fears and considerations concerning possible conflict situations. This is obvious and understandable for the NIS as well as for the former satellite countries in Eastern Europe. In the future, Russia wants to remain a military superpower, which of course requires a strong domestic defence industry. On the other hand this distinct attitude must put the smaller East-central and South-East European countries, and naturally also the non-Russian NIS into great insecurity, particularly as Russian nationalistic overtones become more pronounced. There is no hard currency to purchase the necessary equipment in the West now. Therefore existing capacities must be used for maintaining at least some defence strength. Abrupt privatization can only endanger the preservation of these capacities.

Thus the question arises what and how much of the existing defence industries must remain national (state) property in order to secure national sovereignty and security? It is not at all surprising that the defence industry was at first kept off the lists of enterprises to be privatized in most of the countries. In Bulgaria, for example, a three-year moratorium on privatization of enterprises producing or selling military equipment was imposed by the Parliament[17].

The Warsaw Pact Division of Labour in Arms Production

In the Eastern Bloc the defence industries were organized according to the intra-bloc division of labour. In no other sector was product specialization and cooperation as developed as in the arms industries. However, this specialization entailed first of all an extreme orientation on the needs of the USSR and secondly on intensive intra-CMEA trade. The result was that production for all these countries exceeded their domestic needs by far, causing enormous marketing problems today, after the end of CMEA and Warsaw Pact.

A country like Ukraine, which has a heavy local concentration of the former-Soviet military production, is now almost completely dependent on sales to its larger Russian neighbor in substantial portions of its industrial sector. This is also somewhat dangerous to Ukranian sovereignty. On the other hand Ukraine's military industry is also dependent on deliveries from Russia, which makes it difficult to quickly build up an independent domestic defence industry.

For some of the Eastern countries (Czechoslovakia, Bulgaria and Poland) weapons also were a very profitable export item not only in intra-CMEA trade but also for hard currency trade - in particular in trade with Third World countries (Libya, Iran, Iraq, Syria, etc.).

After the end of the Cold War, the subsequent dissolution of the Warsaw Pact, and the disintegration of the CMEA, the profitability of arms production had disappeared almost completely because all of a sudden intra-CMEA was converted into hard currency trade, and the first area to be to cut was arms purchases from the former allies. But also exports to the Third World became difficult due to international embargoes and payment problems of the customers. The West disapproved arms exports to some former good customer countries because of the ultimate destination (security, terrorism): Iraq, Syria, Libya. For example, in 1987 the USSR exported armament worth US-$ 23 billion, but in

1993 Russia could sell only arms for US-$ 2 billion, whereas capacities would allow an annual export volume of US-$ 30 billion [18]! So, why should foreign or domestic private investors be interested in these industries where almost no market - at least in the immediate and medium-term future - exists?

But even worse, the new competition for arms exports among the former allies began after the break-up of Warsaw Pact and CMEA, affecting prices very negatively. The Czech Republic and Poland competed for deliveries of T-72 tanks to Pakistan, and the Slovak Republic and Poland tried to sell armored vehicles there. Pakistan succeeded in reducing the purchase prices, finally buying only in the Slovak Republic.

Peculiarities of the Eastern Defence Industries Concerning Privatization

As I explained, the defence industry in the former socialist countries is a special case, and cannot be compared with other industries where privatization is already more or less underway. In particular with regard to privatization there are additional features which might create more question marks when speaking about its impact on the labour markets.

First of all it must be considered that the main customers of these factories are the governments which all (except the Czech Republic) are suffering from large deficits in their budgets. Over-capacities have already been, and will be further, on reduced regardless of possible privatization. In Russia it is said that a reduction of more than 50 percent has been achieved, and similar reductions have taken place in the other former Warsaw Pact countries. But it is not clear to what extent these reductions in production have led also to lay-offs in the work force. National security considerations as well as political pressure on the governments have blocked such attempts. This means, however, that these defence enterprises are probably in a worse economic situation (uncertain, hazy future prospects, huge over-employment, enormous debts) than "normal" industrial enterprises, which makes it more difficult to think about privatization.

Another important point is that practically all the smaller former Warsaw Pact countries proclaim the general aim to become incorporated into NATO structures which forces the weapons industries in these countries to restructure their technical equipment according to NATO requirements. However, for this purpose, investment must meet financial means. Normal (domestic) privatization certainly cannot provide this, and foreign investors will be very cautious and selective: So far only engagements in the Czech Republic and in Poland are known (SOFMA, Thompson).

On the other hand it is particularly important that the arms industries have the best qualified workforce available. Layoffs in the course of reducing over-capacities (restructuring) and/or privatization trigger large "brain drains" which already can be observed in some countries today. This is happening in Russia, where an estimated 1.5 to 1.8 million highly skilled scholars and specialists will be lost by the end of the 1990s. Today's main motives for emigration are ethnic (minority) problems and poor financial and material conditions at work and at home[19]. If larger layoffs occur in the defence industries, the brain drain -particularly from the NIS - will accelerate, as these industries employ most of the highly-qualified researchers. Yuri Andreev quoted in his presentation at the Colloquium, that in the fundamental sciences half of all expenditures were connected with the military, and up to 70 percent in space research! Where will these specialists find new jobs, if not abroad in countries trying to develop their own defence capacities, like Pakistan, India, Iran, or Iraq? Already, in South Korea there are 155 Russian scientists employed including special designers for fighter airplanes[20].

Given the fact that the best-qualified and skilled workers are in the arms industries, it should be easier, to draft a retraining and reallocating program for these people than for others. These enterprises could be more attractive to foreign investors because of the better trained labour force, but also for other kinds of non-defence production activities. It is, however, not certain whether this scenario fits the national security considerations of the respective governments described above.

Two additional important points should not be forgotten. Firstly, workers/employees in the military sector have a rather strong lobby: the military. This group will certainly play the national security card in their own vested interest (Russia). Since a rather high number of deputies in these countries' parliaments are either officers or are related to the military-industrial complex, decisions on reductions of the defence industry have difficulty finding the necessary majorities.

Secondly, we must consider the fact that production was very often concentrated in specific regions. Layoffs there can have over-proportional unemployment impacts on entire regions. Andreev told us that in Russia, for example, half of all firms in Moscow and some three quarters in St. Petersburg belong to the military-industrial complex. Russia has ten so-called "secret" towns totally devoted to nuclear defence production, and dozens of other smaller secret towns producing other types of armaments. Names like Chelyabinsk, Sverdlovsk, Krasnoyarsk or Tomsk are well known even in the West in this respect. But also such concentrated regions can be found in other countries, such as Middle Slovakia.

These two special characteristics can become great political barriers against too rapid privatization or restructuring which allegedly will be connected with large-scale layoffs. In 37 regions of the Russian Federation more than 400,000 workers already demonstrated for "constructive measures" of the government in the beginning of June 1994! It is only normal that nationalist and/or conservative politicians and political parties must be extremely interested in supporting such actions, and in wielding the fear of unemployment for counteracting the realization of privatization and restructuring.

Defence privatization may reach even more into basic political issues. In 1990, when Vaclav Havel took the quick decision that the then Czech and Slovak Federative Republic should immediately stop the production of armaments, this became one of the strong arguments for the separation of the Slovaks. They claimed that the negative employment effects hit mainly Slovakia whereas the Czechs harvest the international positive reputation related to the announced closure of the defence industry!

Finally, privatized defence industry will need much more capital for modernization than other industries. Normal domestic voucher privatization, however, cannot provide the necessary fresh capital, whereas foreign investors could - if they are allowed, and are interested find appropriate conditions. But if this does not happen and only domestic attempts of privatization are applied, larger lay-offs will be unavoidable, because without the necessary capital most of the respective industries will certainly be unable to compete on the very demanding international markets. Of course, the lay-offs will differ in size due to the structure and the technological level of production, and will also have differing political impacts in the various countries. It will be certainly much more difficult for Russian factories than for Czech producers. There is an example of a small Czech producer (Ceska Zbrojovka, privatized in 1992) who managed to survive and even now to compete without the infusion of foreign capital!

Conclusions

In this short discussion paper I attempted to underline that the defence industry in the former socialist countries is a very special case indeed, regarding the question of changes on the labour market. Although the dimension of production and thus of employment in these industries varies significantly among the respective countries, some features seem to be common to all of them. This is certainly the regional concentration of the defence industries affecting whole regions in monocultural manners, but also the political dimension and the very probable impacts of closures of defence-related factories on the political environment.

The general security uncertainty which all of the smaller former satellite countries feel - vis-à-vis Russia and also vis-à-vis possible turmoils in some other NIS-states - does not leave room for much contemplation on further and larger reductions of national defence capacities. On the other hand, domestic politics in Russia (i.e. the unstable political situation) allow nationalistic and conservative pressure groups in the military and in politics to bloc any attempt to "weaken" the international military position of the country.

Therefore, we should not expect privatization to progress too rapidly in the Eastern defence industries. But what in the meantime? Other solutions must be found, because restructuring and modernization of the defence industries is unavoidable. Countries, such as the Czech Republic, the Slovak Republic and Hungary, have found their intermediate solutions: state holdings or consortiums with strong state influence of those enterprises which could not be successfully privatized so far.

Footnotes:
1. Douglas L. Clarke: Eastern Europe's Troubled Arms Industries: Part I. In: RFE/RL Research Report, Vol. 3, No. 14, 8 April 1994.
2. Aero chce dodávat L-139 ozbrojeným silám USA. In: Mladá Fronta Dnes, 4 July 1994.
3. Defense News, 15-21 Nov. 1993, p. 25; quoted after D.L.Clarke, op.cit.
4. D.L.Clarke, op. cit.
5. Polska Zbrojna, 8 Dec. 1992; quoted after D.L.Clarke, op. cit.
6. Antoaneta Dimitrova: The Plight of the Bulgarian Arms Industry. In: RFE/RL Research Report, Vol.2, No. 7, 12 Febr. 1993.
7. The smaller figure was given by Miklós Karácsondi: The Defenceless Defence Industry. In: Hungarian Economic Review, No. 17, Dec. 1993. The higher figure is from Douglas L. Clarke: Eastern Europe's Troubled Arms Industries: Part II. In: REFE/RL Research Report, Vol.3, No. 21, 27 May 1994.
8. Magyar Hírlap, 5 Nov. 1993.
9. Ilie Ceausescu: Romania, Vol. 20, Bucharest 1981, p. 510.
10. Jonathan Eyal: Romania - Between Appearances and Realities. In: J. Eyal (Ed.): The Warsaw Pact and the Balkans, RUSI Defence Studies, Houdmills: Macmillan, 1981, p. 80.
11. J. Eyal, op. cit., p. 81, and D. L: Clarke, op. cit. (II), p. 36.
12. Fragmente dintr-un raport cutremurator. In: Romania Mare, No. 203, 27 May 1994. Conversia industriei de aparare. In: Express, No. 17, 3-9 May 1994.
13. Keith Bush: Aspects of Military Conversion in Russia. In: RFE/RL Research Report, Vol. 3, No. 14, 8 April 1994.
14. ITAR-TASS and Interfax, 11 and 12 March 1994.
15. Komsomolskaya prawda and Izvestiya, 16 Sept. 1993, and Krasnaya zvezda, 11 Sept. 1993.
16. Russian TV, 16 June 1994.
17. BTA (in English), 23 June 1993, published in FBIS-EEU-93-141, 16 June 1993, p.4. Quoted from D.L.Clarke, op. cit. (II), p. 31.
18. Vice Premier Oleg Soskovets in a government meeting. DDP/ADN, 12 June 1994.
19. Stanislav Simanovsky: Brain Drain from the Former Soviet Union and the Position of the International Community. In: Osteuropa-Wirtschaft, 1/1994, pp. 17 ff.
20. S. Simanovsky, op.cit., p. 18.

PANEL V

Role of Foreign Investment in Defence Industry Privatization, Taking into Account Privatization Experiences in other Fields

Chair: Daniel George, Director, NATO Economics Directorate

Panelists: Daniel Daianu
Kaja Kell
Robert Watters
Riccardo Iozzo
Thierry Malleret

POST-COMMUNIST DEFENCE INDUSTRY RESTRUCTURING: THE ROLE OF FOREIGN DIRECT INVESTMENT

Daniel Daianu

Privatization won't convert the defence industries by itself, says Daniel Daianu. The slump is what is really cutting them down to size. Meanwhile the world is becoming more unstable, and Eastern European countries feel they're living in a security vacuum. They know they have a saleable commodity of proven value - arms. They also know that Western protectionism is keeping their consumer goods out. The real question is how to get the West to face up to this, and invest politically in Eastern Europe. Countries with the most foreign direct investment do better economically. Why not go for foreign political investment as well?

Dr. Daniel Daianu is the Chief Economic Advisor of the National Bank of Romania.

The Magnitude of Change

What is unique about post-communist transformation in Europe is that it implies several simultaneously evolving processes: large-scale institutional change, economic (industrial) restructuring, structural adjustment and macro-stabilization. When comparisons are made with other countries one should not underestimate the lack of institutional ingredients of a market environment (in post-communist societies) and the enormous inherited distortions in the allocation of resources.

Not infrequently, people — both in the West and the East — do not realize the magnitude of this transformation. This is, perhaps, the main reason for the emergence and persistence of too many false expectations among people, at large, and policy-makers, regarding the feasible speed of real change. These expectations lie behind the development of social tensions and the genesis of wrong macro-policy decisions.

The most telling indicator of the magnitude of post-communist transformation is the extent of required reallocation of resources as compared to the ability of the system to undergo wide range and quick change.

In eastern Europe (and in Russia even more), the structure of the economy and the size of resource misallocation have put the system under exceptional strain once the combination of internal and external shocks occurred. What are major implications of the existence of such strain? One is that these economies

251

can very easily become unstable and that their capacity to absorb shocks is pretty low.

Policy-makers face extremely painful trade-offs and that, in most of the cases, unless sufficient external support is available, the room for manoeuvre is dangerously small. Policy-makers have to sail between the Scylla of high inflation and the Charybdis of high (huge) unemployment.

Resource reallocation and industrial restructuring involve privatization. Moreover, foreign direct investment (FDI) — which can speed up considerably privatization — is essential for fostering restructuring. If one considers the economic slump in the region, as well as the anaemia of domestic savings and investments, the significance of FDI becomes obvious.

The International Environment: Restructuring (Privatization) and National Security

Industrial restructuring - via privatization - with its focus on meeting consumer demands, implies a reallocation of resources from military toward civilian use as well. The zeitgeist of the post-Cold War world would make such a process more than natural — the so-called " peace dividend " would be at work.

This is the rationale which led to the conclusion of the Paris Treaty concerning the reduction of arsenals.

However, one can easily detect worrying trends on the European continent and in the world at large, which increase instability in the emerging democracies and raise serious questions as to how to define national security.

Military conflicts (the war in Bosnia-Hertzegovina, and ongoing (latent), or looming conflicts in other parts of Europe), inter-ethnic tensions, borders which are questioned explicitly, or implicitly, the lack of "perceived", or real adequate security guarantees, rising nationalism and protectionism - all these portray a dynamic reality which is still very confusing to policy-makers. From a certain perspective, ironically, the post-Cold War world looks less stable. To the above mentioned trends one can add the widespread global economic recession, the rise of Islamic fundamentalism and right-wing extremism.

There are three concentric circles of transition in the world: one that comprises the former communist states; a larger one that regards the whole of Europe; and a third one that refers to processes in the world beyond.

Under such circumstances, one could argue that states (including the East European states, which still feel they are in a security vacuum) develop a propensity to get more cautious in downsizing and privatizing their defence apparatus, lest they harm their defence capabilities. There are several additional factors which, in my view, increase this propensity: the existence of highly saleable military goods as against the range of tradeables in the economy, an intensifying western trade protectionism combined with the foreign exchange constraint syndrome afflicting the transforming economies, and a very brisk and tempting world trade in weaponry which is stimulated by world instability.

On the other hand, the economic slump engulfing the post-communist economies can force a substantial — be it temporary — ad hoc curtailment of activity in the defence industry. In the case of Romania, for example, the capacity utilization of many facilities in the defence industry was below 20% in 1993.

There is no doubt that defence industry is a special area, and that irrespective of the size of the private sector (or, of the intensity of privatization), governments have a special relationship with this industry. Basically, national governments strive to make sure that national security needs are safely protected, which means that they need to be able to exert control on domestic military production.

The Case of Romania

The military doctrine of Romania emphasizes self-reliance and the modernization of national defence capabilities, within the context of developing closer links with NATO. Currently, almost 70% of defence equipment needs of the country are covered by domestic industry. The production of most defence-related factories has a dual character (military and civilian). Following the passing of Law 15 in 1990 regarding the corporatization of state enterprises, the defence-related units were turned into three "regies autonomes ", one holding company (for aircraft manufacturing), and 40 commercial companies. Approximately, 100,000 people work in these companies.

The defence industry has not been unaffected by the brutal decline of economic activity and the requirements of fiscal austerity. In 1993, the defence budget represented almost 10% of the state budget; of the defence budget, less than 24% was made up of capital expenditure. This meant that many development and modernization projects were put on hold. Nonetheless, modernization remains a major focus of the defence strategy. The latter has two main purposes: to make the national defence arsenal compatible with NATO structures; and to compensate the deliberate (as envisaged by the provisions of the Paris Treaty) and the forced (due to the decline of overall economic activity) down-sizing of certain military activities.

As far as the defence industry is concerned, privatization is not a major issue for the time being, and, very likely, it will not be for the foreseeable future. Even if privatization were much more intense than it is now, the situation of the defence industry would not change significantly in this respect. At the same time, it should be stressed that improving the management of enterprises in the defence industry should get a very high profile.

The role of foreign direct investment should be judged from a similar perspective. Bucharest is very keen on military cooperation managed at governmental level, and on entering cooperation deals in production with foreign companies in certain key defence sectors where modernization is critical. The best known example of such cooperation is between the Romanian company, Aerostar of Bacau, and the Israelian firm, ELBIT. This cooperation in production involves upgrading the fighter MIG-21, with the foreign partner providing highly sophisticated avionics. At a closer look, this cooperation has the allure of an actual joint venture; the inference would be that the FDI element exists in this case. Other deals in the making include microwave telecommunications and frequency-hopping radio stations.

Foreign Direct Investment

There are two main channels through which resources for productive use can flow into the emerging democracies. One is the private channel. Its utilisation depends, essentially, on the degree of fuzziness, volatility and uncertainty of the area in the eyes of private investors. The countries which evince better economic performances show, also, a relatively substantial inflow of direct investment.

The second channel is public; it refers to the strategic and political involvement of the West, as a stakeholder, in the future of the post-communist societies. In a broad political, social, economic and cultural sense, integration into Europe (into pan-European political, economic and defence structures) is an ultimate goal for the post-communist countries. In an operational sense, the public channel regards concrete steps - undertaken by western governments - that can enhance reforms, the stability and security of the emerging democracies. In this respect, there is much discrepancy between rhetoric and reality.

The need to "strategize" together!

The policy towards eastern Europe has most of the time been reactive. The fact is that the western countries perceive the eastern countries as a highly unstable and contaminating zone. This policy has been shaped more by the desire to contain undesirable events, or by an attempt to set up a sort of a buffer area (with a hard core represented by the Visegrad Group), than by an understanding that western involvement needs to be active and visionary relying on a genuine philosophy of integration. The Copenhagen statement of June, 1993, signalled a major conceptual breakthrough in this respect. However, actual support is still much below what is needed in order to keep alive the momentum of reforms in the East and secure the stability of the continent.

For example, there are plans entertained in Brussels (as EU initiative) of undertaking major public work projects in order to deal with the rising unemployment in the west. At the same time, the similar and more perturbing phenomenon of unemployment can derail reforms in the east. If one considers also the very low investment ratios and the badly needed improvement in infrastructure in the post-communist countries, a logical question comes up: why is there no common strategy to deal with this issue? For, if the vision of a future, stable and prosperous Europe - this would include post-communist states - exists, why should not projected trans-European networks (road, rail, energy and telecommunications) cover the area of an expanded European Union?

Such infrastructure investments would help homogenize the European space, they would mitigate the costs of transformation, they would forge organic links between the West and the East — and, ultimately, they would help the restructuring and conversion of military facilities to civilian use. The West should "strategize' (which means more than consult) with the East!

References

- Polanyi, K., (1944), " The Great Transformation ", New York, Farrar and Reinhart;
- Sachs, J., (1994), " Russia'struggle with stabilization. Conceptual issues and evidence ", paper presented at the World Bank annual Conference on Development Economics, 28-29 April.

FOREIGN INVESTMENT AND PRIVATIZATION IN ESTONIA

Kaja KELL

Estonia is the third most favoured nation in Eastern Europe for foreign investors. Joint ventures and foreign-owned companies are doing good business, and this year, investment from abroad exceeded domestic investment for the first time, says Kaja Kell. Tax breaks are bringing in a lot of money and a big chunk of it comes in from offshore tax havens. As the privatization programme progresses more slowly, it seems that foreign investors would rather start new companies than buy up old ones.

Kaja Kell is Deputy Head of the Information Department with the Bank of Estonia.

Looking at foreign investment (and privatisation) issues in the three Baltic states (Estonia, Latvia and Lithuania) it can be said with reasonable certainty that, besides some very important individual features for each of the three, there seems to be quite a lot of common ground. The following problems will be discussed in a bit more detail below (on mainly Estonian examples).

- Foreign investors prefer new ventures to companies to be privatised (generally ill- equipped and debt-laden).
- Privatisation decisions by politicians cannot always be aimed at maximising economic effect. That can lower the interest of potential investors.
- Ineptness in solving organisational problems and conflicting legislation has turned out to be surprisingly important as a source of problems.
- Country-risk inherent in the geographical position of Estonia and the other Baltic states (and to a smaller extent - risks connected to the rapidly changing economic environment) tend to play a major role in investment decisions.
- Any statistics concerning foreign investment should be handled with caution. Dealing with relatively small economies even a single figure for an individual investment can bring quite substantial changes to the overall picture.

Investment in Estonia - General Background

The number of entities in the Estonian state company register increased from 30,431 in December 1992 to 41,820 in November 1993. By March 1994 the number of registered enterprises was 53,421.

78% of the registered enterprises are private-owned. It should be noted as well, that the overwhelming majority of businesses fall into the categories of small businesses (up to 19 paid workers) and medium-size businesses (20 - 99 paid workers).

The panel used by the Estonian State Statistics Board for its company-finance survey, consists of 17,553 companies divided into the following groups (see Table 1).

Table 1.

	Number	%
Individuals	5163	29.4
1-19 paid workers	9078	51.7
20-99 paid workers	2530	14.4
100-499 paid workers	686	3.9
> 500 paid workers	96	0.6

Approximately 54% of the total sales fall to the companies considered "large" according to Estonian conditions (100 and more paid workers).

During the first quarter of 1994 the share capital of Estonian companies increased by 1,125,8 million kroon.

Bank credits and foreign capital have gained in importance as sources of real investment. The table below shows the importance of different sources of financing in real investment.

Table 2 - Various sources of financing real investment

	1992 million kroons	1992 %	1993 million kroons	1993 %
Companies' own capital	1174	74.0	2140	61.6
Local budget	119	7.5	201	5.8
Bank credits	72	4.6	316	9.1
of which foreign banks			117	
Foreign capital	55	3.5	258	7.4
Private capital	42	2.7	169	4.9
Other	40	2.5	122	3.5
TOTAL	1581	100.0	3473	100.0

No significant changes in the above proportions have been predicted for 1994. There have been some changes during 1993 in the structure of real investment, however.

The importance of the following sectors of the economy as investment targets has fallen (1993 compared to 1992):
- agriculture and forestry 2.4% (6.4%)
- housing construction 3.3% (8.3%)
- property, renting, business services 0.9% (2.1%).

The importance of the following sectors has increased (compared to 1992):
- government, defense, welfare 6.4% (0.5%)
- finance, insurance 5% (0.9%)
- hotels, catering 3.4% (1.3%)

The bulk of the real investment has been used by manufacturing industries - 26% (31.1% in 1992), transport-storage-communications - 22.8% (23.2% in 1992).

Foreign Investment in Estonia

The bulk of the foreign investment in Estonia so far has come in the form of capital for new joint ventures or foreign-owned companies set up. Joint ventures in Estonia date back to 1987, when 13 were established between 1987 and 1988. The law was liberalised in 1988 to allow full foreign ownership as opposed to the previous 40% maximum stake, while the following year laws were passed concerning joint-stock companies and the opening of foreign representative offices. Foreign investment is governed by the law on Foreign Investments. Up to January 1, 1994 firms with a minimum 30% foreign capital received a two-year holiday on profit tax, followed by further reductions for another two years. Those with a minimum of 50% foreign capital investment (USD1 million and more) received a three-year tax holiday and a 50% reduction for the following five years.

Unlike the other two Baltic states, foreign businesses can buy land outright. With the growing external convertibility of the kroon, foreign currency regulations were gradually relaxed during 1993. The last restrictions remaining from the time of the 1992 monetary reform, concerning private individuals' foreign currency accounts, was abolished in April 1994. Both foreign and local companies have been able to open accounts in any currency from January 1993 and there are no restrictions (besides an obligation to adhere to customs formalities) for exporting/importing cash or securities (see appendix to this paper for a short summary of changes in foreign exchange regulations).

The regions of Central and East Europe used only about 3% of the total foreign investment made in the world in 1993 (i.e. about USD6 billion of the total USD200 billion).

Within that framework it could be said that Estonia used approximately 0,01% of the total foreign investment made in the world in 1993. Estonia has so far been generally somewhat more successful in attracting foreign investments than its two Baltic neighbours, Latvia and Lithuania, and took the third place in East Europe (after Hungary and the Czech Republic) for foreign direct investment per head of population.

It should be stressed immediately, that statements and calculations like the above must not be taken without a certain caution. Some possible sources for the quite large variation in basic figures are shown below on Estonian examples and it is reasonable to suspect that the problems might be very similar in other East European countries as well.

The following table shows the foreign investment figures according to the balance of payments compiled by the central bank.

Table 3.

The structure of direct foreign investment in Estonia, calculated according to the methods used for compiling the balance of payments (million kroons)

	1993 Q1	1993 Q2	1993 Q3	1993 Q4	1994 Q1
1. Equity capital	334.0	119.2	354.3	425.5	356.2
- of which new ventures	280.0	98.0	166.0	220.0	268.2
- of which privatisation	0.0	11.9	5.2	63.3	6.5
- of which additional investments into existing companies	54.0	9.3	183.1		
	142.2	81.5			
2. Reinvested profits	49.2	94.7	122.8	97.9	92.3
3. Liabilities to direct investor (i.e. long & short-term credit granted by investors minus loan payments)	101.1	167.3	162.6	203.8	125.0
4. Claims on direct investor (i.e. long & short-term credit granted to investors)	-8.6	-14.5	-31.7	-27.0	-21.0
TOTAL	475.7	336.7	608.0	700.2	552.5

The figures for 1993 have been adapted to the version V of the Balance of Payments

As seen below, the figures can look somewhat different if based on different sources and data-gathering methods (the state company register, for instance).

Foreign Investment in Estonia During the First Quarter of 1994

During the first three months of 1994 630 new companies with mixed or foreign ownership were registered in Estonia (total foreign investments of 607 million kroon according to the state company register - the corresponding figure in the balance of payments is 268.2 million).

It should be noted here that according to expert estimates only 60-70% of the sums declared for the company register are really invested in Estonia. Part of the companies registered will never start their activities at all.

The significant increase in the interest shown by foreign capital in new ventures in Estonia during the first months of 1994 can be explained, to a large extent, by the fact that from 1 January 1994 the tax holidays and reductions for new companies with a share of foreign capital have been abolished. For that reason as many enterprises of this type as possible were registered at the end of 1993. (In Estonia the companies registered by local authorities are included in the state company register only after a delay of several months).

Besides that, the figures for the month of January include one exceptionally large foreign investment from Egypt made into a new company named Monir El Noba & Abu Simbl As whose registered share capital amounts to 250 million kroon. This investment alone covered 45% of the total for January 1994. (By May 1994 the registered amount of foreign capital had not really been paid in and consequently the figures for the balance of payments compiled by the Bank of Estonia do not include this amount.)

Table 4.
Total foreign investments in new ventures by countries

	1994 Q1 (thousand kroons)	1994 Q1 %	1993 (thousand kroons)	1993 %
Egypt	273 000	45	0	0
Finland	80 720	13	195 547	22
Sweden	78 461	13	284 953	31
USA	50 141	8	145 511	16
Germany	33 079	5	35.524	4
Bahamas	25 316	4	12 342	1
United Kingdom	12 677	2	22 110	2
Russia	10 815	2	53 289	6
Other	43 596	7	157 690	17
Total	607 805	100	906 966	100

More than 3 million kroon each has been invested in new Estonian ventures by investors from Denmark (7 million EEK), Ireland (5.5 million) China (5.2 million), Pakistan (4.1 million), Turkey (3.2 million) and Kazakhstan (3.2 million).

Disregarding the exceptionally large investment from Egypt mentioned above, Finland and Sweden continue to remain the most important sources of foreign investment for Estonia.

It should be noted that several (relatively) large foreign investments have come to Estonia from tax havens (i.e. Bahamas, Panama, Cyprus, Vanuatu etc.). The volume of investments from Russia has decreased, to some extent.

There have been instances where Estonian capital comes back to Estonia under the guise of foreign investment via various tax havens. It can be partially explained by the lucrative tax reductions until recently offered to foreign companies. Money laundering might well count for a second reason, and the possibility of transferring profits earned by local branches to mother companies set up in tax havens, thus avoiding income tax in Estonia is a third consideration worth mentioning.

Besides the tax havens, countries like Ireland, Turkey, Sweden, USA, Hungary and Poland have been used both by Estonian and Russian capital for this type of operations.

The influence of the recent changes in taxation of new foreign-owned companies can be clearly traced in the figures for the average size of foreign investment. While the average foreign investment into the share capital of a new company registered in January 1994 amounted to 1.148 million kroon, the average for the whole 1993 was only 0.308 million, the average for February 1994 - 0.264 million and March 1994 - 0.324 million.

Table 5.
Average foreign investment in new ventures by countries

	1994 Q1		1993	
	Enterprises	Average investment (thousand kroons)	Enterprises	Average investment (thousand kroons)
Egypt	1	273 000	0	-
Finland	355	189	1 364	119
Sweden	48	1 427	284	866
USA	40	1 206	86	1 516
Germany	37	807	111	286
Bahamas	7	3 617	9	1 371
United Kingdom	24	528	42	503
Russia	46	152	237	191
Total	630	758	2 416	308

A significant (and increasing) part of the new enterprises based on foreign capital - 53% in 1994 - can be characterised as 100% foreign-owned companies with a single owner. The average share of foreign capital in a joint venture amounts to 85% (65% in 1993).

52% of the capital of new companies entered in the state register in the first quarter of 1994 is foreign capital. It is the first time the volume of foreign investment has exceeded the volume of domestic investment.

Manufacturing industries have lost some of their attractiveness for foreign investors, wholesale and retail trade gaining at the same time.

Table 6.
Foreign investments in new ventures by sectors of economy

	1994 Q1			1993	
	Number of enterprises	Capital (thousand kroons)	%	Number of enterprises	Capital (thousand kroons)
Wholesale & retail trade	351	394 940	65	1 311	235 961
Industry	113	141 996	23	423	409 525
Finance	9	45 610	8	30	74 455
Property, renting, business services	63	6 875	1	296	67 423
Transport, warehouses, communications	29	4 774	1	117	55 576
Hotels, restaurants	10	4 194	1	59	20 956
Agriculture, forestry	15	1 912	0	42	28 184
Other	40	7 504	1	138	14 886
TOTAL	630	607 805		2 416	906 966

The bulk of the foreign investment (80% in all) was made in Tallinn in the first quarter of 1994. (In 1993 the share of Tallinn in total foreign investment had been 65%). A few large foreign investments have been made in the counties of Jôgeva (31 million kroon) and Vôru (20 million) and in the town of Narva (20 million).

According to the latest estimates by the Estonian Ministry of Economy there should be a modest increase in foreign investment during the second quarter of 1994, the average amount invested remaining modest as well.

In a longer perspective, the recent decision by Eesti Pank/Bank of Estonia to make Estonian kroon - Deutschmark futures and swaps of up to 7 years maturity available to the banking sector might well play a significant role. The new instruments offer an additional way to the foreign investor to hedge the possible currency risks.

It is a mark of the success of joint ventures and 100% foreign-owned companies that although only 6% of the total workforce was engaged by these companies in 1993, their share in total wages paid was 9%, their share in value-added tax revenues - 14%, net turnover (sales) - 16%, and total net profit - 13% in 1993. The fact that foreign-owned companies have taken an especially active role in foreign trade operations is reflected by the fact that their share in the total customs tariffs paid in 1993 amounted to more than a third.

Privatization in Estonia

The Estonian press has from time to time published rather gloomy warnings that Estonia's assets would all be sold out to foreign investors, This danger is strongly exaggerated. The results of the first two privatisation tenders show that only 18.5% of the sales contracts of large enterprises were awarded to foreign buyers. According to the balance of payments quarterly figures, privatisation revenues have amounted to approximately 10% of the total foreign investment in Estonia for the last three quarters.

Despite having had the only systematic privatisation programme in the Baltic states for a long time, Estonia's attempts to dispose of its public enterprises, particularly the larger ones, have been fraught with difficulties. Since August 1993 the programme has been directed by the Estonia Privatisation Agency formed by merging two former bodies, one of which had been responsible for large enterprises, the other for small privatisation.

By January 1, 1994 the privatisation authorities had sold off 54 large-scale enterprises. Small-scale privatisation having been more successful, an estimated 80% of small businesses had been privatised by the end of 1993 according to the Ministry of Economy. (54% of the country's retail outlets were in private hands and another 30% were run by cooperatives while 8% had remained state-owned, for instance). By mid-1994 the government hopes to introduce public share offerings, retaining a 25% stake which will subsequently be sold off for vouchers.

The privatisation programme for 1993 of the Government of Estonia stressed the following:
- choosing the best method for privatisation in every individual case (tenders with preliminary negotiations, public offer of shares, auction);
- auctions should be used more often (for the relative speediness and resource-effectiveness of this method);
- tenders with preliminary negotiations should be used mainly for large- and middle-sized enterprises; international tenders should be used only in case it is realistic to hope that there would be sufficient interest and additional stipulations should be used with great care.

In the Estonian Ministry of Economy quarterly review for QI 1994 the Privatisation Agency is criticised for having not followed the above principles to the full. The Ministry of Economy has noted that the interest of foreign investors in enterprises to be privatised has, in general, fallen: there are more competitive investment possibilities available, and the political instability in Estonia's neighbouring regions (i.e. potential markets) seems to be on the increase.

It is in this context that the results for the three international tenders for the sale of state-owned enterprises should be looked at.

Tender 1
- 38 enterprises, 180 offers (of which 53 or 51.5% from foreigners)

Tender II
- 52 enterprises, 180 offers (of which 77 or 42.8% from foreigners)

Tender III
- 40 enterprises, 109 offers (of which 12 or 11% from foreigners).

Privatization Results for 1993 in Estonia

A) so-called large-scale privatisation (tenders)

54 contracts were signed for 353,194,951 kroons in all. The buyers guaranteed total investments of 237,755,964 kroons. The buyers took over old debts for 195,562,292 kroon. 9,099 jobs were guaranteed (see table in the appendices to the present paper for individual contracts).

b) so-called small privatisation (auctions)

243 entities were sold for 124,178,100 kroon in all (it must be noted that 169 entities were sold for the initial price).

Privatization Results for Q1 1994 in Estonia

A) so-called large-scale privatisation (tenders)

30 contracts were signed for 137,706,601 kroons in all. The buyers guaranteed total investments of 120,868,000 kroon. 4,294 jobs were guaranteed (see table in the appendices to the present paper for individual contracts).

B) so-called small privatisation (auctions)

Only 29 entities were sold for 23,643,500 kroon in all (it must be noted that only 9 entities were sold for a price higher than the initial price).

In its latest quarterly review the Estonian Ministry of Economy had to admit that from "a purely business point of view" it must be recognised that the (privatisation) ideology chosen and the slowness of reform (especially in solving issues of restitution and compensation) is "continuously lessening the interest of foreign investors in Estonian privatisation". It seems that there have been similar feelings in Latvia as well.

It is quite natural that the foreign investor would prefer a new firm without inherited liabilities or problems.

Both the Estonian and the Latvian experience show that it is necessary to balance the renewal of ownership rights which existed before the occupation by the USSR with the interests of the present users as well - and even more important - to direct the process in such a manner that it not impede the transition towards a market economy.

265

APPENDIX I: Estonian companies privatized, 1993-94

DATE	COMPANY PRIVATISED	BUYER	PRICE	SPECIAL CONDITIONS
01.06.96	RAS Mistra-Autex	AS A.S.M.A. Estonia and Hydnum OY, Finland	3,000,000 EEK (initial price)	jobs for 130 investments 9,240,000 EEK
01.06.93	RAS Sulev (textiles)	AS Sule, Estonia	3,100,000 EEK (initial price)	jobs for 290 investments 5,500,000 EEK
03.06.93	RAS Suva (hosiery factory)	AS Sukktokk, Estonia	5,200,000 EEK (initial price)	jobs for 600 investments 5,000,000 EEK
29.06.93	RAS Noorus (sewing factory)	AS P.N.P., Estonia	1,200,000 EEK (initial price)	jobs for 300 investments 4,860,000 EEK
01.07.93	RAS "Sangar" (sewing factory)	AS Sangar, STC Estonia	5,200,000 EEK (initial price)	jobs for 425 investments 2,000,000 EEK
02.07.93	Puka branch of RAS "Valge MÖÖbel" (furniture)	Gomab Möbel AB, Sweden	3,200,000 EEK (initial price)	jobs for 300 investments 2,425,000 EEK
06.07.93	Engineering unit of RAS Mistra	AS Mistra Met, Estonia	250,000 EEK (initial price)	jobs for 12
15.07.93	RAS VGT	AS EVGT	1,100,000 EEK (initial price)	jobs for 120 investments 3,456,800 EEK
23.07.93	Branch of RAS Estoplast (plastics)	AS Tarvikud	110,000 EEK	jobs for 20 investments 12,000 EEK
27.07.93	Avinurme branch of Auto VAZ	AS Aviko, Estonia	160,000 EEK	jobs for 9 investments 200,000 EEK
27.07.93	Sillamäe branch of Auto VAZ	AS Universal Service	500,000 EEK	jobs for 31 investments 216,000 EEK
31.07.93	Tartu branch of Auto VAZ	AS Auto Kommerts, Estonia	500,000 EEK	jobs for 25 investments 300,000 EEK
30.07.93	Tallinn branch of RAS Tondi Elektroonika (electronics)	TTK Avers	1,000,000 EEK	jobs for 120 investments 950,000 EEK
02.08.93	Tartu branch of RAS Vasar (metal)	AS Mekre	45,000 EEK	jobs for 4
16.08.93	Elva branch of RAS Sangar (clothing)	AB Ludvig Svensson and AB Stenströme Skjortfabrik, Sweden	1,625,000 EEK	jobs for 30 investments 6,000,000 EEK

DATE	COMPANY PRIVATISED	BUYER	PRICE	SPECIAL CONDITIONS
22.09.93	RE Tallinna Vineeri-ja Mööblikkombinaat (furniture)	AS Marlekor	56,000,000 EEK	jobs for 1000 investments 48,000,000 EEK
28.09.93	RAS Wendre	AS Vely & CO	4,000,000 EEK	jobs for 160 investments 2,400,000 EEK
04.10.93	RE Painküla Treacle plant (part of the assets)	Pepsico Eesti AS	3,600,000 EEK	investments 2,400,000 EEK
05.10.93	RAS Mistra (part of the assets)	AS Mivar, Estonia	5,000,000 EEK	jobs for 150 investments 2,100,000 EEK
07.10.93	Antela branch of RAS Villak	AS Saldre,Estonia	300,000 EEK	jobs for 25 investments 1,021,000 EEK
15.10.93	Garage of RAS Klementi	Eesti Helkama Auto AS, Estonia	1,800,000 EEK	jobs for 14 investments 1,400,000 EEK
22.10.93	Eesti Energomontaazh (small business)	AS Monteeria, Estonia	1,500,000 EEK	jobs for 174 investments 540,000 EEK
25.10.93	Warehouse of RAS Kommunaar	AS Kington, Estonia	380,000 EEK	jobs for 12
28.10.93	RAS Kommunaar footwear factory	AS Polaria	600,000 EEK	jobs for 70 investments 300,000 EEK
02.11.93	Tallinna Masinatehas (engineering plant)	AS SIF-D	5,000,000 EEK	jobs for 620 investments 1,600,000 EEK
05.11.93	RAS Polümeer (plastics)	PSS Projekt	10,900,000 EEK	jobs for 155 investments 1,500,000 EEK
05.11.93	Tartu branch of RAS Areng (textiles)	AS MTP	1,000,000 EEK	jobs for 110 investments 2,700,000 EEK
08.11.93	RAS Flora (chemicals, cosmetics)	AS Flora Liit (80% of the shares), Estonia	36,500,000 EEK	jobs for 450 investments 21,015,000 EEK
09.11.93	Kohtla-Järve baskery	AS Järle, Estonia	15,000,000 EEK	jobs for 290 investments 3,830,000 EEK
11.11.93	Pärnu Sewing Factory of RAS Klementi	AS Zigmund	4,500,000 EEK	jobs for 267 investments 3,000,000 EEK
12.11.93	Türi-Alliku branch of Volta (metal)	AS Masi, Estonia	1,000,000 EEK	jobs for 100 investments 1,400,000 EEK

DATE	COMPANY PRIVATISED	BUYER	PRICE	SPECIAL CONDITIONS
19.11.93	Mäealuse branch of Tehnoprojekt	AS Ergon, Estonia	2,000,000 EEK	jobs for 32 investments 300,000 EEK
17.11.93 competition	Wood processing unit of RAS Kommunaar	AS GMPP Disain, Estonia	270,000 EEK (initial price)	jobs for 17 investments 625,000 EEK
17.11.93 competition	Population shelter of Pärnu Fish processing plant	AS Esox, Estonia	60,000 EEK (initial price)	jobs for 20 investments 225,000 EEK
17.11.93 competition	Valga branch of Auto VAZ	AS Transoil Service, Estonia	1,200,000 EEK (initial price)	jobs for 35 investments 5,000,000 EEK
17.11.93 competition	RAS Põhjala (rubber footwear)	AS Kuldkumm, Estonia	1,000,000 EEK (initial price)	jobs for 200 investments 400,000 EEK
17.11.93 competition	Haljala branch of Auto VAZ	AS Kommerts Service, Estonia	190,000 EEK (initial price)	jobs for 17 investments 320,000 EEK
17.11.93 competition	Branch of RAS Iimarine (incinerators etc.)	Bergemann Gmbh, Germany	1,600,000 EEK (initial price)	jobs for 57 investments 3,800,000 EEK
14.12.93	Tallinn branch of "Ajakirjanduslevi" (mailing of periodicals)	AS "Päevaleht", "Hommikuleht", "Lõuna-Eesti Sõnumid", "Maaleht", "Postimees", "Croneos" and "Levileht", Estonia	3,000,030 EEK	
29.11.93	RAS Kiviter (fertiliser plant)	Lentransgaz (subsidiary of Gasprom), Russia	3,990,815 USD + 3,161,618 EEK	jobs for 529 investments 5,250,000 USD by the end of 1998 liquid assets bought for 5,034,980.85 EEK
30.11.93	"Thomesto" warehouse of RAS Kommunaar	AS Reester, Estonia	450,000 EEK	jobs for 50 investments 400,000 EEK
20.12.93	RE Tartu Bakery	AS Pere Leib, Estonia	30,000,000 EEK	jobs for 293 investments 8,000,000 EEK
21.12.93	RAS Võru Jalats (footwear)	AS Abris	200,000 EEK	jobs for 120 investments 490,000 EEK
21.12.93	Assets of Rakvere Cinema Company	AS Monika, Estonia	1,500,000 EEK	
21.12.93	Rakvere service shop of "Orbita Service"	AS Triiton, Estonia	8,500 EEK	
27.12.93	RAS Leibur (bakery)	AS Offero	71,000,000 EEK	jobs for 706 investments 38,900,000 EEK
28.12.93	RAS Valumehaanika (metal casting)	AS Valumalm, Estonia	1,827,000 EEK	jobs for 130 investments 2,500,000 EEK

DATE	COMPANY PRIVATISED	BUYER	PRICE	SPECIAL CONDITIONS
28.12.93	Kiiingi-Nõmme branch of RAS Kordu	AS TMP	300,000 EEK	jobs for 30 investments 291,000 EEK
29.12.93	RAS Flora (chemicals, cosmetics)	AS Flora Liit (20% of the shares	9,125,000 EEK	
04.01.94	RAS Areng (part of the assets)	AS K.A.S.	500,000 EEK	jobs for 50 investments 2,000,000 EEK
06.01.93	RE Pärnu Fish Processing (part of the assets)	AS Maseko	18,500,000 EEK	jobs for 130 investments 7,200,000 EEK
20.01.94	RAS Mistra laboratory (part of the assets)	AS Pakett	500,000 EEK	jobs for 10 investments 90,000 EEK
27.01.94	RAS Virulane (all shares)	AS Wirulane	4,000,000 EEK	jobs for 480 investments 4,000,000 EEK
27.01.94	Rassiku branch (all shares)	AS Viidest	610,000 EEK	jobs for 16 investments 700,000 EEK
28.01.94	RAS Tarbeklaas (part of the assets)	Denos AB, Lindahl AB, Ramco AB	8,679,000 EEK	jobs for 64 investments 22,000,000 EEK
28.01.94	RAS Galantex (all shares)	AS Fobar	5,500,000 EEK	jobs for 160 investments 2,200,000 EEK
31.01.94	RAS Standard Madara Furniture Factory (part of the assets)	AS UNIVER International Eesti	1,100,000 EEK	jobs for 60 investments 1,500,000 EEK
07.02.94	RAS Tondi Elektroonika (whole shares)	AS Mikrel	18,000,000 EEK	jobs for 1050 investments 18,000,000 EEK
11.02.94	RAS Vasar (part of the assets)	AS Finmec	6,300,000 EEK	jobs for 20 investments 4,000,000 EEK
11.02.94	RAS Vasar (all shares)	AS Erivasar	19,800,000 EEK	jobs for 305 investments 1,500,000 EEK
14.02.94	RAS Villak (all shares)	AS Klementi Kaubandus	1,000,000 EEK	jobs for 50 investments 1,000,000 EEK
14.02.94	RAS Sangar (all shares)	AS Klementi Kaubandus	1,100,000 EEK	jobs for 40 investments 1,100,000 EEK
14.02.94	Räpina branch of RAS Areng (textiles)	AS Klementi Kaubandus	1 EEK	jobs for 20 investments 60,000 EEK

DATE	COMPANY PRIVATISED	BUYER	PRICE	SPECIAL CONDITIONS
14.02.94	RAS Nordek (all shares)	AS Estpuud	2,300,000 EEK	jobs for 85 investments 1,550,000 EEK
21.02.94	RE Keile (part the assets)	AS Aldus	5,100,000 EEK	
01.03.04	RAS Valumehaanika (part of the assets)	AS MTP	360,000 EEK	jobs for 20 investments 900,000 EEK
07.03.94	RAS Standard (all shares)	AS Eripuu	13,500,000 EEK	jobs for 490 investments 6,000,000 EEK
07.03.94	RAS Mahtra Metsamajand (all shares)	AS Iris	800,000 EEK	jobs for 35 investments 6,500,000 EEK
07.03.94	RAS Kodu (part of the assets)	AS Kena Kudum	550,000 EEK	jobs for 41 investments 180,000 EEK
07.03.94	RAS Estoplast (part of the assets)	AS Eswind	3,000,000 EEK	jobs for 100 investments 1,345,000 EEK
11.03.94	RAS Stamp (all assets)	AS Tamp	2,300,000 EEK	jobs for 90 investments 1,712,000 EEK
16.03.94	RAS Puiteks (all shares)	AS Silvest	1,000,000 EEK	jobs for 85 investments 5,550,000 EEK
17.03.94	RAS Säilis Tartu (all shares)	AS Salvest	4,000,000 EEK	jobs for 200 investments 10,000,000 EEK
17.03.94	RAS Kommunaar (part of the assets)	AS Style Wear	700,000 EEK	jobs for 35 investments 600,000 EEK
17.03.94	RAS Kommunaar (part of the assets)	AS Vatu	1,800,000 EEK	jobs for 21 investments 1,000,000 EEK
17.03.94	RAS Kommunaar (part of the assets)	AS Kington	7,500 EEK	
18.03.94	RAS Pärnu Fish Processing (part of the assets)	AS Kampol	600,000 EEK	jobs for 5 investments 281,000 EEK
28.03.94	RE Keila (part of the assets)	AS Evilkan	2,000,000 EEK	jobs for 56 investments 1,800,000 EEK
30.03.94	RAS Koil (all shares)	AS Kohila Paberivabrik	1,100,000 EEK	jobs for 132 investments 8,000,000 EEK
30.03.94	RAS Klementi (80% of the shares) (clothing)	AS Klementi Kaubandus	15,000,000 EEK	jobs for 500 investments 7,500,000 EEK
31.03.94	RAS Kommunaar Narva mnt.5a (part of the assets)	AS Schmidt & Ko	2,000,000 EEK	jobs for 100 investments 3,000,000 EEK

DATE	COMPANY PRIVATISED	BUYER	PRICE	SPECIAL CONDITIONS
04.04.94	RAS Alutaguse Foresty (all shares)	AS Ware	700,000 EEK	jobs for 40 investments 300,000 EEK
04.04.94	RAS Elva Forestry (all shares)	AS Alnus	2,575,000 EEK	jobs for 76 investments 1,700,000 EEK investments after 3 years 800,000 EEK
11.04.94	RAS ABT (2/3 state-owned, 1/3 Tallinn municipality) (all shares)	AS KAR	26,100,000 EEK (state-17,400,000EEK Tallinn -8,700,000 EEK)	jobs for 120 investments 3,060,000 EEK
11.04.94	RAS Saaremaa Foresty (all shares)	AS Norman	2,200,000 EEK	jobs for 77 investments 2,490,000 EEK investments after 3 years 450,000 EEK
14.04.94	RAS Estjal (all shares)	AS Kaveli	4,500,000 EEK	jobs for 36 investments 400,000 EEK
14.04.94	RE Pärnu Fish Processing Liiva Plant (part of the assets)	AS Waldhof	575,000 EEK	jobs for 15 investments 500,000 EEK
18.04.94	RE Paide Meat Processing Plant Järva Lihaühistu (all assets)	Eesti Teraviljaühistu	500,000 EEK	jobs for 65 investments 1,500,000 EEK
18.04.94	RAS Viljar (all shares)		400,000 EEK	jobs for 32 investments 175,000 EEK
18.04.94	RAS Harju Asfalbtetoonitehas (all shares)	AS Harbet	6,000,000 EEK	jobs for 46 investments 2,045,200 EEK
20.04.94	RAS Folia (all shares)	OÜ Wenders Timber	480,000 EEK	jobs for 32 investments 640,000 EEK
22.04.94	RAS Tarbeklaas (part of the assets) (glassware)	AS Kurmet	950,000 EEK	
02.05.94	VE Raudval (all shares)	AS Radlik	3,500,000 EEK	jobs for 100 investments 3,000,000 EEK
02.05.94	RE Tartu Piimatoodete Kombinaat (dairy) (all assets)	Keskpiimaühistu "Tartu Piim"	3,000,000 EEK	jobs for 348 investments 3,111,000 EEK

DATE	COMPANY PRIVATISED	BUYER	PRICE	SPECIAL CONDITIONS
05.05.94	RE Rakvere Viljasalv Jõhvi Grain Purchase Branch (all shares)	Jõhvi Teraviljaühistu	250,000 EEK	jobs for 13 investments 250,000 EEK
10.05.94	RAS Loksa Ship Repair Plant (all shares)	AS OSF Portfolio Investment V	20,000,000 EEK	jobs for 63 investments 25,000,000 EEK
11.05.94	RE Haapsalu Viljasalv Haspsalu assets	Läänemaa Teraviljaühistu	600,000 EEK	jobs for 30 investments 350,000 EEK
16.05.94	RAS Eesti Tekstiil	AS ET-Riie	13,000,000 EEK	jobs for 130 investments 3,200,000 EEK investments after 3 years 2,300,000 EEK

Eesti Pank/Bank of Estonia Information Service (source: Estonian Government Agency for Privatization of State Property)

APPENDIX II

CHANGES LIBERALISING THE RULES REGULATING FOREIGN CURRENCY USE DURING 1993 AND 1994

In 1993, the following documents were formulated and imposed:

1. On February 4, the Estonian President signed "The Law on Changing the Foreign Currency Law of the Republic of Estonia" adopted by the parliament on January 26.
2. The Bank of Estonia regulations No 39 (March 1, 1993) imposed the procedures of opening foreign currency accounts in Estonian authorised banks for legal entities.
3. The Bank of Estonia regulations No 40 (March 1, 1993) imposed the procedures of opening foreign currency accounts abroad for legal entities.
4. The Bank of Estonia regulations No 49 (March 31, 1993) imposed the amended rules "On the registration of foreign loans in the Bank of Estonia" that took effect on April 1. The old rules imposed with the Bank regulations No 82 of July 20, 1992, were invalidated.
5. The Board of the Bank of Estonia, on June 7, adopted the amended "Rules of issuing licences for independent foreign currency transactions to Estonian banks", and invalidated the former rules passed by the Bank Board on June 18, 1992.
6. The Bank of Estonia regulations No 90 (August 2, 1993) imposed the amended "Procedures of opening foreign currency accounts in Estonian banks", invalidating the old procedures imposed with regulations No 39 of March 1.
7. The Bank of Estonia regulations No 91 (August 2, 1993) changed the procedures of opening and using foreign currency accounts abroad, imposing the amended "Procedures of opening and using foreign currency accounts abroad", invalidating the procedures imposed with regulations No 40 of March 1.
8. The Bank of Estonia regulations No 99 (August 18, 1993) imposed the amended "Procedures of determining the foreign currency position of authorised banks", invalidating the procedures imposed by the Bank Board on June 18, 1992.
9. The Bank of Estonia regulations No 132 (December 1, 1993) "On transactions with non-convertible foreign cash" lifted the restrictions on transactions with foreign non-convertible cash, invalidating the Bank regulations No 164 of November 24, 1992.
10 The Bank of Estonia regulations No 133 (December 1, 1993) imposed new procedures on opening foreign currency accounts in Estonian and foreign banks, invalidating the Bank regulations No 90 and 91 of August 2.
11. The Bank of Estonia regulations No 139 (December 16, 1993) that took effect on December 15 invalidated the regulations No 69 (July 6, 1992). That means abolishing any restrictions concerning the exchange rates used for commercial banking operations.
12. Decision of the Board of the Bank of Estonia (December 21, 1993) cancelled all restrictions on import and export of cash, invalidating the Bank Board decision of June 18, 1992.
    In 1994, the following documents were formulated and imposed:
13. The Bank of Estonia regulations No 16 (March 16, 1994): invalidated articles 3 and 8 of the regulations No 85 (July 24, 1992). That meant abolishing any restrictions concerning opening correspondent accounts with banks of the former rouble zone and opening rouble accounts for clients.
14. The Bank of Estonia regulations No 17 (March 18, 1994): Procedure of recording foreign currency and securities at customs.
15. The "Foreign Currency Law of the Republic of Estonia" was declared invalid by the Parliament (March 23, 1994). That means lifting the last of the existing restrictions set at the time of the 1992 monetary reform.
    From April 7, 1994 private individuals can open foreign currency accounts with Estonian commercial banks.
16. The Bank of Estonia regulations No 29 (April 18, 1994): The procedures for registering foreign loans (Regulations No 49, March 31, 1993) were declared invalid.
17. Decision of the Board of the Bank of Estonia No 5-2 (May 3, 1994): The foreign currency statutes (approved by the Board on March 30, 1993) were declared invalid.

PRACTICAL SOLUTIONS FOR STIMULATING RUSSIA'S PRIVATE SECTOR

Robert Watters

The business of politics and the politics of business in Russia have received their fair share of negative press in recent months. But Robert Watters says that this country is ripe for investment. He offers three practical solutions to help kick-start this country's private sector. Firstly, encourage training and education, secondly press governments to focus technical assistance money directly at the developing Russian private sector - not on another feasibility study. And thirdly, he urges western governments and companies to be patient and look at Russia as a long term investment.

Robert Watters is President of the Information Systems Company, American International Trading, Brussels/Moscow

When, at midday on the second day of the meeting of NATO foreign ministers in December 1991, Ambassador Nikolai Nikolkaiyevich Afanasyevskiy was obliged to report to the North Atlantic Cooperation Council that the Soviet Union had dissolved and that he no longer had the authority to speak for the USSR, no one would have thought that 30 months later we would be meeting at an official NATO Colloquium to discuss the subject of defense conversion. Many of those who were in Room 16 of the NATO Headquarters that rainy afternoon believed that the USSR and Russia were on the verge of collapse. The political and economic structures were so uncertain that many doubted that Russia would survive without falling into civil disorder and possible civil war.

Yet - two and one-half years later - Boris Nikolaevich Yeltsin has visited Naples to press again for Russian admission into the Group of Seven.

The Setting

Although by living and working in Russia on a daily basis we sometimes are tempted to do otherwise, we must admit that there has been an incredible, irreversible, and (with the exception of the events of October 1993) a mostly peaceful revolution in Russia. Yes, obstacles remain - loads of them - in completing the transition to a full market economy. Many Western companies are evaluating daily their investment tactics and strategies.

Some small companies are leaving. Others are consolidating their present positions and have decided to maintain, though not necessarily strengthen, their positions over the next six months. But others have decided to come in strong, to take advantage of what they consider to be a real, and perhaps temporarily open, window of opportunity. For them, even though the dangers of Russia's falling back into a period of tumultuous inflation are present, they believe that the climate for foreign investment has improved, and they are willing to take the plunge.

The Role of Privatization

One constant impulse for this movement forward - and against stiff odds - has been the privatization effort. And among others, there has been one consistent reason for its success: the Russian leadership which pioneered the privatization effort listened to Western advice. Anatoly Chubais's inner circle of Maxim Boyko, Vassilyev and others, working closely with experts from Western governments and financial institutions - some seconded to their staffs, and others not - and backed by an energetic International Finance Corporation/World Bank team, kept the program moving ahead.

The model three-step program they introduced is well known, as is the fact that they chose to begin the installation of the program in the city of Nizhni Novgorod, thanks to the initiative and imagination of the political leadership of Nizhni - the young and dynamic oblast' governor, Boris Nemtsov; his deputy for international affairs Evgeniy Gorkov, and the then Nizhni mayor, Dmitriy Bednyakov.

This group, backed by the IFC/World Bank Development team, began the privatization of small and medium enterprises in March, 1992, introduced the privatization of the transport sector with the first public auction of trucks in October, 1992, and followed with subsequent land auctions in 1993.

As part of the governmental effort to encourage progress in the defense conversion area, the U.S. government sent to Nizhni - through the auspices of the International Executive Service Corps - advisors to assist the local government in its defense conversion efforts. These men, and their wives, surveyed 43 defense-related enterprises, and finally selected eight for further cooperation in defense conversion projects.

This description is not to say that it has been easy. There are problems in this conversion effort - many of them. One particular problem in the process, which has surfaced repeatedly, concerns the process in which the property is privatised. Many of the investment funds now active in Moscow - the Russian - American Enterprise Fund, The Paine Webber Fund, the funds from the European Bank for Reconstruction and Development, the U.S. Ex-Im Bank and others - are often finding in researching the applications of Russian enterprises for this investment money that factories have merely been taken (or stolen) from the State in the name of privatization. Consequently, in working with these newly privatized companies, foreign investors must remain diligent to insure that their Russian foundation is solid.

Among Western observers resident in Moscow there is a wide range in the forecasts of ow the future will develop. Over the last month we have talked with Moscow-based representatives of several investment funds, whose combined available capital is in the range of 800 million dollars over the next two-to-three years.

The Pessimists

The pessimists - many of whom have been in country for less than one year - charge that in terms of economic planning there is no plan, there are no clear goals or objectives, no-one is in charge. They argue that President Yeltsin sits above the fray, and that Alexander Shokhin often is out of Russia attending international conferences. When he is in town, they say, his predilection is to avoid, rather than take, the hard decisions necessary to steer a defined and predictable course. The pessimists also say that absent firm course (almost in any direction) Western investment planners lack the foundation on which to base either tactical or strategic investment decisions, as the planning cycles are more often measured in months rather than years.

On the other hand, many of the representatives who have been in Russia for two or more years are much more optimistic. They note that great progress has been made since December 1991. They use the image that Russia is building a causeway from one side of a river to the other. Over the last two years the building blocks have been put in place, and though that foundation may not yet be above the water's flow, if Prime Minister Chernomyrdin continues to push the privatization program aggressively, the causeway will soon emerge. Foreign investors, they continue, should focus on the great progress in the transition to a full and free market economy that has been achieved, not concentrate on the obstacles that remain.

Continuing Concerns

From our experience in Moscow we see three main areas that the Russian government must address if they are to continue to make Russia attractive to Western investment.

The first is that the privatization process - in fact the evolution of political and economic reform in Russia - is outrunning the government's ability to control, never mind lead, it. The government's proclivity to produce decrees - at the rate of 600 plus per year - in an attempt to catch up to the reality of change is counterproductive, especially as the decrees adopted are contradictory and seldom enforced. This is also a reflection of the reality that over the last three years the authority of the central government has to a large degree vanished, so that enterprise directors or association directors away from Moscow pay little or no direction to the central authorities.

The second concern is that even given the attempts of Western governments and institutions to encourage the development of the necessary legal underpinning, one is not yet in place. There still is no understandable or stable tax regime, and there has not been sufficient progress in establishing the rules and procedures for licensing property and granting titles. But more importantly, there still is a severe lack of understanding of Western business practices and procedures at the enterprise level.

Thirdly, of course, there is the problem of widespread corruption. Russia now offers a combination of the Alaskan Klondike one hundred years ago and the Chicago of the 1930s. And although in our view the problems are overstated in the Western press, this factor must be taken into account, as one local mafia or another out of the twelve such groups operating presently in Moscow controls much of the banking and public service sectors.

Three Solutions for Russia

To paraphrase the words of a former NATO Assistant Secretary General, what the West must do first to help Russia move forward in the business development sector is to develop the world's largest business school. This need not be at the level of the Harvard Business School or Wharton or Kellogg - but it should address the basic finance and accounting principles that all Western corporations accept and work by.

We should encourage and develop exchanges at all levels so that practical day-to-day experience is learned and shared. The U.S. Government program to bring 10,000 young Russian entrepreneurs to U.S. banks and corporations is one step in the right direction, but it is just a start. The results are clear: if Russian enterprise directors can talk the same business language as interested potential Western partners, both sides would benefit and the flow of western capital and investment would increase.

Secondly, governments should be pressed at every level to direct technical assistance money directly into the developing Russian private sector. Governments no longer need to fund the second and third tiers of feasibility studies - there have been enough such studies written to paper over Red Square. Instead governments should be looking at ways to stimulate directly the private sector. That approach would pay dividends in the sector we should be aiming to encourage.

Thirdly, western governments and enterprises should show patience and resolve, and come to Russia for the long term. The investment climate is improving, the rate of inflation is dropping dramatically; the rouble is now essentially convertible; the Russian government has promised they would seek legislation to grant foreign investors a five-year tax holiday on taxes on profits, the building blocks are slowly being put into place. From the point of view of a small company which has been in Russia since 1989, the political and economic prospects in Russia are brighter now than they have been in the last five years.

FOREIGN INVESTMENTS
IN THE BANKING SECTOR

Riccardo Iozzo

Eastern Europe's money moved about in a financial Neverland where state-owned banks lent to state-owned companies. Today many positive steps have been taken to undo this situation, says Riccardo Iozzo, but more foreign capital, and more foreign know-how are needed. Mr. Iozzo suggests a mix-and-match approach. The American model will create more flexible money markets that are ready to take more risks - which could be crucial in restructuring the defence industry. And the Italian experience shows that the state can help prime the pump.

Dr. Riccardo Iozzo is the Brussels representative of the Istituto Bancario San Paolo di Torino.

It is now common to think that the economic reform process and the privatization programs in the Eastern European countries need the presence of a solid banking and financial system.

Such a system guarantees an efficient allocation of the financial resources and allows an overall control of the firms' profitability. It also favours the development of the financial markets and payment systems, and facilitates the privatization programs either through financial reform assistance, the redistribution of the property rights or financial intervention for the programs themselves on behalf of the private investors.

When Eastern European countries abandoned the planned system, absolute priority that had to be given to banking system reform. Actually those countries, unlike the less developed countries and in some way opposite to them, started out in a situation that can be considered as industrially advanced (even allowing for the obsolete plants, the excessive importance of heavy industry,and the technological backwardness, etc.) but certainly underdeveloped from the banking and financial point of view.

In fact an important effort and considerable financial commitments have been diverted into the banking and financial system reform process in those countries. The foreign private capital contribution has probably been less important than expected. But it can have a very important role in the reform process, and not only of the banking system - especially if it is conducted in a coordinated and a complementary way with regard to the national resources.

In an historical perspective, we can nevertheless say that some Eastern European countries have already achieved substantial results compared to the decades it took to build efficient and extensive financial markets in Western Europe. But the complex economic and political situation in the area makes it necessary to speed up the reform process.

Privatization of the Banking System

Privatization is generally acknowledged as the engine of such a reform process. However, the banking system itself has to strengthen its privatization programs and maybe even carry them out before the privatization of state-owned companies. It is sufficient to think of what happens in the huge programs based on the voucher system. They are gathered by investment funds usually created by the banks themselves and so there are vicious circles of control transfers from state-owned companies to state-owned banks.

The privatization of the financial system therefore assumes a primary role in the development of the market economy in the Eastern European countries. From this point of view, the problem of "bad loans" (which not only represents an aspect of the vicious circle between state-owned banks and state-owned companies) should also be solved in the short term. In fact the bad loans phenomenon seems to have extended also to the new private banks created recently.

Several solutions were put forward. Bank re-capitalization would involve a temporary growth of the public quota in them but it is also an essential condition to attract foreign investors. Bad loans could be concentrated in a new single body, or the debt could simply be cancelled.

Some useful information can be taken from the Italian experience, during the years that followed the First World War. At that period the assets of the three national banks included credits and control shares in companies that had great difficulties which were increased by the conversion crisis of war production. To deal with this, a single public entity took upon itself the risk and loss responsibility, and financial support in favor of both banks and companies was agreed upon.

This kind of intervention led to the setting-up of companies with government participation. The characteristics of such firms (which are different from the services offered by the public administration) are that they carry out an economic activity for which at the moment there is no private capital available, and where there is the possibility of a future return of the private capital through the partial withdrawal of the state shares. They operated in different sectors with multi-sectorial holdings.

It was a fifteen-year-long process that took place in different phases and brought about the recovery and the reorganization of the big public industries.

Today in Italy, we are at the end of this phase and we are going through an opposite process. However we cannot deny that state intervention had a very important role not only in the rescue of the Italian banking system but also in the recovery and the development of the Italian economy.

The Role of Foreign Capital

The role of foreign capital in the economy of Eastern Europe is a delicate question. History shows that foreign investment is essential for the development of industrialization. And the changes in the contemporary world economy demonstrate that internationalization enables development at high rates.

In Italy, in the Fifties, the first investments were made by multinational companies and in particular by Americans. They allowed the import of the know-how which produced, in the Sixties, the impressive development of the Italian entrepreneurship and in particular of small and medium-size companies.

In the financial sector, the entry of foreign capital is seen with even more suspicion. This is understandable with regards to some experiences encountered with foreign banks, especially for the creation of joint-ventures banks operating mainly as offshore banks. These banks made substantial profits but had no effect on the transfers of know how to the domestic market of such countries. Nevertheless it has to be stressed that foreign investment in the banking sector, if correctly made, is not only desirable, but absolutely necessary.

The "debt to equity swap", has not been sufficiently utilized in East European countries. This instrument helps debt reduction, increases foreign investments, and gives support to the privatization of the banking system. Chile had a very positive experience in that field in the late Eighties which contributed significantly to the economic recovery of the country.

The role of foreign investors has great importance in the creation of efficient banking systems. Technical assistance programs, such as those provided in a massive way by various international organizations, even if praiseworthy, are not able to substitute entirely for foreign banks in transferring managerial and technical know-how, providing an organizational and managerial model, and bringing in efficient payment systems and risk analysis.

An interesting experiment that links technical assistance and private investment is the one set up in Poland and financed by the World Bank in the so called "Twinning exercise". The technical assistance provided by a certain number of western banks for a parallel number of Polish banks can develop into a shareholding. A similar program will be set up in favour of a certain group of Russian banks.

The creation of an efficient banking system is a precondition for spread of a managerial mentality in the whole economy. Think of the effects that are reproduced in the entire economy when the banks have recourse to a correct and reliable credit analysis.

Therefore the first objective of reforming the financial systems is to develop markets and agents who are able to estimate the credit worthiness of the potential entrepreneur, and thereby allocate financial resources and monitor their usage.

Foreign Participation and the Italian Banking System

In a parallel way, the role of foreign investors in banks is important in the modernization and the development of the industrial sector. Again it can be useful to take into account the Italian experience in another historical phase (from the end of the 19th Century till the First World War) when the presence of foreign financial institutions in the capital of the main Italian banks enabled a rapid development of the industrial process. It has been said that, in Italy, the history of the evolution of the banking system coincides with the history of industrialization.

It is interesting to point out the role of German investments which took, in Italy, various forms such as capital inflow, and human resources when Germany was the major commercial partner of Italy. In particular, next to the commercial firms and financial companies which made investments in industrial activities, the presence of the German capital was considerable in share investments in the two main mixed Italian banks: Banca Commerciale Italiana and Credito Italiano.

When they were founded (a few years before 1900 - this year is the hundredth anniversary of Banca Commerciale Italiana) the presence of German banks capital was massive, especially in the Banca Commerciale. Other foreign banks present included the Swiss and, later, the French.

The presence of the capital corresponded to an even more massive presence of German representatives in the administration and management bodies of the two banks. Foreign investments in these specific cases were diverted to the creation of new banks and therefore avoided taking over the high credit risk burden of the already existing banks. The presence of foreign management in Italy was decisive in introducing a management system based on the criteria used in the big German banks It stimulated Italian industry and in the process, from 1896 till 1914, there followed one of the most rapid industrialization process in Europe.

The presence of foreign management continued even when foreign participation in the capital was considerably reduced. In 1914 the board of directors of the Banca Commerciale was composed of 15 Italians and 18 foreigners (8 Germans, 4 French, 3 Swiss and 3 Austrians). Foreign capital amounted to a little more than 30%.

This example appears to be the result of the international cooperation based on market mechanisms. The two banks operated as mixed banks with a decisive role in the development of several strategic industrial sectors. Later on, due to the difficulties in the bank-industry relationship, the two banks were put under the control of the State, and a new banking law was set up in 1936 that imposed the separation of the credit activities.

1994 is, for the Italian banking system a year of radical changes coming back to the institutional situation of the beginning of the century. Starting from this year the new Italian banking law increases the opportunity for the banking institutions to operate as mixed banks. In the last months Banca Commerciale Italiana and Credito Italiano have been privatized. Foreign investors ,and namely German banks, have become important shareholders of the two Italian banks

One aspect that appears to be almost absent in East European countries is an internationalization process with a regional basis. The Polish investments made in Hungary are not significant and the same could be said for all the other countries of that area.

It is important to favour the development of regional markets - though obviously in a different way with respect to the past. This also represents a precondition for more efficient integration in the whole European economy. Therefore it is important to set up instruments that link these markets.

Apart from commercial agreements a greater integration of the banking system of this area is desirable.

Integration means both good relations, reciprocity and creditworthiness but also possible shareholding. It means the development of a regional financial center where investments in banking and financial institutions could be channelled. Budapest could play this role owing to its relatively well advanced banking and financial system.

Besides, it is very important to create an efficient and modern payment system between commercial banks of the area. Last April an interesting project became operational. It is supported by the European Community and links several banks of Eastern Europe in order to help hard currency payments between these countries.

Some aspects could also concern the privatization and restructuring process of defence industry. The question is to find out the most effective answers that the banking and financial system can give to this problem. Contrary to the first expectations the restructuring process of military industry has proved a long and difficult task and it has not produced the hoped for results of giving new vitality chiefly to the economies of Eastern European countries but also to Western Europe. In a more general way, it appears that the restructuring and privatization of military industry reflects the modernization of the industry as a whole.

With reference to the role of banks and financial markets it remains to be ascertained whether the model consisting in a high rate of financial intermediation through banks and in a low level role of financial markets, which is prevailing in Europe (especially in Germany) can adequately cope with the problem. Such a model shows its limits as regards to innovation, to the need to set up new methods, productions and new ways having a higher level of risk compared to those already tried.

The American model in which the role of the banks is more specialized and the saving allocation is assured through a more flexible financial market seems more capable of answering correctly to the necessity arising from the restructuring of defence industry as it can offer funds for more complex and risky activities.

THE ROLE OF FOREIGN INVESTMENT IN DEFENCE PRIVATIZATION: THE RUSSIAN CASE

Sven Hegstad and Thierry Malleret*

There are many theories about what should and should not be done to privatize the Russian defence complex, and Sven Hegstad and Thierry Malleret offer an interesting external perspective. According to these experts, if you look beyond today's immediate crisis situation, the Russian case offers great possibilities. The long term prospects here are something of an economist's dream: the absorption potential of the Russian internal market is huge, while the entry cost is virtually zero.

Sven Hegstad is Director, and Dr. Thierry Malleret a member, of the Privatization and Restructuring Team at the European Bank for Reconstruction and Development.

This paper describes the principles that determine the way in which the European Bank operates in the area of defence industry privatisation. The EBRD has been created to support the transition process to the market economy. Therefore, every single transaction concluded by the Bank, whatever the sector, is ultimately aimed at developing the private economic activity. Defence conversion is no exception to that rule, although we recognise that the defence industry constitutes an unusual case because it represents one of the few sectors where the state governance may be maintained for reasons of national sovereignty. However, one may assume that this justification ceases de facto to be relevant when the facility is converted.

How do we tackle the conversion issue? We will not elaborate on the titanic difficulties the conversion process is currently facing in the former Soviet Union. We will just highlight a very simple but crucial fact which illustrates why the process - if only for this reason - is worthwhile: in the long run, the conversion from defence to civilian production will be very profitable because the absorption capacity of the internal market is huge, while the cost of entry is virtually nil. This is why we support defence conversion. We would like also to point out that we use the word conversion, but what we really mean is diversification. Conversion per se is extremely difficult to realise and examples abound all

* *The oral presentation during the conference was made by Thierry Malleret.*

around the world of conversion failures. By contrast, diversification allows expansion of the civilian core business in a military enterprise which may devote only 10-20% of its total production to the military activity. This is the case today in Russia.

The conversion needs in the Bank's 25 countries of operation are so considerable that the resources of one or even several institutions would not be sufficient to meet them. Even if the European Bank were to devote all its resources to foster the conversion process in the former Soviet Union only, this would represent in the end an infinitesimal contribution (to make a comparison, President Clinton decided to allocate in the next few years US$ 20 billion - twice the capital of the EBRD - for conversion in the United States).

Therefore, the most sensible way to proceed is to create a critical mass of replicable conversion cases. In other words, the aim is to register a few "success stories" which could then exercise a snowball effect on the conversion process itself, with a spin-off effect on the business environment. In that respect, attracting and gaining the support of foreign joint venture partners constitutes the cornerstone of the Bank's conversion policy. In effect, joint ventures offer many advantages: they enable us to carve out a fraction of the production facilities which can then be privatised; they provide the expertise and the know-how, they train the local workforce along Western lines and improve managerial methods; they establish in the local economy some development poles; they help in de-monopolizing the economy; and finally, they accelerate the transition process.

Obviously, domestic investment opportunities for conversion abound, but most of them are beyond the current means of the Bank because of its commitment to sound banking principles and the constraints on its equity investment portfolio. In particular, principles approved by the Board require the Bank to equity invest only when it:

(1) invests under terms it considers fair;
(2) perceives clear potential exit strategies;
(3) projects an acceptable internal rate of return.

You may notice that immediate privatisation does not constitute an absolute prerequisite. Obviously, the Bank favours those projects which offer a clear prospect of privatisation, but will not systematically exclude state-owned companies. In the field of defence conversion, one cannot afford to be too demanding because bankable opportunities are very limited indeed. Therefore, conditions which should be met before a project is seriously considered derive from common sense rather than "religious dogma". However, defence enterprises in the former Soviet Union do not - or very rarely - meet these criteria since many of them are currently in danger of further deterioration and collapse.

In fact, none of them is yet in a position to borrow money on commercial or any other terms from an international bank. Why? To put it in a nutshell, any bankable project encounters the following general problems (setting aside the economic and political difficulties): uncertain legal framework, no audited financial statements, liquidity crisis, uncertainty about ownership rights, and lack of knowledge in preparing business proposals. Furthermore, and this is particularly relevant to the defence industry, the transformation of these big conglomerates into stock companies and their subsidiaries into companies with limited liabilities proves to be a nightmare, exactly as it was in East Germany when the Treuhand found that for most companies, total liabilities exceeded the realisable value of their assets.

These "kombinates" would be due for liquidation if normal economic rules were applied. However, some of them possess a strong potential for surviving and prospering if they are given the proper assistance (both financial and technical). Therefore, the privatisation-restructuring team concentrates on:
- Stabilising enterprises currently in a critical condition, but potentially viable, so that they might be able to operate profitably in a market economy.
- Attracting, and sharing the financial risk with local and foreign corporate investors who would otherwise have scaled down or cancelled their investment plans.

For the time being, the European Bank has about 20 conversion projects in the pipeline. The majority of these are at an exploratory stage while a few are more advanced. They cover several countries (with a strong emphasis on Russia) and a wide range of industrial products from satellite launching rockets and integrated circuits to refitting of railway cars, forklifts and furniture production. Twenty is simultaneously very few and very many. Very few in the light of what needs to be done, but many when one considers the constraints faced when tackling conversion.

To give an order of magnitude, at the end of 1992, about 220 joint-ventures were directly involved in conversion and diversification in the former Soviet Union, of which 180 were for Russia alone. However, the role played by the European Bank cannot be measured in terms of figures alone. As a direct result of its policy to stabilise, restructure and privatise certain companies, the Bank, in reality, is making a contribution to a positive and irreversible transformation of these economies. We understand that we are just putting a drop in the ocean, but this may be a drop of ink which might colour the sea. If I have time, or if you should have questions, I would be happy to expand on a few projects already launched by the Bank in some very large enterprises such as Lomo or Perm or entire sectors such as the Air-Traffic Control.

Before concluding, I would like to stress a methodological point. The main problems associated with the state governance of enterprises are well known: ex-ante control (leading to meddling) rather than ex-post (that is to say, judging results), multiple objectives (i.e. non-commercial objectives such as employment combined with profit maximisation), multiple principals, and lack of competition. However, privatisation works efficiently only when it modifies the behaviour of the firm. In that respect, one could redefine the role of the state and its articulation with free initiative. When the cold war came to an end, we heard about the end of history proclaimed by Francis Fukuyama, which was to be followed by the natural emergence of the market and democracy.

Clearly, the creation of a proper entrepreneurial climate relies upon the promotion of entrepreneurs, in other words upon the creation of a situation where individuals shoulder their own responsibilities. However, the state also has a number of crucial responsibilities, since there are many areas such as the creation of a legal framework, a viable and fair taxation system, an effective competition policy, a decent social security system, an efficient education system, the acceptance of public order, etc. where the state has a fundamental role to play. To put it very simply, the market and democracy will only thrive where and when the state has the means to protect them.

In the end, there is no miracle or quick solution. This reminds me of an apt metaphor used by Vaclav Havel when he was welcomed by the Académie des Sciences Morales et Politiques in Paris last October. Referring to Beckett's famous play "Waiting for Godot" and analyzing the phenomenon of waiting in post-communist societies, he noted that people should not wait for Godot. Godot will not come because he does not exist.

RAPPORTEUR'S SUMMARY
OF THE 1994 NATO ECONOMICS
COLLOQUIUM

Richard F. Kaufman

The politics of privatization in Central and Eastern Europe are as important as its economic motivations, says Richard Kaufman. For the governments of these post-communist states, a variety of approaches to the 'destatification' of key industries are possible. They include transferral of ownership to company employees or managers, selling or giving away shares to the public, or opening to bids from foreign investors. There is no 'right way' to privatization, only a responsible one - which for each country depends on a different set of factors.

In this report Mr. Kaufman offers an overview of all the speakers' views and experiences at the 1994 NATO Economics Colloquium.

Richard F. Kaufman is a 1993-1994 Fellow of the Woodrow Wilson International Center for Scholars and Director of the Bethesda Research Institute.

What is meant by "privatization" and what is the rationale for it? Although privatization can be defined in several ways, it is generally agreed that it involves the transfer of assets from state ownership and control to private ownership and control. For the change to be meaningful with respect to state-owned enterprises, production and pricing decisions must also be placed in private hands. A variety of approaches are possible, including transferring all or part of the ownership to employees and managers, selling or giving away shares to the general public, and inviting offers from domestic and foreign investors.

There are political as well as economic reasons for privatizing state properties. The economic argument is that the economy functions more efficiently when production facilities are in the private sector where incentives for private gain promote innovation and higher productivity. These attributes, in turn, contribute to sustained economic growth and make possible improvements in living standards. Privatization is also a means for restructuring industries in which there is excess capacity or which are not competitive in world markets.

The politics of privatization in Central and East Europe are as important as the economic motivations. The comprehensive transformations underway in the countries of this region include a reduction in many aspects of the role of the state. Thus, even where a state owned enterprise has been managed efficiently it may be deemed desirable to privatize it as part of a policy of change from the period when the state dominated economic activities. It can also be argued that privatization can achieve a more just distribution of wealth and is likely to benefit the emerging middle class. At the same time, there are often political factors that slow or prevent privatization, such as the response of governments to concerns that workers in state-owned enterprises will lose jobs or, in the case of strategic industries, that national security will be impaired.

Marvin Jackson's analysis of the experiences in 14 post communist countries shows that in most of them there has been substantial progress in the privatization of state-owned enterprises. The percentages of enterprises privatized by the end of the first quarter of 1994 was nearly 60 percent in the Czech Republic, 30 percent in Russia, Lithuania and Estonia, 27 percent in Poland and Hungary, 15 percent in Belarus and Ukraine,and lesser amounts in the other countries. Although it is too soon to evaluate the actual effects of privatization on economic behavior, Jackson correlates the figures with increases in thes hare of the private sector in the gross domestic product (GDP) of each of the countries.

Progress, in terms of sheer numbers, is confirmed by reports from individual countries. In Russia, for example, privatization is credited by Andrey Loginov with having brought about a revolution in property relations. Under the voucher privatization approach used there, 94.3 thousand enterprises were privatized by April 1994. Of the 19 thousand largestenterprises, 15 thousand were transformed into joint-stockcompanies, and 12 thousand had been privatized. Keith Bush concludes that since the removal of price controls in January1992, the privatization program in Russia has been President Yeltsin's most important economic reform..

However, a closer examination reveals uncertain and uneven results in important respects. Several participants in the conference qualify the apparent progress reflected in the figures by pointing to the need to go behind the statistics. Marvin Jackson points out that there are no common statistical standards in the region for reporting privatization, and Yuri V. Andreev discusses the shortcomings in Russian official statistics generally. There is uncertainty, Andreev states, even about the number of factories in the Russian military industrial complex.

In Russia and other countries official statistics are still designed to report primarily on government activities and much of the private sector is not included. What used to be the "hidden"economy, comprising what was then questionable or illegal activities because they were not sanctioned by the state, is still not visible in official statistics. As Eva Ehrlich shows, for tax avoidance and other reasons a considerable portion of private production activities are left off the books. In addition, an estimated 40 percent of registered small businesses are "dummy" organizations or "phantom firms" that are established for various reasons but never actually start operations. Thus, estimates of the private share of GDP and the economic consequences of privatization may have a wide range of uncertainty.

In most countries, privatization has been more successful for small enterprises than for the larger ones. Salvatore Zecchini finds that only Russia and the Czech

Republic have made substantial progress in privatizing large enterprises. In effect, heavy industries, energy, motor transport, major chemical industries banks and other financial institutions, and agricultural land (except in Poland) have been largely excluded from the process.

The effects of privatization will vary depending upon the approach that is employed. Typically, a state owned enterprise is turned into a joint-stock company whose shares are owned by the state and may be privatized through sale or otherwise. The most common approach is mass privatization in which one or more entities are transferred to the general public through auction orsale, often with the aid of vouchers that are distributed to potential buyers. A second approach is to permit a buy-out by the managers or employees of the enterprise being privatized. A third approach is to seek domestic or foreign investors.

Mass privatization has the advantages of rapid transfers of ownership and satisfaction of public demands for a portion of the wealth created under communism. It also gives large segments of the public a vested interest in the emerging market economy. Manager-employee buyouts have the advantage of continuity in management and work force, but that may also be a disadvantage.In Russia and other countries buyouts have been accompanied by charges of favoritism to the former nomenclatura and criminal elements. One of the weaknesses of both of these approaches is that the transfers of ownership do not produce new management,capital or expertise.

Many economists prefer a third approach, "trade" sales to investors. This approach is a source of needed revenue to the government and, more importantly, is likely to be followed by infusions of capital and entrepreneurial skills into the enterprise. But trade sales require extensive preparation by the government, which may need to restructure an entity before it can be sold, and are often difficult to justify to a skeptical public.

It is useful, for a number of reasons, to know how western governments have dealt with the issue of privatization generally and, in particular, with the privatization of defense enterprises and their conversion to commercial activities. The East German case is, at first glance, the most applicable as it, too, is a former communist country. With the end of communist rule, East Germans found themselves with many inefficient, non-competitive industries and arms production facilities that were excessive to the needs of national security. The decision of the German government soon after unification was to privatize or liquidate much of the former East German industrial structure.

Wolfgang Vehse's paper provides a detailed account of Germany's successful privatization of East Germany. There are many lessons in the German experience worth recording. Unfortunately, most of them do not appear to be applicable in the other former communist countries. For one thing, the costs of the German approach would be prohibitive elsewhere. By mid 1994 the German government had spent 150 billion DMs and it is estimated that the full costs will be 275 billion DMs.

Secondly, Vehse makes the point that the transformation of a command economy into a market economy cannot be forced. He lists the basic conditions that he believes such a transformation necessitates: (1) a consensus about the economic policy to be followed; (2) a proven and uncomplicated legal system; (3)competent and loyal government administrations at the local level; (4) a welfare system capable of absorbing moderateun employment; and (5) a well organized and trustworthy financial system and currency. It is precisely the absence of most of these conditions in the former communist countries that reforms are attempting to remedy.

Presentations were made at the colloquium about recent efforts in the United Kingdom, the United States, and France to privatize, diversify, or convert their defense industries. Each has employed a somewhat different approach. In the UK, the government in 1979 began privatizing broad sectors of industry such as aerospace and most of the defense industry, shipbuildingand state owned housing. The US has not had notable success in past efforts to convert defense firms to other activities. More recently it put in place a program to cushion the industrial effects of reduced defense orders, to preserve certain technological capabilities, and to retrain defense workers. But it is expected that many defense firms will go under and that some of the larger firms will be absorbed in corporate mergers.In France a policy of diversification has been adopted for a segment of the defense industry, rather than privatization. The presence of Vehse's preconditions in these countries has facilitated the changes there.

Another way of distinguishing the privatization and defense conversion problems of the West with those of the post communist countries is to point out that the western nations are liberal democracies with market systems. The western nations also have relatively balanced and advanced economies. Alexander Kennaway demonstrates that the defense industries in the western countries are a small part of the manufacturing base, and the economies can easily absorb restructuring and closures in the defense sector. Nevertheless, even in the West the adjustment process has not been without political and social difficulties. The fact that the countries of Central and East Europe do not yet possess the political and economic advantages of the West is, in part, what makes the privatization and conversion problems so much more difficult in this region.

There are several types of special problems surrounding the efforts to privatize and convert or diversify defense industries. The most serious problems are in the former Soviet Union where the military establishment had grown to enormous proportions. In Russia and the newly independent states the demand for arms has been sharply curtailed domestically and in foreign markets. The defense industry no longer enjoys the privileged status that gave it the highest priorities for supplies, manpower and technology. Many defense plants were located in cities whose economies were highly dependent upon them and are now depressed areas. Large numbers of the youngest and more skilled workers have left to find other jobs. Defense production skills and equipment are often not convertible to commercial products.

Moscow's attitude towards the problem of privatizing and converting substantial portions of its defense industry has been ambivalent. Defense procurement has been drastically reduced but factories have not been closed and there is much hidden defense unemployment. Although there has been recent progress in the mass voucher privatization of defense enterprises, it is not clear how this will lead to increased investment or a restructuring of the defense industry.

Some of the same problems exist in the former Warsaw Pact countries where defense industrial structure and end products were determined by the former Soviet Union, where there also has been a collapse in demand for arms and equipment, and where there is now substantial excess capacity. The task for these countries is to reorient defense to their own requirements and dispose of the unneeded portions of their defense industries. The former Czechoslovakia and Poland had the largest defense industries inthe region in absolute terms and relative to the size of their economies. Consequently, the more serious adjustment problems are in those countries.

Most of the defense industry in the former Czechoslovakia is located in Slovakia and the reduction in arms production and employment there has been the sharpest in the region. Cuts in arms spending have also been severe in the Czech Republic. Government efforts to assist defense firms in Slovakia and the Czech Republic to diversify and to attract foreign investment seem to have had only limited success. To the extent that defense firms have been privatized it appears to have occurred within the framework of overall privatization rather than as a result of actions directed at the defense industry.

The Polish government adopted in 1992 a defense industry restructuring program prepared by the Department of Defense Affairs. Under the plan, as explained in Edward Gorczynski's paper, a certain number of defense enterprises will remain under government ownership and control. The remainder are to be converted to civilian activities and privatized, or their assets will be sold. As of mid 1994, defense employment in Poland had been reduced by 50 percent.

Of course, the unemployment accompanying defense privatization and conversion is a matter of deep concern throughout the region. Franz-Lothar Altmann calls attention to the fact that the loss of jobs is caused by the downsizing of defense and the excess capacity in the defense industry rather than by privatization per se. The unemployment consequences can be eased by the privatization and conversion process. For this reason, foreign investment is preferable to voucher privatization because of the fresh capital that foreign investors can provide.Without an infusion of capital into privatized firms large layoffs are unavoidable.

The subject of defense conversion in the post communist countries could not be discussed adequately without reference to the broader issues of national security and future relations with the West. In fact, these issues were raised at numerous times during the colloquium. There are several interrelated concerns.

One is that although the Cold War is over, there are still security threats to all the nations in the region. Although it is recognized that self-sufficiency in arms and equipment is not practical, all express a need to retain some defense capabilities. Yuri V. Andreev argues that the part of the Russian military-industrial complex necessary for the maintenanceof national security should be identified before the rest is converted to civilian production and privatized. Some of the participants state that efforts are underway in some countries to redefine security requirements. Others, including Salvatore Zecchini, express doubt that the countries with large defense industries have drawn a demarcation line between the core defense activities to be retained for security reasons and those that can be privatized.

A second issue is about relations with NATO. Secretary General Manfred Worner mentions in the opening remarks prepared for the colloquium the dynamic nature of NATO's cooperation with the states of the former Soviet Union and the other Central and East European countries. The Secretary General states that the aim is to use the framework of the North Atlantic Cooperation Council (NACC) to facilitate and promote work on common problems, like defense conversion. He goes on to state: "We aim to advance on practical cooperation on defense conversion and on security-related economic issues, including those related to defense budgets." Daniel George, Director of the Economics Directorate, states in his opening remarks that this colloquium itself is part of the work of the NACC.

The Central and East European nations welcome the idea of international cooperation. Katarzyna Zukrowska and Leon Turcynski state in their paper that defense production cannot be left out of international economic cooperation and that the Central and East European countries need to catch up with the structures and equipment of the NATO partnership countries. They and other participants mention efforts by countries in the region to achieve standardization and interoperability with NATO weapons. Zukrowska and Turcynski conclude by noting that all the countries of the region want to become members of NATO. However, at the West's insistence the Central and East European countries"have to proceed through a transition period which resembles a quarantine during which they will restructure their defence systems" to bring them closer to NATO requirements.

Finally, some of the papers presented at the colloquium broach the subject of European integration. Igor Kosir views the present transition period as a challenge not only for the postcommunist countries but for all of Europe and its integrated future. Daniel Daianu states the issue most succinctly: "In a broad political, social, economic and cultural sense, integration into Europe (into pan-European political, economic and defense structures) is an ultimate goal for the post-communist countries." Most of the participants of the colloquium appear to agree with that statement.

L'INCIDENCE DE LA PRIVATISATION DES INDUSTRIES DE DEFENSE SUR LE MARCHE DE L'EMPLOI - UN POINT DE VUE OCCIDENTAL

Franz-Lothar Altmann

Il est pratiquement impossible de comparer de façon rigoureuse les infrastructures de défense des différents pays de l'ancien bloc de l'Est et de l'ex-Union soviétique, mais elles présentent cependant certains traits communs qui nous aident à mieux comprendre le défi que suppose la privatisation du secteur de la défense. Evoquant l'implantation régionale et "monoculturale" de ces industries de défense et les risques qu'une privatisation trop précipitée présenterait sur le plan politique et du point de vue de la sécurite, Franz-Lothar Altmann indique que telle est la réalité à laquelle l'Est et l'Ouest doivent faire face.

LA SITUATION VUE DE RUSSIE

Iouri V. Andreev

En Union soviétique, la connaissance était liée au pouvoir et le parti accaparait les deux. Selon Iouri Andreev, le principal obstacle à la restructuration de l'industrie de défense russe est que personne ne connait ses véritables dimensions. Le culte du secret, conjugué à une piètre efficacité, ont fait que les statistiques ne sont pas fiables. La sécurité nationale commande que l'Etat ait encore amplement son mot à dire quant à l'avenir de l'industrie de défense, mais il faut néanmoins que le secteur privé prenne pied dans cette dernière - et il se gardera de le faire tant qu'il ne saura pas exactement dans quoi il s'engage.

THE FUTURE OF DEFENCE INDUSTRIES

Thierry Baumgart

In a world context which has changed greatly over the last decade, it is necessary to reconsider the future of defence industries. For this purpose, the Commissariat général du Plan in France has established an industrial strategy group comprising all the interested parties. Thierry Baumgart explains how French defence industries, which for a long time contributed to the equilibrium of the trade balance, must now adjust to a rapid shrinking of markets. The establishment of powerful international groupings through restructuring, reconversion and durable cooperation frameworks, as well as the efficient valorization of technologies and the rationalization of budget expenditure, are indispensable conditions for the perpetuation of activities in which France has become particularly prominent since the beginning of the seventies.

LA PRIVATISATION DES INDUSTRIES DE DEFENSE : L'EXEMPLE DE LA CONSTRUCTION NAVALE

Fredrik Behrens

Lorsque, dans les années 80, les Etats occidentaux ont vendu leurs chantiers navals, ceux-ci ont été repris par un secteur privé prospère qui pouvait les aider à se diversifier en absorbant de nouveaux produits et en créant de nouveaux marchés. Pourtant, même ainsi, l'opération ne s'est pas faite sans douleur. Les chantiers ont dû se morceler pour survivre et un grand nombre d'entre eux ne sont devenus compétitifs que récemment. Les chantiers russes travaillent sans filet, indique Fredrik Behrens, en ajoutant que soit l'Etat, soit des investisseurs étrangers, devront prévoir un dispositif de protection.

LA PRIVATISATION DES INDUSTRIES DE DEFENSE : L'EXEMPLE DU ROYAUME-UNI

Michael Bell

Les entreprises de défense n'ont pas été traitées différemment des autres firmes du secteur nationalisé dans le cadre du programme de privatisation britannique. Elles ont été vendues ou mises sur le marché boursier, certaines comme un tout, d'autres par fragments. L'Etat détient une "action spécifique" dans trois entreprises clés afin de protéger l'intérêt national, mais la règle de base est de laisser jouer les lois du marché.

Cette orientation a encore été renforcée avec l'adoption par le ministère de la défense d'une politique d'acquisitions fondée sur la concurrence.

Pareille mutation ne pouvait être indolore à une époque où les budgets de la défense sont en baisse : des emplois ont été supprimés et des sites fermés, mais les entreprises ont diminué de taille et se sont mises davantage à l'écoute du client - comme en témoigne le niveau record des commandes à l'exportation enregistré l'an dernier - sans qu'il en coûte rien au contribuable.

LA CONVERSION ET LA PRIVATISATION DES ENTREPRISES DE DEFENSE EN RUSSIE

Keith Bush

La conversion ne va pas sans difficultés à l'Ouest, mais les problèmes sont encore bien plus vastes en Russie. La pratique des monopoles d'Etat dans le secteur de la production pour la défense remonte à l'époque des tsars. Mais le temps des privilèges est révolu. Les usines d'armement, habituées depuis toujours à un traitement de faveur, doivent désormais acheter leurs matières premières aux prix du marché et appliquer les barèmes salariaux du marché. Par ailleurs, la Russie, privée de ses partenaires du Pacte de Varsovie, se voit contrainte de fabriquer elle-même tous ses armements. Dans ces conditions, observe Keith Bush, il n'est guère étonnant que la conversion n'ait suscité jusqu'ici qu'un enthousiasme très mitigé. La situation évolue peu à peu, mais tout le processus pourrait être compromis si le climat politique venait à changer.

QUELQUES REFLEXIONS SUR LA POLITIQUE DE PRIVATISATION ET DE RESTRUCTURATION DE L'INDUSTRIE DE L'ARMEMENT EN ROUMANIE

Mircea Cosea

Pour que le processus de privatisation des industries de défense aboutisse, il faut d'abord et surtout penser en termes de sociologie appliquée et non de reconfiguration industrielle, indique Mircea Cosea. En septembre 1994, les autorités roumaines ont lancé un programme de privatisation à marche forcée portant sur quelque 3.000 sociétés d'Etat, mais aucune n'appartenait au secteur de l'armement. La conversion des industries de defense est très délicate à gérer sur les plans démographique et politique et sur celui de l'emploi, aussi ses aspects sociaux doivent-ils être soigneusement planifiés pour que la transition s'opère sans heurt. La Roumanie entamera la conversion de son appareil de défense à la mi-1995.

LA RESTRUCTURATION DES INDUSTRIES DE DEFENSE DANS L'ERE POSTCOMMUNISTE : QUEL EST LE ROLE DES INVESTISSEMENTS ETRANGERS DIRECTS?

Daniel Daianu

La privatisation en soi ne transformera pas les industries de défense, avertit Daniel Daianu. En réalité, c'est la crise qui ramène peu à peu celles-ci à de justes dimensions. Entretemps, le monde devient plus instable et les pays d'Europe de l'Est ont l'impression de vivre dans un vide de sécurité. Ils savent qu'ils possèdent avec les armes un produit négociable dont la valeur est avérée - tout comme ils savent que les frontières des pays occidentaux sont fermées à leurs biens de consommation en raison de la politique protectionniste appliquée par ces pays.

La vraie question est de savoir comment amener l'Ouest à affronter cette situation et à investir politiquement en Europe de l'Est.

Les pays qui reçoivent le plus d'investissements étrangers directs sont ceux qui enregistrent les meilleurs résultats économiques.

Pourquoi ne pas envisager aussi des investissements étrangers "politiques"?

LE SECTEUR PRIVE ET LA PRIVATISATION DANS CERTAINS PAYS D'EUROPE CENTRALE ET ORIENTALE : PARTICULARITES DU CAS HONGROIS

Éva Ehrlich

La Hongrie, la Pologne et la République tchèque sont déjà bien avancées sur la voie de la privatisation des activités économiques et commerciales tandis que la Slovaquie est à la traîne, indique Éva Ehrlich, tout en précisant que même dans les trois premiers pays, il faudra sans doute compter une dizaine d'années au moins pour que le phénomène se généralise. La privatisation marque le pas à présent que les sociétés les plus intéressantes ont été vendues. Par ailleurs, ceux qui sont chargés de mener à bien l'opération, c'est-à-dire les gestionnaires et les dirigeants de l'ancien régime, freinent le mouvement car ils sont inquiets. Seule une reprise économique parviendra à calmer leurs appréhensions.

LA PRIVATISATION DES INDUSTRIES DE DEFENSE ET LES EXIGENCES DE LA SECURITE NATIONALE : L'EXEMPLE DES ETATS-UNIS

Robert Farrand

De tous temps s'est posé à l'humanité un problème crucial : comment forger des socs de ses épées au lendemain des conflits armés de grande envergure? Evoquant l'exemple de la privatisation de l'industrie de défense aux Etats-Unis, l'Ambassadeur Robert Farrand et ses collègues font observer que l'objectif des pays est aujourd'hui d'assurer la défense nationale le plus efficacement possible au coût minimum. La question n'est pas : "devons-nous privatiser?", mais bien : "dans quelle mesure pouvons-nous compter sur le complexe de défense privatisé en temps de guerre?".

LA RESTRUCTURATION DE L'INDUSTRIE DE DEFENSE DE LA POLOGNE

Edward Gorczynski

Avant la chute du communisme, l'industrie de défense polonaise était au service de l'Union soviétique et du Pacte de Varsovie plutôt que de la Pologne elle-même. Edward Gorczynski explique comment le gouvernement a procédé pour en réduire la taille en vue d'une plus grande efficience et pour affecter davantage de ressources à la production civile. Les autorités polonaises envisagent aussi de rendre à l'industrie de défense un rôle plus traditionnel, à savoir fabriquer des armes et du matériel destinés à la défense nationale.

LA PRIVATISATION DANS LES ECONOMIES POSTCOMMUNISTES, UNE ANALYSE THEORIQUE

Bülent Gültekin et Michael Goldstein

Chacun des pays anciennement communistes trouve peu à peu sa propre voie vers le marché et il devrait en aller de même des entreprises, observe Bülent Gültekin. Les petites sociétés devraient être vendues ou cédées le plus vite possible. Les plus grandes posent un problème plus délicat. Elles doivent être d'une taille suffisante pour pouvoir réaliser des économies d'échelle, sans toutefois devenir impossibles à gérer. Et le professeur Gültekin ajoute, à propos des grandes entreprises, que la principale question à se poser n'est pas "comment", mais bien "pourquoi" privatiser. La privatisation est un moyen et non une fin. L'objectif recherché est en définitive d'accroître l'efficience et le rendement et d'élever le niveau de vie.

LE ROLE DES INVESTISSEMENTS ETRANGERS DANS LA PRIVATISATION DES INDUSTRIES DE DEFENSE : L'EXEMPLE DE LA RUSSIE

Sven Hegstad et Thierry Malleret

De nombreuses théories ont cours quant à ce qu'il convient de faire - et de ne pas faire - pour privatiser l'appareil de défense de la Russie. Sven Hegstad et Thierry Malleret présentent ici un point de vue extérieur qui ne manque pas d'intérêt. La Russie offre selon eux de vastes possibilités pour peu que l'on ne s'arrête pas à la situation de crise immédiate.

Les perspectives à long terme sont de nature à faire rêver les économistes : le marché intérieur russe a une immense capacité d'absorption pour un coût de pénétration pratiquement nul.

L'EMPLOI, LA PRIVATISATION ET LA RESTRUCTURATION DANS LES PAYS D'EUROPE CENTRALE ET ORIENTALE

Lajos Hethy

Dans les années à venir, l'une des tâches essentielles des gouvernements consistera à trouver des solutions créatives pour combattre les pertes d'emplois qui se multiplient dans toute l'Europe centrale et orientale, déclare Lajos Hethy. Même dans des pays tels que la Pologne, où le déclin économique a été enrayé, une aggravation future du chômage n'est pas à exclure du fait des processus de privatisation et de restructuration en cours. A ce jour, la solution la plus novatrice est peut-être celle qui a été imaginée en République tchèque, où l'on encourage les chômeurs à s'installer à leur compte en leur offrant des subventions appréciables.

LES INVESTISSEMENTS ETRANGERS DANS LE SECTEUR BANCAIRE

Riccardo Iozzo

Les capitaux des pays d'Europe de l'Est évoluaient autrefois dans une espèce d'Eden financier où des banques d'Etat prêtaient de l'argent à des sociétés d'Etat. De nombreuses mesures concrètes ont été prises pour remédier à cette situation, note Riccardo Iozzo, mais il faudrait que l'étranger fournisse davantage de capitaux et de savoir-faire. M. Iozzo suggère une démarche composite. Le modèle américain créera des marchés monétaires plus souples, prêts à prendre plus de risques, ce qui pourrait se révéler extrêmement utile pour la restructuration des industries de défense. L'expérience italienne démontre par ailleurs que l'Etat peut aider au démarrage.

PROBLEMES FONDAMENTAUX LIES A LA PRIVATISATION : L'EXPERIENCE DES PAYS D'EUROPE CENTRALE ET ORIENTALE

Marvin Jackson

Tous les pays d'Europe centrale et orientale se sont lancés dans des programmes de privatisation massive d'un type ou d'un autre. Le problème, explique Marvin Jackson, est que chacun a des attentes différentes et que les résultats varient selon la méthode choisie. Le système des coupons a l'avantage d'accélérer la vente, mais les sociétés risquent d'avoir de trop nombreux actionnaires et la gestion risque de laisser à désirer. De leur côté, les programmes centralisés sont lents à mettre en oeuvre.

Ils font appel à des consultants dont les services sont très onéreux et avantagent au départ les dirigeants en place, ce qui est assez mal reçu. Le mieux semble qu'il y ait un seul gros investisseur ou que ce soient les propriétaires qui gèrent l'entreprise.

COMPTE RENDU DU COLLOQUE ÉCONOMIQUE DE L'OTAN 1994 ÉTABLI PAR LE RAPPORTEUR

Richard F. Kaufman

Selon Richard Kaufman, les stratégies de privatisation adoptées en Europe centrale et orientale importent autant que les raisons économiques qui sont à l'origine du processus. Diverses solutions s'offrent aux gouvernements des Etats anciennement communistes pour "désétatiser" les industries clés. M. Kaufman cite par exemple le transfert de la propriété des entreprises à leurs employés ou à leurs dirigeants, la vente ou la cession d'actions à la population et le lancement d'appels d'offres s'adressant aux investisseurs étrangers. Il n'existe pas une "bonne" méthode de privatisation qui l'emporte sur toutes les autres; il y a seulement pour chaque pays une méthode réaliste, dépendant de toute une série de facteurs.

M. Kaufman présente dans son rapport une synthèse des réflexions et des témoignages de tous les orateurs qui se sont exprimés au Colloque économique de l'OTAN 1994.

LES INVESTISSEMENTS ETRANGERS ET LA PRIVATISATION EN ESTONIE

Kaja Kell

L'Estonie se classe troisième parmi les pays d'Europe de l'Est les plus prisés des investisseurs étrangers. Kaja Kell indique que les entreprises mixtes et les sociétés étrangères prospèrent et que, cette année, les investissements étrangers ont pour la première fois dépassé les investissements nationaux. Les allégements fiscaux attirent beaucoup de capitaux, dont une bonne part en provenance des paradis fiscaux extraterritoriaux. Avec le ralentissement du programme de privatisation, les investisseurs étrangers semblent avoir plutôt tendance à créer de nouvelles sociétés qu'à en racheter d'anciennes.

LA PRIVATISATION DES INDUSTRIES DE DEFENSE DANS LE CADRE GENERAL DE LA PRIVATISATION

Alexander Kennaway

Selon le professeur Kennaway, la difficulté de mener à bien la privatisation des industries de défense est peut-être essentiellement liée à un problème de perspective. Les pays occidentaux devraient oublier leurs modèles macro-économiques ainsi que les scénarios décrits dans leurs manuels et les producteurs de l'Est cesser de leur côté de nourrir l'illusion que la production peut rester telle quelle ou "revenir bientôt à la normale". La seule voie possible est celle du pragmatisme : les pays occidentaux devraient aider les industries de défense de l'Est de leurs conseils, leur offrir de multiples possibilités de formation et rechercher avant tout des succès économiques modestes, mais concrets.

LA CONVERSION DE L'INDUSTRIE DE DEFENSE SLOVAQUE, ELEMENT MOTEUR DE LA TRANSFORMATION ECONOMIQUE ET SOCIALE DU PAYS

Igor Kosir

Après la Révolution de velours, la Tchécoslovaquie s'est scindée, selon un processus pacifique en deux Etats distincts : les Républiques tchèque et slovaque. Pour la République slovaque, qui a hérité de 60% de la capacité de production militaire de l'ex-Tchécoslovaquie, le plus ambitieux des défis consiste à gérer aussi efficacement que possible la mutation du secteur de la défense. Actuellement, les progrès sont lents et la Slovaquie a grand besoin d'investissements extérieurs, mais ses efforts de privatisation sont stimulés par son objectif numéro 1 : l'intégration à part entière dans l'Union européenne comme objectif stratégique final.

LA PRIVATISATION DE L'INDUSTRIE DE DEFENSE ET LES EXIGENCES DE LA SECURITE NATIONALE : L'EXEMPLE DE L'UKRAINE

Nikolai Koulinitch

La conversion du secteur de la défense ukrainien a démarré alors que le pays faisait encore partie de l'URSS et abritait sur son territoire un tiers du complexe militaire soviétique. L'Ukraine, observe Nikolai Koulinitch, s'est ainsi trouvée en possession d'un arsenal supérieur à ses besoins et d'une industrie de défense restant tributaire de l'ex-Union soviétique.

La conversion n'en est pas moins menée à un bon rythme et la production de biens de consommation se développe. Cependant, les vieilles habitudes sont tenaces : aucune entreprise de défense n'a été mise en vente lors de la première vague de privatisations et aucune ne le sera non plus lors de la deuxième. L'Ukraine souhaite que la communauté internationale contribue au financement de son programme de conversion.

LA PRIVATISATION EN RUSSIE : BILAN ET PERSPECTIVES

Andrei N. Loginov

En Russie, la culture économique évolue lentement mais sûrement sous l'effet de la privatisation. La population surmonte peu à peu sa défiance initiale. La demande de conseils juridiques et commerciaux a augmenté de façon spectaculaire et les cours de commerce connaissent un succès sans précédent. Un retour en arrière est désormais inconcevable, surtout si l'économie se redresse en 1994-1995. La démarche à l'égard de l'industrie de défense est plus circonspecte. Une grande partie des sociétés du secteur seront vendues cette année, mais l'Etat protège les plus stratégiques d'entre elles et conserve une participation majoritaire dans d'autres. Il faut compter que le coût de la conversion des industries de défense russes sera de l'ordre de $ EU 150-300 milliards.

CHANGE IN STATUS OF GIAT -
WHY, HOW AND WITH WHAT RESULTS?

Jean-Hughes Monier

21 Defence industry structures have changed a great deal during recent years in France. The most significant development was probably the denationalization of GIAT (Groupement Industriel des Armements Terrestres) which was formalized on 1st July 1990 with the establishment of GIAT Industries. How and why this was done, and the results four and a half years later, were described to the NATO Economics Colloquium by Jean-Hughes Monier. It is an experiment which should mainly interest the countries of Eastern Europe, where several defence enterprises still remain state arsenals.

LA PRIVATISATION ET LA CONVERSION DES
INDUSTRIES MILITAIRES EN LITUANIE

Gediminas Rainys

Les gouvernements des pays baltes s'emploient à faire en sorte que l'Etat ne s'occupe plus désormais que des affaires le concernant et qu'il tente ainsi de vendre au plus vite les entreprises publiques. Comment? La distribution de coupons permet d'intéresser financièrement au système un plus grand nombre d'individus; les actions, quant à elles, procurent davantage de capitaux à mesure qu'un marché boursier se développe. La Lituanie a opté pour la méthode des coupons tandis que ses voisines, la Lettonie et l'Estonie, ont préféré la seconde formule, davantage axée sur le marché. Selon Gediminas Raynis, les trois pays ont cependant deux problèmes en commun : ils doivent trouver de nouveaux débouchés pour les biens qu'ils vendaient autrefois à l'Union soviétique et ils ont besoin de savoir-faire et d'investissements étrangers.

LA CONVERSION ET LA PRIVATISATION EN REPUBLIQUE TCHEQUE

Radomir Sabela

Les changements politiques intervenus en Europe ont entraîné des réductions substantielles de la production d'armements. En République tchèque, la taille même du secteur de la défense a contraint les autorités à engager un programme de conversion massive parallèlement à leur programme de privatisation.

Le gouvernement a créé en 1991 un fonds spécial destiné à atténuer au maximum les effets douloureux de la conversion. Certaines entreprises ont tout simplement cessé leurs activités; d'autres ont été adaptées à la production de biens de consommation.

Radomir Sabela explique comment son pays a procédé pour transformer ses industries de guerre en industries de paix.

PRIVATISATION A L'ALLEMANDE
Aperçu de la stratégie et des méthodes de la Treuhandanstalt

Wolfgang Vehse

La privatisation est loin de se résumer à la vente d'entreprises au plus offrant, indique M. Wolfgang Vehse. La Treuhandanstalt tente de trouver pour chaque société d'Etat de l'ex-Allemagne de l'Est l'acheteur idéal et évalue à cette fin les repreneurs potentiels en fonction de plusieurs critères : montant et destination des investissements prévus; capacité de présenter des garanties d'emploi; politique d'assainissement de l'environnement; analyse de marche; stratégie de redressement; stratégie pour la production future et prix d'achat. Trois ans après sa création, la Treuhand a mené à bien quelque 35.000 opérations de privatisation et est sur le point d'avoir achevé sa mission et atteint ses objectifs.

SOLUTIONS PRATIQUES PROPOSEES POUR STIMULER LE SECTEUR PRIVE EN RUSSIE

Robert Watters

Au cours des derniers mois, la presse n'a pas ménagé ses critiques à l'encontre de la classe politique et des milieux d'affaires de Russie, accusés de confondre affaires publiques et affaires privées, mais Robert Watters pense que le pays est mûr pour l'investissement. Il propose trois solutions pratiques pour aider au démarrage du secteur privé russe : premièrement, encourager la formation théorique et pratique; deuxièmement, inciter les gouvernements à consacrer directement l'essentiel des fonds d'assistance technique au développement du secteur privé et non à de nouvelles études de faisabilité; troisièmement, exhorter les autorités publiques et les entreprises occidentales à la patience, en les invitant à considérer la Russie comme un investissement à long terme.

LA PRIVATISATION DANS LES PAYS ANCIENNEMENT COMMUNISTES, PROBLEMES ET PERSPECTIVES

Salvatore Zecchini

Pour Salvatore Zecchini, ce n'est pas un hasard si les gouvernements - à l'Est comme à l'Ouest - choisissent aujourd'hui d'accorder la priorité à la privatisation des entreprises publiques. Ils commencent en effet à s'apercevoir que la privatisation peut puissamment contribuer à la relance de l'économie et au maintien d'une croissance soutenue. La privatisation pourrait de même faciliter la réduction des déficits budgétaires et aider certains secteurs nationalisés de l'économie à devenir financièrement autonomes.

LES TRANSFERTS DE PROPRIETE DANS L'INDUSTRIE POLONAISE DES ARMEMENTS ET LES PROBLEMES DE SECURITE QU'ILS SOULEVENT

Katarzyna Zukrowska et Léon Turczynski

Pour les nombreux fabricants d'armes polonais qui produisaient également des biens à usage civil, il a été relativement facile de s'orienter vers la production de biens de consommation, mais les grandes sociétés se sont toutefois heurtées à de plus gros problèmes. Sur le plan économique, elles font face aux mêmes difficultés que leurs homologues du secteur civil, avec une demande intérieure et extérieure en régression, tandis que, sur le plan politique, il leur faut s'adapter aux changements qui interviennent sur la scène internationale et tenir compte de leurs incidences sur la sécurité nationale. Katarzyna Zukrowska et Léon Turczynski énoncent clairement les objectifs à long terme de leur pays : devenir membre à part entière de l'OTAN et coopérer plus étroitement avec les pays occidentaux dans le domaine de la fabrication des armements pour faire en sorte que les systèmes de défense de l'Europe orientale et de l'Europe occidentale soient pleinement compatibles. Patience et planification : tels sont, indiquent-ils, les maîtres mots dans la situation actuelle.